P9-APC-424

SCIENCE, DEVELOPMENT, AND SOVEREIGNTY IN THE ARAB WORLD

SCIENCE, DEVELOPMENT, AND SOVEREIGNTY IN THE ARAB WORLD

A. B. Zahlan

palgrave
macmillan

SCIENCE, DEVELOPMENT, AND SOVEREIGNTY IN THE ARAB WORLD
Copyright © A. B. Zahlan, 2012.

First published in 2012 by
PALGRAVE MACMILLAN®
in the United States—a division of St. Martin's Press LLC,
175 Fifth Avenue, New York, NY 10010.

Where this book is distributed in the UK, Europe and the rest of the world,
this is by Palgrave Macmillan, a division of Macmillan Publishers Limited,
registered in England, company number 785998, of Houndmills,
Basingstoke, Hampshire RG21 6XS.

Palgrave Macmillan is the global academic imprint of the above companies
and has companies and representatives throughout the world.

Palgrave® and Macmillan® are registered trademarks in the United States,
the United Kingdom, Europe and other countries.

ISBN: 978–1–137–02097–0

Library of Congress Cataloging-in-Publication Data

Zahlan, A. B. (Antoine Benjamin), 1928–
    Science, development, and sovereignty in the Arab world /
  A. B. Zahlan.
      p. cm.
    Includes index.
    ISBN 978–1–137–02097–0 (alk. paper)
      1. Science—Arab countries. 2. Economic development—
  Arab countries. 3. Science and state—Arab countries. I. Title.

Q127.A5Z33 2012
303.48'309174927—dc23   2011052935

A catalogue record of the book is available from the British Library.

Design by Newgen Imaging Systems (P) Ltd., Chennai, India.

First edition: July 2012

10 9 8 7 6 5 4 3 2 1

Printed in the United States of America.

To Rosemarie

CONTENTS

FIGURES AND TABLES

Figures

Tables

*These tables can be found online, no login or subscription necessary, at
http://us.macmillan.com/sciencedevelopmentandsovereigntyinthearabworld
/ABZahlan. They have not been printed in this book.

PREFACE

When I was a child growing up in Haifa, Palestine, it was very obvious to me that our lives were enmeshed in science, its applications, and products. The elementary school and high school I attended in Haifa did not teach science. Yet the events around me told a different story. Nobody in my family knew or cared much about science, and there were no libraries available to borrow books from, except that of the British Council, which had no section for children.

Neither children nor adults could avoid seeing that we, "the natives," lacked the ability to resist the tsunami of invasion engulfing us. Although we never had any weapons, our home was searched, several times, by British soldiers. My mother was very upset, but there was nothing that she could do except to call my father, who could also not do anything to stop this invasion of our privacy. So by the age of eight I had become familiar with a profound sense of helplessness.

My first acquaintance with technology change was when I learnt that Akka (Acre) had previously been the main city of northern Palestine. It is a great historical fortress set in a beautiful location. When in the nineteenth century the construction of a railway system with a terminal in Akka was proposed, the people who managed camel caravans opposed the move. So the railway line ended in Haifa. This led to the downgrading of Akka and the upgrading of Haifa. Akka slowly died, and Haifa took over as the major economic center of northern Palestine.

I learnt later that resistance to technology change and to the discoveries of science is a well-established phenomenon. For example, after the Second World War, when containerization began, London stevedores who earned their living loading cargo ships opposed the arrival of container ships. So the shipping companies serving London built a new harbor at Felixstowe, which is now the largest container harbor in Europe. London ceased to be a sea transport hub. Resistance to change is still continuing in the United States, with the antievolution fundamentalists and others playing an active role.

It was obvious that we Arabs of Palestine lacked important capabilities, making it possible for others to invade our country and destroy our way of life. During the process of ethnic cleansing in Palestine, we of course heard a lot from the perpetrators of these injustices and their supporters about values, democracy, and human rights.

Once I bought a rather obsolete book that discussed nineteenth-century chemistry. It had a discussion of Volta and his voltaic cell. I decided to duplicate his experiment. I found a copper sheet and a carbon rod, wires, and a torch bulb. I still needed some acid, so I went to the pharmacist to buy sulfuric acid. The pharmacist did not ask me what I needed the acid for, but told me to take a seat. A few minutes later my father walked in. The pharmacist had called him and told him that I wanted to commit suicide by consuming sulfuric acid! I was able to find an alternative source of acid and performed the experiment.

My father and his brothers had established small water and electricity companies serving the old city of Haifa. By the late 1930s, well-funded German Jews were able to provide Haifa with high quality water in substantial quantities, as well as with modern methods of power generation. Needless to say, this was the end of my father's attempt to adopt new technologies, and it was also a lesson in facing competition.

With the beginning of the Palestinian uprising in 1936, things deteriorated rapidly. One day, Um Ahmad, who used to supply us with her delicious goat's milk yoghurt, said that British soldiers had come to their village the day before and shot on sight her two sons who were running home from the field to see what was going on in their village. The British troops then destroyed the food supplies that the villagers had in their homes. She was helpless, we were all helpless.

A group of Palestinian leaders headed by Hajj Amin el-Husseini organized a resistance movement. But it was obvious to me that what they did would lead us nowhere.

By 1940 I began to visit the British Council library with my sister, who was an avid reader—but not of scientific books. She kindly used to borrow books for me too. Unfortunately they were too advanced for me to understand properly. Toward the end of the war I recall that I read a book about nuclear physics. There were points in it that I did not understand, so I wrote to its British author. It was a great pleasure for me to receive a long reply with detailed explanations. It was a wonderful experience, and somehow it made me realize that science is universal and scientists have to respond to enquiries, no matter from what source.

My father was a businessman. He imported a large range of European products—in the 1920s he dealt in men's and women's clothes, perfumes, and household appliances. He had a large store with some 30 employees, but as the years progressed the deterioration in the political situation shrank his business. By the beginning of the Second World War his business had shrunk and there was only one employee, and he dealt in men's clothes only.

My father thought that my reading habit was a nuisance and that it did not bode well for my future.

Around the 1940s I had a friend, Khalil Muhaishem, whose French mother brought him the Jules Verne series of science fiction books from France. He kindly lent me the books to read. It was a wonderful revelation. Alas, after the Palestinian exodus of 1948 Khalil went to France with his mother, who wanted him to be French, and afterward he was drafted into the French army, and I was told that he died in Vietnam. He too was helpless.

When Italy joined Germany in the Second World War, the war zone was extended to North Africa, and Italian forces occupied Greece. So Haifa, which was a terminal for oil from Iraq, became a viable strategic target for Italian war planes.

One bright sunny day, a couple of Italian bombers flew over the oil tanks near the city of Haifa and dropped their bombs. British forces were unprepared for the attack and had no antiaircraft weapons to fight back. In fact, as I recall, the fire went on for months because they did not even have the means to put out such a large fire.

When the Germans reached El Alamein, the strategic importance of Haifa increased immensely. The headquarters of the British fleet in the eastern Mediterranean was moved from Alexandria to Haifa.

The Italian air force did not attempt any more raids on Haifa after the British brought in modest antiaircraft defenses. The German air force, however, made spectacular air raids on the massed British fleet in Haifa bay. We used to watch hours of ground-to-air combat between the British navy and the German air force. These were massive and spectacular displays of a wide variety of technologies, courage, and skill.

Numerous heroic dives by German pilots and unrelenting resistance by the British navy resulted in one German plane being shot down but no ships being sunk. This is not based on any examination of military reports, but rather on direct observation by me sitting on a balcony with a magnificent view of Haifa bay. I have subsequently been deprived of both home and view.

These displays of power taught me about what we lacked to defend ourselves. It was clear that the Palestinian leadership seeking to find a way to avoid the destruction of our country were not aware of the nature of industrial power. Since my society had little idea about the nature of such power, they failed to take appropriate measures to acquire enough knowledge about it in order to—at least—reduce the destructiveness caused because of the technology gap with the adversary.

We rejoiced when we learnt that the Arab League had been formed and that the Arab states were concerned with what was happening in Palestine. Little did I know that the leaders of the Arab states were no better off than my leaders in Palestine.

My late wife, Rosemarie Said, was a historian of the Arab Gulf countries. She wrote a book on how wonderful and supportive the Gulf populations were at the time. Alas, Gulf populations were even more helpless than we were in Palestine. Despite all their faith in justice and their sustained efforts over the past many years, they have had limited influence on the events that took place. Arab governments did not, and still do not, appreciate the nature of industrial power.

The childhood lessons that I learnt from this overwhelming scientific hegemony resulted in a desire to devote myself to science in order to help change conditions in the Arab world. The lesson from Palestine is that nobody can be trusted. Wilsonian, American, and European commitments to the most basic principles of justice are falsehoods when it does not concern their own people.

The trouble with science is that it is value-neutral. It is simply a beautiful knowledge. Countries, societies, and nations have to derive values and morality from elsewhere. But having values without science leads us nowhere. Having science without values leads to situations similar to Nazi Germany, the Balfour Declaration, and imperialism.

What one also learns is that science is a beginning but not an end. Unless a society learns how to manage its sociopolitical and cultural affairs in a manner that can sustain an innovative technological culture, it will neither support the pursuit of science nor learn how to benefit from the associated technologies.

A society that tolerates patronage, sectarian principles, gender inequalities, and corruption can neither benefit from technology nor achieve a secure homeland.

The challenges that have emerged out of the Industrial Revolution and successive developments have shown that every member of society is important. This is why a society, to be able to defend itself, has to seek a good education for its children and high quality health services for its entire population; it must also establish economic principles that enable all of its citizens to earn enough to be able to live in dignity and contribute to sustaining a just and equitable society. Science and technology are vital inputs to achieve this; however, without justice and human rights, science and technology become instruments of oppression, exploitation, and dispossession. This is why much of this book is devoted to poverty, national security, building organizations, and municipalities.

The past two hundred years have been steeped in human misery and rich in human experience. There are enough studies to satisfy the most avid learner on all aspects of the issues that confront humanity today.

Whether we like it or not, responsibility to save ourselves falls on all members of society. Those who fail to wake up and take note of the challenges are doomed. Those who are clever and learn quickly to oppress and exploit certainly benefit in the short term. But we know that all past empires have collapsed and disappeared. It is likely that the new empires will fare alike. Of course, this is little consolation to the individuals who are crushed and whose lives are destroyed.

The reason I am giving all of this information is merely to illustrate the fact that one does not need a college education to realize that science is all around us, and that it is an irresistible force. It is obviously not enough to just be positively inclined toward science; one has to be enabled to use it competitively and effectively. The challenge is how to become so enabled.

The problems that the people of the Arab world face today are not unique. Many others have faced similar problems before the Arabs. Those groups who were not clever enough disappeared, others survived. Arabs feel that being so numerous and inhabiting such a large area makes them indestructible. This may or may not be so. Wisdom commands us to plan for the worst scenario.

I have been monitoring scientific output from the Arab world for more than 50 years and have been looking for positive signs that the Arab world is waking up. There are certainly signs of change.

Saudi Arabia, Tunisia, Iran, and Turkey have shown signs of life in recent years, not enough to be optimistic about but enough to have expectations of better things to come. Of course, Iran and Turkey are not part of the Arab world, but perhaps the attainments of our neighbors will be contagious.

Delays in publication of this book provided me opportunities to review the manuscript and make some additions regarding some recent occurrences. These concerned events of titanic proportions that took place in the Arab world and Japan during the early part of 2011.

The helpless conditions that prevailed in the Arab countries were suddenly challenged by mass uprisings that sprouted everywhere. Having been around for more than 80 years, I cannot be as optimistic about these events as my young friends.

The mere sight of so many excited, bright, optimistic, and energetic youth is enough to renew hope. I hope, however, that the young, once moved, will not easily give up when confronted with difficulties. It also made me feel that this book on science and sovereignty came at the right time: may be it will find readers who will be interested in its contents.

The earthquake and tsunami that hit Japan reminded mankind of the power of nature and the need to be always conscious of this power. Our science cannot dominate nature; at best, we can understand and adapt ourselves to live in harmony with it. But Japan suffered doubly: being the object of this uncontrollable power's fury, and having mistakenly choosing nuclear power.

During my student days in the United States in the early 1950s, I did a bit of what may be called nuclear chemistry, and attended at least one exercise in preparation for nuclear war. The United States was mobilizing for "better dead than red" and people were building silly nuclear shelters and training for the evacuation of cities in the event of a nuclear attack. It was rather obvious that all of these efforts were trivial in the face of nuclear bombs.

I became convinced at the time that nuclear power was like a tiger and it would be infantile to try to ride it. I was very surprised to see intelligent societies adopt nuclear energy. Since I was not involved in this science, I did not follow up the news of the nuclear industry. I hoped that no Arab country would go nuclear. I feel that we neither have the labor discipline, skills, nor the resources to handle such a complex industry in the foreseeable future. I am saddened that the UAE agreed to build nuclear reactors on its soil. It is also very worrying that Israel, Turkey, and Iran have built, or are building, nuclear reactors within the orbit of the region.

There is no end to reasons for a human to feel helpless.

ACKNOWLEDGMENTS

This book has been long in preparation. I intended, some time ago, to prepare it as a complement to two of my previous books on the subject of science in the Arab world.[1]

When a study takes such a long time, one incurs many debts to numerous discussions that inspire the effort. I first acknowledge with thanks the benefits that I acquired from the cited references in the notes.

I have benefited considerably from the assistance of a number of libraries in both London and Beirut. I was fortunate to use, for 35 years, both the old and the new British Library. It was always a pleasure to work there and to benefit from its enormous range of resources and services. Unfortunately, I am unable to thank the library staff by name.

In Beirut, I benefited from the librarians of the UN ESCWA library. Malak Tannir, the head librarian, is an encyclopedic source of knowledge. Zeinab Bumalhem, assistant librarian, was always knowledgeable and helpful. At the American University of Beirut, I am grateful to Helen Bikhazi, head librarian (now retired), for her assistance and advice. Myrna Tabet was extremely resourceful, and always helpful, in managing databases and sources of information.

I also benefited from Elizabeth Bouri who generously made available her expertise in scientific and statistical information. Moza al-Rabban, director of the Arab Scientific Community Organization, became a regular Internet discussant on numerous topics concerning Arab scientific activity and on data on scientific activities in the Arab world.

Then there were friends with whom I frequently discussed issues and problems. Among these I would like to thank Sami' el-Banna, Omar Bizri, Ashraf el-Bayoumi, Hassan Cherif, George Doumani, Hocine Khelfaoui, Mohammad Mikdashi, Isam Naqib, Abdalla Najjar, Usama Al-Khalidi, Geoffrey Oldham, Roshdi Rashed, and Mohammed Amin El-Tom. Muneer Bashshur was always a source of useful information on Arab higher education.

As for my efforts to improve my understanding of the mysterious working of Arab economies, I must thank George Corm, Zeki Fatah, Atef Kubursi, Samir Makdisi, and Khairi eldin Haseeb. Roulla Majdalani kindly clarified some aspects of Arab municipalities. Thanks to Saeb Jaroudi for many discussions of the problems and issues of Arab economic development.

From Soheir Morsi Al-Bayoumi, Claire Nader, Laura Nader, Nayla Nauphal, Soraya al-Turki, Mayssun Succarie, George Kosseifi, and Shelagh Weir I tried to learn about the sociology of Arab societies.

I benefited greatly from reading the works of Clement Henry on political economy, and from discussions to clarify aspects that were still vague in my mind.

Kaoru Makhlouf has been a rich source of information on Japan, and she kindly commented on the manuscript. Imen Jeridi Bachellerie and Clement Henry read and commented extensively on the manuscript.

Thanks also to Helga Graham for the many discussions on national security, the oil industry, and for extensive comments on some of the chapters. I thank Rebecca Foote for her insights and knowledge of early Arab water history. Ali Al-Assam generously (and often) gave his valuable time to help improve my use of my computer. I am especially grateful to Shawki Ahmad Ibrahim of Team International for his assistance with preparing the graphs.

Midway through the work on this book I suffered the loss of my wife, Rosemarie Said, who had been a critical and inspiring partner. Her balanced views and wisdom have always been a regulator of my thoughts. Her inputs were sorely missed in the end phase of the work.

Dana Abou Chakra has been my research associate for almost two years and a steadfast and cheerful worker. Last, but not least, I thank Mary Starkey for her expert editorial assistance, despite her heavy workloads, which made the text more readable.

ABBREVIATIONS

ACSAD	Arab Centre for the Study of Arid Zones and Dry Lands
ALECSO	Arab League Educational, Cultural and Scientific Organization
ARSCO	Arab Scientific Community Organization
ASTF	Arab Scientific and Technological Foundation
AUB	American University of Beirut
AUH	American University Hospital
BNL	Brookhaven National Laboratory
CAUS	Centre for Arab Unity Studies
CCC	Consolidated Contracting Company
CERN	Conseil Europeén pour la Recherche Nucléaire
CGIAR	Consultative Group on International Agricultural Research
CIRS	International Centre for Scientific Research
CNRS	Conseil National de la Recherche Scientifique—Liban also NCSR: National Council for Scientific Research
CMEA	Council for Mutual Economic Assistance
EU	European Community
FDI	foreign direct investment
Fermilab	Fermi National Accelerator Laboratory
GCC	Gulf Cooperation Council
GFCF	gross fixed capital formation
GNP	gross national product
GOIC	Gulf Organization for Industrial Chemicals
HDI	human development index
HSP	high-skilled personnel
ICARDA	International Centre for Agricultural Research in the Dry Areas
ICTP	International Centre of Theoretical Physics
IRFED	Institut de Recherches et de Formation en vue de Development

ISI	Institute of Scientific Information
KAM	knowledge assessment methodology
KISR	Kuwait Institute for Scientific Research
KSA	Kingdom of Saudi Arabia
LAU	Lebanese American University
MENA	Middle East and North Africa
NCSR	National Council for Scientific Research—Lebanon
OECD	Organization for Economic Cooperation and Development
R&D	research and development
SOC	self-organized criticality
S&T	science and technology
SME	small and medium enterprise
TFP	total factor productivity
UAE	United Arab Emirates
USJ	Université St Joseph
WEF	World Economic Forum

CHAPTER 1

BACKGROUND

Introduction

During the past four decades, Arab countries increased their R&D output between 40- and 60-fold as a result of expanding scientific research.[1] I thought it would be useful to reflect on these efforts in the context of international science.

Scientific activity in any country is affected by what scientists elsewhere achieve. This is true whether we are concerned with basic science, the treatment of a disease, or the manufacture of a desired product. Ever since the nineteenth century, improved global communications have increasingly enhanced the universality of science.

In industry, it is not enough to invent a new device, such as a TV; it is also necessary to be able to produce one that is as good as those made by competitors elsewhere. It is well known that the TV industry in the United States and Europe was decimated in the 1960s when the Japanese succeeded in making TV sets that were more reliable and less prone to breakdown.

Different countries in the world have selected different objectives for their science policies. Some, such as the United States, seek to excel in all fields. Others have opted for more limited scientific fields in which they seek to excel.

The Arab countries do not appear to have defined any particular objective. What I hope to do in this book is to show that the Arab world already has considerable, though modest, capabilities. If these capabilities are to become useful to society, they must be enabled and managed to yield definite outputs.

The Utility of Knowledge

Societies capable of converting knowledge into useful and appropriate outputs are constantly distancing themselves from other countries that are not able to do so. This increasing gap between nations has, since 1800, dominated cultures, economies, and power relationships. Advances in knowledge have given rise to new forms of colonialism and imperialism, two world wars, and the current systems of international relations. This has led to the globalization of the world economy. Those countries that have not been able to manage their relationship with knowledge production and consumption have been left behind, with diminished sovereignty and increased dependence.

The international pursuit of scientific knowledge is occurring on a massive scale. Expenditure, or rather investment, on this activity is in excess of $1 trillion per year. The United States invests half this sum; hence it has a dominant military and economic position in the world. The United States, the EU, China, and Japan account for about 95 percent of global investment in R&D.

It is very likely that expenditure on R&D will grow at the rate of 7 percent annually as more nations join the "knowledge club" and competition intensifies. The commitment of a country to scientific research is equivalent to its commitment to be sovereign and independent.

The evolution of scientific knowledge in any society occurs because of learning from others ("standing on the shoulders of giants") and a culturally generated drive to understand better the working of nature. Both of these driving forces have been of paramount importance in history.

The ability of a country to benefit from the discoveries of others depends on the efforts it deploys to learn about these advances in time and to possess the capability of understanding them. The production of knowledge, its dissemination, and use require a wide variety of organizations and services. This is a complex system that has to provide an enabling environment to the scientists to facilitate and encourage communication and cooperation among them, and between the scientists, society, and the economy.

The capabilities of the individual scientist are central to the process and, thus, to the overall political culture, and also to the management of the scientific infrastructure of each country. The motivation of the individual scientist and the freedom to explore and investigate are of great essence. Science does not grow in countries and cultures that do not give a priority to the creativity of their youth. The freedom to explore, discover, and invent is an integral part of this process.

Collaboration and cooperation among scientists themselves are of paramount importance. The freedom of association to form scientific societies and to travel and participate in national, regional, and international conferences is an integral part of the process of scientific production. Clearly, the provision of economic means to travel and participate in all relevant activities is crucial.

International activity in science is highly decentralized and strongly competitive, and it affects every scientist in the world. A major discovery anywhere changes the global scientific landscape in that field.

Scientists are engaged in the solution of problems and in the discovery of new facts and principles. Thus, once the solution to a problem has been discovered, there is no need to continue that particular research. Scientists then have to move on and benefit from the discovery and/or investigate other problems.

The speed with which scientists can work depends on their organization and resources. Clearly, those in the slow lane end up missing out on most major discoveries.

The acceleration in the rate of scientific advancement makes it nearly impossible for countries that are not actively involved in research to learn about new advances in time, to benefit from them, and to avoid collateral damage due to ignorance. Massive damage was suffered by Asian and African countries during the nineteenth century as a result of their ignorance of the scientific and technological advancements that were under way elsewhere.

Applied Sciences and Dematerialization of the Economy

The modern economy has become heavily based on "dematerialized" products, such as software, or materials that possess some low-cost material contents, such as chips, pharmaceutical products, fashion products, solar energy devices, and others. Even the means of production of "raw materials" are heavily dependent on scientific advancements in these fields.

Every year, an American periodical, *Technology Review*, chooses ten leading technologies with "potential to change the world" during the next few years.[2] Their choices for 2009 include, as may be expected, technologies that have no significant material content. The ten technologies chosen for 2009 involve the following:

- biological machines;
- memory units that possess considerably increased storage capacity;

- new methods to analyze DNA for as low as $100 per human genome, compared to current costs, which exceed $1,000 per genome;
- a new nuclear reactor design that makes reactors safer and less expensive;
- paper diagnostic tests that promise to make medical tests simpler and less costly, and can be done without complex electronic equipment;
- a battery with enormously enhanced capacity;
- intelligent personal software capable of learning about the tastes and interests of its owner in order to undertake complex searches and able to communicate with sources of information to make reservations and commitments;
- nano-piezotronics that can undertake medical and other measurements remotely and routinely;
- computer information storage methods for use in developing countries where Internet bandwidth is limited; and
- Internet software that contributes to improving the management of the routing of messages to suit the user.

Thus, as industrial countries continue to transfer sunset/old technologies to the Third World, they themselves are moving into new technology areas that are more knowledge intensive. These technologies also will eventually be transferred, with their countries of origin retaining, as at present, the income from royalties.[3]

Economics has not yet caught up with the knowledge revolution. Estimates of the economic returns from investment in research are still primitive. Nevertheless, it is estimated by some that every dollar the US government has invested in space research (that is, by NASA and associated organizations) adds $9 annually to the US economy![4] The multiplier effect may turn out to be even larger when more sophisticated methods of estimating this return are developed. Naturally, different types of advances in technology will be associated with different multiplier effects.

The Increasing Importance of Prosuming

The Tofflers have highlighted the increasing importance of activities that are generally outside the economy. Cooking our meals, curing each other, taking care of the sick in the family, working for charities, and entertaining ourselves without the exchange of money are all activities that the Tofflers call "prosuming": the consumption of our own production without it having become part of the money economy.[5]

The Tofflers estimate that the monetary value of these prosumed activities is equal to a monetized production of $50 trillion. But they also predict that the tendency of these activities is toward an increase, thanks to technology change.

The relevance of these tendencies to developing countries is immediately obvious: unless they develop the appropriate enabling infrastructures and organizations, they will not be able to benefit from such a development.

For example, several of the research projects selected by *Technology Review* for their immediate importance and noted above will enhance this prosuming tendency. Take, for example, the development of paper diagnostic tests. This is an extension of activities that are already under way. Today, most people who suffer from diabetes treat themselves: they carry out tests and administer the treatment depending on the results of the test.

A combination of tests that are simple to carry out, combined with question/answer Internet services, should enable people to take care of a great part of their health problems by themselves.

The only reason I am mentioning prosuming here is to emphasize the changing nature of the services that a modern society needs. Arab societies have, to date, failed to develop the capacity to invent and design simple, and low cost, do-it-yourself (DIY) responses to some of the problems it faces.

Determinism, Randomness, Flexibility, and Appreciation

It is generally taken for granted that scientific and technological activities are subject to planning. It is thus assumed that clear targets, detailed planning, and the adoption of research programs in logical and deterministic ways lead to desired outcomes.

However, when we study the past advances of societies and nations, we find that, although planning did play an important role, there has always been a strong element of randomness and chance.

Gavin Weightman, in a delightful account of industrial development, recounts how a vast number of persons emerged out of nowhere to make important contributions.[6] He discusses the ways and means invented to utilize coal, iron, steam engines, dyes, chemicals, naval ships, torpedoes, bicycles, motor cars, communication systems, and so on. In all cases, he shows how a combination of skills and chance events combined to bring about useful outcomes, and how this process was spread over many countries and over time.

What one finds is that totally unexpected persons from unlikely social and educational backgrounds made important and unexpected contributions. These led to useful results because there was flexibility in the system, which facilitated appreciation of such developments by key individuals, and a society that was able to adapt its plans when an unexpected development took place.

Unless we allow ourselves to benefit from chance events, we will miss important opportunities. Our plans should not restrict us to a single road, and they must contain the flexibility to enable us to examine and benefit from all possibilities at all times. Does this mean that we should not plan? No, planning is still a useful tool and, if well done, it prepares us to benefit from favorable chance events when they do occur.

How do we prepare ourselves to benefit from all possibilities? Many of the principles that underpin central, governmental, and personal planning in the Arab world essentially eliminate the possibility of benefiting from these "random" processes.

For example, in many Arab countries, appointment of university professors is subject first to the "acceptance" of the degree of the candidate, rather than being based on an assessment of his capabilities and creativity. Some great scientists do not possess doctorates, some eminent economists have scientific backgrounds, and so on. Furthermore, in some Arab universities, a professor can only teach a course that he or she took as a student. A person who obtained a degree in chemistry may not be appointed in a physics department.

There are no places in the Arab world where a gifted person can develop and benefit from his or her technical expertise. Some of the great inventors in Silicon Valley never went to university. Many others developed completely new and unexpected ideas while at university and where able to implement them. Some of their ideas were initially laughed at, yet these inventors were enabled to try them out and succeed.

The obsession in the Arab world with loyalty to leadership, the near absolute importance of personal relations (the *wasta* system) in securing employment, the politicization of most activities by making it essential for participants to be members of a political party or a confessional group all abort the possibility of success for many. There are no correlations between scientific capabilities and the factors that rule Arab society. By their addiction to all these constraints in their societies, Arab societies are committing developmental suicide.

Needless to say, many young and creative persons in the Arab world, when confronted by these obstacles, either fossilize at home or join the brain drain and succeed elsewhere.

Current scientific activity and technological progress are heavily based on the capabilities of individuals working in teams and supported in relation to the quality and creativity of their work. An individual's qualities are generally obvious to other scientists, though these may not at all be clear to politicians and bureaucrats. Of course, if the person in question is young, it is even more difficult to recognize her or his talents.

It is important to realize that university degrees are poor measures of scientific creativity. A PhD qualification shows that somebody has completed a set course or a defined piece of research. Some of the people who are awarded PhDs in science do not make any creative contributions in later life. On the other hand, there are very creative persons who were unable to even complete their studies.

Much of what has been achieved during the past century in computer sciences, solid state physics, and electronics has been accomplished both by brilliant scientists who continued their studies, such as Alan Turing and substantial numbers of BS graduates, such as William Hewlett and David Packard, as well as by high school graduates such as Bill Gates and Steve Jobs. The infrastructure for promoting and managing such cooperation fruitfully is nonexistent in the Arab countries. Such cooperation cannot survive bureaucratic rules, addiction to confessional favoritism, and the dominance of the *wasta* system.

The Assessment of Creativity

In scientific research, creativity and performance are the order of the day. Thus, over the past two centuries, methods have been evolved to enable planners and scientists to assess their own performance and that of their colleagues, as well as that of organizations and countries. Enormous effort is exerted in countries that are seriously striving to stay ahead, or to move ahead, to assess and improve their own standing in the world.

My purpose in highlighting this aspect of science and technology is to alert the reader to the fact that though what is presented appears to be logical and deterministic, the underlying reality is more complex.

Furthermore, there are many dichotomies that one encounters in science, such as that of pure science and applied science. These two fields are complementary to each other and one cannot exist without the other. Yet, this dichotomy has plagued the scientific community in the Arab world since the 1950s on the ground that "pure" science is not useful but applied science is. People concentrating on pure science were therefore considered to be wasting their time. As a result, there is a dangerously low level of basic scientific research going on in the Arab world today.

For a society to succeed, its national political culture has to facilitate and support the undertaking of scientific activities. Societies that are unable to arrive at a felicitous cohabitation between their political culture and their scientific population are unable to develop and sustain scientific activity.

Science, Culture, and Survival

Despite the universal characteristics of scientific knowledge, scientific development is subject to local cultural influences. There are several aspects to this interesting relationship.

The mutual influences between science and culture do not affect the nature of scientific facts or the laws of nature; however, economic factors or the availability of some specific resources can play a role. Some particular cultures may also favor priorities that reflect their existential requirements. This is why we see different civilizations emphasizing different fields of science.

Interestingly, the Arabs, both before and after the advent of Islam, responded to the constraints imposed by their location and resources, and they managed to develop world-class and competitive systems of trade and transport as well as arid zone agriculture throughout the Arabian Peninsula. By contrast, since 1800 the Arab world has (with the exception of the emirate of Dubai) failed to respond to the economic imperatives imposed by the possession of a geostrategic resource and enormous natural resources in oil, gas, and phosphates.

Sadly, any immoral, oppressive nation will have the same opportunities as any other to benefit from research and to find better ways to subjugate and oppress other nations and populations, while the latter will also seek to develop ways to retaliate.

Thus, we see that the people of Gaza, subjected to the imposition of brutal and inhuman oppression by their neighbors, have sought to develop capabilities in tunnelling technology. At the same time, the Gazans feel culturally bound to reflect their anger at the treatment that they are receiving and have developed small rockets to enable them to express their disgust. This grassroots R&D that the people of Gaza are seeking signals their desperate desire for a way out from under their oppressors. The fact that their neighbors are more powerful and can destroy these efforts has not weakened their resolve. Technological development springs from economic need and the need for national security.

Clearly, a vital form of defense for the oppressed is to be creative and research oriented. In other words, no society, no matter how poor, weak, and destitute, can afford not to be engaged in relevant research. The Vietnamese, the Cubans, and others have also pursued similar strategies during periods of their recent history.

Technology is dependent on science, despite the fact that its progress is also driven by applications and economics. For example, the invention of the steam engine by Hero of Alexandria[7] some 2,000 years ago did not lead to its significant practical application for a long time. The steam engine was of limited significance until Sadi Carnot in the early nineteenth century sought to understand the determinants of its efficiency in converting heat energy to mechanical work. Carnot discovered the science of thermodynamics in the course of his efforts to understand how the steam engine functioned.

What Motivates Countries to Sponsor Research?

A great deal of the drive to undertake research originates in our natural inquisitiveness about our surroundings. However, the high cost of this exercise calls for substantial commitments and investments by society and government. Why would governments throughout history have devoted funds to support such efforts by scientists? And what difference does it make to a country if it did so?

Instruments of War and Advances in Technology

As early as the Stone Age, it became clear to humans that people who possessed certain tools, methods, and capabilities were stronger in resisting aggression and more powerful in confrontations. Warfare and the tools needed to conduct it have been a dominant force in the development of a whole range of technologies, from better iron weapons to nuclear bombs.

Thus, national military establishments and their technological requirements became a factor in technological progress. Science was often developed as a collateral of the technologies that were needed for military purposes. We know little about the relationships that existed between the two in ancient times.

However, there is little doubt of strong relationships existing between the two in modern times. We know, for example, that Galileo and Leonardo da Vinci both contributed to military technologies. It is not that they were warmongers, but this was a way for them to earn a living, since at the time, as we well know, few were sympathetic to their interests in the basic sciences. In fact, Galileo was penalized by the Catholic Church for his interest in astronomy.

A great deal more is known concerning this matter in modern times. Since the First World War, the relationships between the military and science and technology have become more explicit and transparent.

The Socioeconomic and Political Independence of Nations

Countries that espoused learning and sought to develop their national capabilities may be considered autonomous. In other words, these countries could adopt policies based on national objectives, capabilities, and organizations.

Even in ancient times, some societies were able to display such self-reliant policies. For example, the priests in the temples of ancient Egypt were a combination of scientific researchers, teachers, bureaucrats, and religious officials.

It is known that, because of the cyclical nature of the Nile's water supply, Egypt used to suffer years of plenty followed by famine. Obviously, when the supply of water was very limited, the Egyptians could not produce enough food to feed the entire population. This resulted in famine during the low flood years. (Building the high dam at Aswan was eventually to enable Egypt to overcome this affliction.)

Naturally, the ancient Egyptians thought of keeping a stock of grain from the years during which they had plentiful supply of water, for use in the famine years. However, these stocks were attacked by mice and rats, and the grain could not be maintained long enough to be used during the years when needed. An observant "temple scientist" discovered the capabilities of cats in eliminating rats and mice, and this discovery enabled the Egyptians to protect their grain stocks.

This discovery was of strategic importance because it enabled the country to avoid famine, which had led to social unrest and often weakened the defenses of Egypt against its aggressive neighbors. Thus, the cats enabled Egypt to resist its belligerent neighbors. Obviously, this knowledge affected the balance of power between Egypt and its neighbors, and the Egyptians kept their new "secret weapon" shielded from their neighbors for a long time.[8]

Countries that do not seek to be autonomous will become derivative and dependent nations. Such countries have fared badly when the technology gap between countries grew rapidly after 1500: the technological dependence of such countries increased and they were reduced to importing their weapons from the countries that were essentially their adversaries.

The behavior of dependent people is typical. For example, the Egyptian fleet of the early nineteenth century was manned by French officers,

who "gracefully" withdrew from their posts in the Egyptian navy before
the battle of Navarino. The officer-less fleet was sunk by the combined
Western (British, French, and Russian) navies in the ensuing battle, which
took place on October 20, 1827.

Undeterred by this experience, Muhammad Ali resorted to assistance
from the French (the enemy that had sunk his fleet) to rebuild his fleet at
his Alexandria naval base. Being totally oblivious of the rapid and con-
temporary technological changes, he built a fleet based on wind power,
thanks to the advice of the "French expert" employed for the job. The
battle of Navarino was, in fact, the last battle in history fought by sail
ships.[9] Subsequently, all navies converted to steam power. Thus a backward and dependent nation not only loses the battle of today but also
adopts policies that guarantee that it will lose its future battles.

This pattern of behavior recurs often in the Arab world. For example,
in the 1950s, an Arab country imported a factory to manufacture radio
tubes, even after the transistor began to replace radio tubes. A similar
situation arose after the June war of 1967: a frontline state imported sub-
sonic antiaircraft rockets at a time when all fighter planes had become
supersonic.

Self-reliant countries are constantly alert to scientific change anywhere. For example, much of the post-Renaissance scientific and technological progress was initiated at various times in a small number of
countries (such as Portugal, Spain, Italy, Holland, Britain, and France).
Yet, their European neighbors, including Russia, quickly sensed what
was taking place and deployed massive efforts to "catch up."

By contrast, in the non-European world of Asia and Africa (including
the Ottoman Empire) the reaction was to pursue technological dependence: the development of a national technology base called for unac-
ceptable cultural and political change. The creativity required by the
new sciences demanded a more liberal political culture, which was not
forthcoming.

As a result, all of these countries became colonies or semicolonies. In
Asia, only Japan, when forced to, had an effective reaction, because it
decided from the outset that it did not wish to be a derivative culture.

Possibility of Change of Policies

Fortunately, every society has the opportunity to change its attitude
toward science. Thus, during the twentieth century a number of countries in Asia adopted strong strategies to attain technological self-reliance.
We now see that Korea (both North and South), China, India, Malaysia,

Taiwan, and others are successfully pursuing such strategies, and that they are rapidly gaining ground.

In all of these cases, whether eighteenth-century European countries, nineteenth-century Japan, or twentieth-century latecomers, one finds that the first step taken by government is to pursue self-reliance and insist on being a nonderivative culture. They all took strong measures not only to be learners from others but also to be contributors to their own efforts. On a much smaller scale, this is what the people of Gaza are trying to achieve.

In the Arab world, we know of three attempts during the past two centuries to acquire military technology; all of them were made without any significant effort to develop a science base to support such technologies. However, in all three cases (Muhammad Ali, Gamal Abdel Nasser, and Saddam Hussein) they allowed themselves to be dragged into military confrontations for which they were not ready, and all three lost out. Clearly, we live in a dangerous world, and setting up facilities to build a capability that may affect the balance of power will be resisted by those who seek to benefit from the present imbalance. An intelligent response to visible danger is a necessity.

Needless to say, the longer a country waits to realize what is happening in the world of science, the larger is the ensuing knowledge gap, and the greater the effort needed to catch up. In all such cases we note that the later the country takes the decision to become self-reliant, the greater is the speed required for developing its research capabilities.

Research in national organizations is the most authentic sign of self-reliance, and it is the only secure route from derivative status to sovereignty. This is true of countries from Cuba to China. The fact that in 2008 China became the second biggest spender on R&D (superseding Japan) is a sign of Chinese determination. The fact that the Arab countries are among the lowest spenders on R&D is a guarantee of a state of dependence.

No Limits to Destruction in a Derivative Culture

Edward Said, in his studies of orientalism and imperialism, has shown how European intellectuals played a critical role in the design and promotion of the concepts and instruments needed to spread colonialism. Technology also played an important role in these conquests.

In the cases that Said studied, the role of the intellectual was to justify and facilitate the adoption of colonial and racist behavior. The Western intellectual was an essential tool for making colonialism acceptable to the conquering population (who would not otherwise have made the "sacrifices" necessary to undertake the conquests), as well as to plan the conquests and manage the resulting empires.

Recently, two important studies have been published that discuss further the role of intellectuals in colonial domination. These studies are especially important in understanding how foreign education and "appropriate" concepts can be combined to mobilize selected elites in specific countries to turn them against their national interests in order to serve colonial interests.

The first of these studies, *The Shock Doctrine*, is the seminal work of Naomi Klein.[10] Klein dissected the consequences of the violent and obsessive application of Milton Friedman's Chicago School concepts in Latin America, Indonesia, Iraq, and other countries. Klein explicates the manner in which a combination of international consultants (IMF, World Bank, Western consulting firms), together with the CIA and US business organizations, secured consequences that were devastating to the targeted countries.

The Washington Consensus, which was an embodiment of the Chicago theology, brought havoc to the compliant Third World and emerging countries. The applications of these concepts, in the words of Klein, "shared the policy trinity—the elimination of the public sphere, total liberation for corporations and skeletal social spending."[11]

In Argentina, Chile, Indonesia, and Iraq, the applications of the Chicago theology and the Washington Consensus were associated with massive violence. In the case of New Orleans, where the city was destroyed by natural events, the efforts to apply these concepts did not need the application of additional violence but sought to benefit from the "opportunities" provided by nature.

The special importance to us here is how the students of Milton Friedman and the University of Chicago (as well as staff of international organizations) became effective agents for inflicting this violence on the selected countries.

In the account provided by Klein concerning Iraq, such students were not needed, since the United States used its armed forces to create the "opportunities." But in Iraq, despite the massive economic and social destruction effected by the "liberating forces of freedom," the occupiers did not fully succeed (at the time of Klein's writing) in creating the desired opportunities for American capitalism, because resistance was partially effective in paralyzing the economy.

Needless to say, there is nothing wrong in studying abroad and learning new concepts and ideas—whether good or bad. However, the ability to have these ideas adopted without examination and evaluation is the point emphasized here.

In a nonderivative culture, all new ideas and concepts would be publicly discussed and evaluated. Society then has the ability to adopt new ideas and concepts by choice, and subject to its own self-interest. By contrast, in all the cases where the Friedman logic was enforced, this was not the case. Here, it was through violence and subterfuge, against a freely elected national government in Chile and in the other cases against rather popular governments, that "the liberating ideas" of Milton Friedman were enforced. None of the affected countries had intellectual and research organizations capable of evaluating and assessing the relevance of the imposed concepts.

The second seminal study is the PhD dissertation of Mayssun Succarie entitled *Winning Hearts and Minds: Education, Culture and Control*.[12]

Succarie discusses the programs that the US government, and its many affiliated NGOs, are implementing in the Arab world with a view to indoctrinate the youth. The program is "in the open" and supported by several Arab governments. The Arab Middle East has been increasingly addicted to American education, to the point that American universities are being set up throughout the region at a substantial speed.

Of course, the most spectacular manifestation of the derivative nature of today's Arab societies and cultures is their technological dependence. This dependence can be seen in all areas of life. A region whose oil resources were known long before Western geologists arrived and whose resources have been exploited now for more than a century is still totally dependent for every associated oil and gas technological activity.

In another equally important area, one finds that after 212 years of direct and extensive contact with the West, the Arab countries do not possess a single world-class academic center or center for scientific research.[13] There is no sign of any effort in any Arab country to secure national control over socioeconomic life and national security.

The Perspective of the Book

What I plan to discuss in this book are the relationships between science and a host of other vital concepts and organizations. Science in its many ramifications will be the focal point.

Higher education and universities, the labor force, the economy, national security, IT, and municipalities are topics addressed daily in books, periodicals, and newspapers. But what I will be trying to focus on in the chapters of this book are the systemic relationships among these factors. I will not be concerned with whether we have illiterate people in the Arab world, but rather with what we do with the more than 200 million literate people and with more than 200,000 PhD holders.

I will try and show that, in comparison with successful developing countries, the Arab countries already possess considerable human capital. They do not need to wait another 30 or 50 years until a new generation of Arab scientists are trained in new commercial, private, or American universities to move forward.

I will argue that a massive change of economic policy can be adopted through the enabling of existing Arab human capital.

There is a great deal that the individual Arab scientist can do to improve the current state of affairs in the Arab world. Though the individual scientist or engineer or medical doctor may be a public- or private-sector employee, there is a range of activities that fall completely within his/her scope, and thus he/she can make valuable contributions to the total effort.

Thus the individual scientist or engineer on the faculty of a university, or as an employee in a ministry, or in a factory or consulting company can contribute in many ways to changing prevailing conditions.

Many years ago the US General Electric Company (GE) approached its own problems in an interesting manner, which may be relevant to the Arab world. The management of the company decided that almost every worker had opportunities to increase the quality of the work for which he is responsible. So GE initiated a program of inviting its employees to recommend improved processes. Any suggestion that succeeded was rewarded proportionally to the contribution that it made to output and company profit. The company wisely gave the reward in company shares, thus making the worker a shareholder and more permanently interested in the fate of GE. The program was a great success, and it led to annual decline in waste and steady improvements in productivity.

Arab scientists and technologists can adopt a similar attitude; however, they will have to do without the reward for some time. Whether they are employed in a municipality or responsible for road maintenance, or university professors teaching in a school of engineering, or surgeons in a hospital, these Arab scientists and technologists should be able to improve some of the activities by 5 percent, 10 percent, or more, with little help.

Naturally, the ability of professionals to convince and secure additional resources to undertake more ambitious reforms will be taken more seriously after they demonstrate their abilities.

There is a pressing need for greater appreciation of the efforts needed to increase our understanding of obstacles to development and how to overcome them.

Many developing countries, which were in a worse condition than the Arab countries, were able through determined effort to join the industrialized countries in output and performance in some 30 years.

CHAPTER 2

R&D IN THE ARAB WORLD

Introduction[1]

It is useful to begin with some facts to locate the Arab countries in the world of science. How do they stand in relation to each other, the industrial countries, the developing countries, and to the Tiger countries?

There are many different methods for comparing countries. Each method emphasizes some aspects of its scientific standing. Some methods are simple and provide a limited, though meaningful, assessment. For example, one simple method is to compare the number of persons who earned a Nobel Prize for work done in that country, on the assumption that the most advanced countries would be the ones that enable the largest number of scientists to obtain a Nobel Prize. Since only few countries have Nobel Prize winners, this rating leaves us in ignorance of the capabilities of most of the world.

A more elaborate approach would compare the performance of countries in different fields of science and technology. It would compare their research and patent output, and the quality and performance of the agricultural sector, the health sector, the industrial sector, and the service industries. Many organizations, especially UN agencies, publish sets of indicators annually. It is therefore not difficult for any country to secure a reasonably accurate idea of its international standing.

For our purposes here, it is adequate to utilize the number of research publications generated by scientific workers in each country to determine one facet of its international standing. The best sources for such information would be the individual scientists and/or national scientific organizations. Unfortunately, most Arab organizations have not established accessible websites where such information may be found. There are, however, organizations that do the recording of the number of publications published under different assumptions. We have to resort to these sources, because their output is standardized and useful for comparative purposes.

The original purpose for undertaking these compilations of articles and citations was to enable scientists to

- rank scientific publications through the use of the citation index,
- search the literature rapidly,
- learn of advances in science that are of interest to them, and
- link current advances to previous research.

There are large numbers of publications that appear in a wide variety of periodicals classified by some bibliographers as science and technology. In fact, anyone can publish a book or a periodical and classify it as a science publication. Does this make it a scientific publication? Fortunately, it does not.

Science is a decentralized and competitive activity. There is no universal organization in the scientific world that stamps a publication as a "science" or a "nonscience" publication. Essentially, a publication "becomes" a science publication when scientists consider it to be discussing science. In this process, a key factor is citation: when scientists cite a scientific paper by referring to its contents, it becomes "recognized" as a science paper. Naturally, papers that lead to important new discoveries have large numbers of citations; others have much less. It sometimes happens that the scientific status of a paper is discovered late. So, this process of recognition is not problem-free.

The ranking of scientific journals is based on the proportion of their published papers that are cited, and on the frequency of these citations. A periodical whose papers are never cited does not, for all practical purposes, "exist" in the world of science. Unfortunately, many Arab periodicals claiming to publish scientific papers are in this category. Once a periodical acquires a reputation as marginal, nobody will look at it, even if it occasionally publishes excellent articles. Most scientists are aware of these issues and seek, when they can, to avoid such periodicals.

Thus, citation of a scientific paper is crucial to the author and to the periodical: it is the acid test to prove that the scientific community has admitted the periodical and its contents. The citation of a paper does not mean that it is important; all it means is that some scientists have found it useful in some way. Sustained collective interest from the scientific community for a scientific paper is a measure of its importance.

Needless to say, there are many scientific periodicals that have had excellent editors for a long time and have established a reputation for excellence.

Industrial countries, and aspiring developing countries such as China, devote considerable effort and resources to publish and compile citations, abstracts, and bibliographies. Regretfully, no Arab organization feels any responsibility to undertake similar activities with respect to publications from the Arab world.

The citation and bibliographical information on the research output of a country informs us about its ability to

- relate to international science,
- acquire and apply science and technology,
- provide its students with quality education,
- make tentative forecasts of its future development,
- plan and develop sound national science policies, and
- assess the scientific health of the country.

Needless to say, industrial and aspiring developing countries devote considerable effort to evaluate their standing in the fields that interest them. The usual objectives are to determine

- the quality of ongoing research in the country,
- the quality of their graduate programs,
- their international standing in science, and
- whether they are keeping sufficiently abreast in fields of critical importance to their national economy and security.

The R&D Output of the Arab World

Figure 2.1 shows the growth of research output of the Arab world since 1967. ★Table A in ★Appendix 1 gives the numerical value of the output for each Arab country separately over this same period of time.[2] The available data for the period before 1967 was neither standardized nor comprehensive.[3] It is clear from the data that there has been a steady increase in research output from Egypt, Jordan, Lebanon, the GCC, and Maghreb countries, but not from the rest of the Arab countries.

★Table 2.1 shows the different constituents that make up the number of records for each country cited by the Institute of Scientific Information (ISI)[4] for the Arab countries in 1990 and 1995. This table shows that the proportion of notes, meeting abstracts, and other documents amount to 10–15 percent of the total number of records.[5]

Most of the tables presented in this book cite the number of scientific papers and exclude the number of meeting abstracts, notes, and other documents. Thus, the totals in most of the tables in the text are slightly different from the totals in ★Table A (in ★Appendix 1). The reason that ★Table A includes all records is that this makes it less time consuming to compare countries. ★Table A was constructed by using ISI data for the period 1967 to 1995 and SCOPUS data for the period 1996 to 2010. The differences per country per year for the same year between the two sources are taken here as indicating the range of uncertainty in the data.[6]

It is difficult to estimate the range of error in the number of records and papers. There are errors in the assignment of records to countries and in the classification of papers by scientific field. There are differences in the number of records cited in studies by ISI and SCOPUS, both of which had to be used because of availability. The databases are not always in symmetrical order to facilitate searches by country and by names. Furthermore, the search engines used are imperfect and may include entries that do not originate in the searched country.[7] Manual

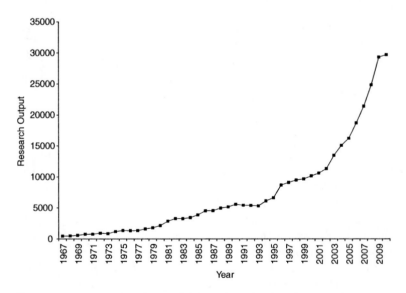

Figure 2.1   Research output of the Arab countries, 1967–2010
Source: ISI until 1995; Scopus 1996–2010.

corrections are tedious but possible and have been made in the tables of this book.

Despite these limitations, the data is adequate for present purposes. Obviously, the only way to obtain clean data without any errors is when the authors themselves, and their affiliated organizations, compile, edit, and publish such information.

Figure 2.1 shows the research output from the Arab countries over the period 1967 to 2010. The output of the Arab world tripled between 2000 and 2010. Egypt, Kuwait, and UAE showed a marked increase in output. But four countries exhibited an unusually high surge after 2003–2004: Algeria, Qatar, Saudi Arabia, and Tunisia. During this surge, Saudi Arabian and Algerian output increased by 1.38 and 1.84 respectively; and Qatari and Tunisian outputs increased by 2.66 and 2.21, respectively. It is clear that there are important changes taking place in some of these countries.

There are clear differentiations between the Arab countries. Egypt, Saudi Arabia, and Tunisia are, at the moment, in the lead. Algeria, Tunisia, and Saudi Arabia have announced plans to expand research activity. Changes in output may be driven by the availability of funding (e.g., sudden increases in national and/or EU funding of joint R&D projects) or changes in faculty recruitment practices.

So far, no Arab country has given the relationship between scientific capabilities and the economy adequate attention. Nevertheless, several Arab countries are rapidly approaching a condition in which they should be able to derive substantial economic benefits from R&D performed in the Arab world. As we will show later, the R&D output of the entire Arab world is already substantial, but severely underutilized.

Economic activities in agriculture, food industries, construction, phosphate, water, electricity production, transport, service industries, and others could improve rapidly, with an increase in productivity and output, if planning and consulting capabilities were better integrated with national and regional R&D.

Figure 2.2 shows the same data as that of figure 2.1 but plotted logarithmically to demonstrate the near exponential growth of research output. One finds that the exponential (base ten) annual rate of growth (that is, the slope of the curve) over this period was 0.033 per year. This is not a high rate of growth.

Wars, civil wars, and economic change are averaged out when the output of all the Arab countries is combined. However, when each Arab country is examined separately (see figures 2.3 to 2.8), national events can be seen to influence output.

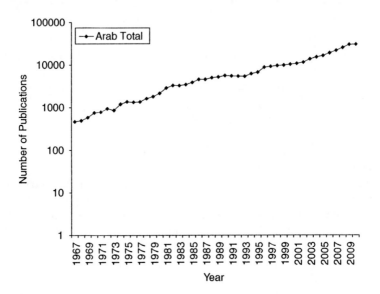

Figure 2.2 A plot of log (total research output of the Arab world) per year, 1967–2010

Source: ISI until 1995; Scopus 1996–2010.

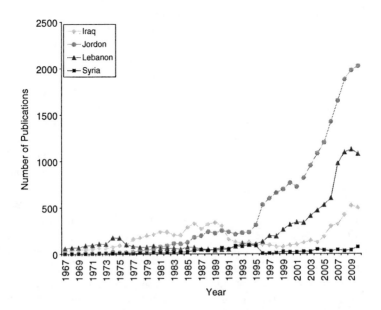

Figure 2.3 The research output of Iraq, Jordan, Lebanon, and Syria, 1967–2010

Source: ISI until 1995; Scopus 1996–2010.

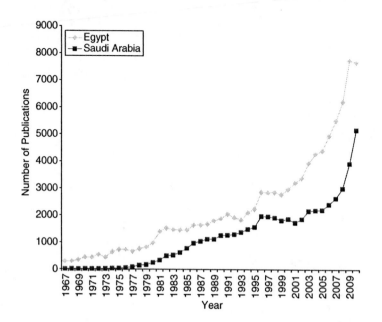

Figure 2.4 The research output of Egypt and Saudi Arabia, 1967–2010

Source: ISI until 1995; Scopus 1996–2010.

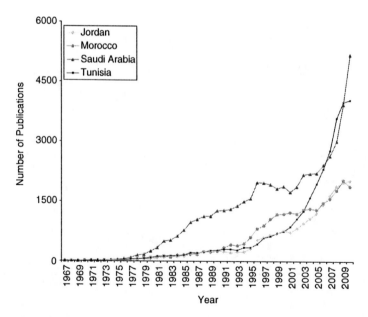

Figure 2.5 The research output of Jordan, Morocco, Saudi Arabia, and Tunisia, 1967–2010

Source: ISI until 1995; Scopus 1996–2010.

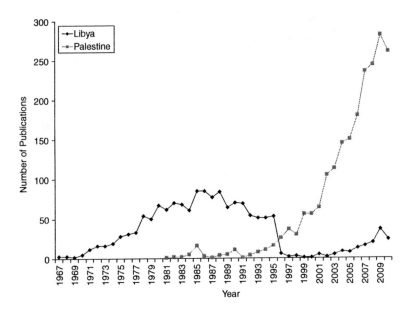

Figure 2.6 The research output of Palestine and Libya, 1967–2010

Source: ISI until 1995; Scopus 1996–2010.

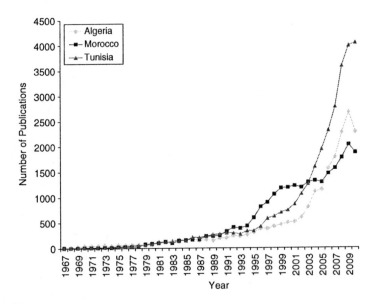

Figure 2.7 The research output of Algeria, Morocco, and Tunisia, 1967–2010

Source: ISI until 1995; Scopus 1996–2010.

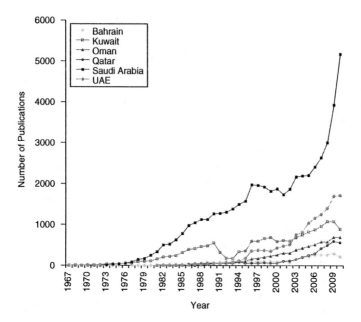

Figure 2.8   The research output of the GCC countries, 1967–2010
Source: ISI until 1995; Scopus 1996–2010.

The impact of the dramatic rise in oil revenues after 1973 (figure 2.4) shows clearly in the performance of Saudi Arabia. Its R&D was insignificant before 1973; however, one notes a rapid increase after 1973 to reach a plateau in 1987. A modest rate of expansion was then resumed in 1990. Figure 2.8 shows the performance of all the GCC countries together. It is clear from figure 2.8 that Kuwait had significant R&D activity before 1973. Other GCC countries began to sponsor R&D only after 1973.

The UAE embarked on a moderate increase in research output in 1980, which stalled in 1996. Rapid increase (as noted earlier) was then resumed in 2004. Research activity in Oman started in 1982 with the founding of its first university, and Oman has maintained a steady rate of growth ever since.

On the other hand, Libya (figure 2.5) showed a very modest growth beginning in 1969, and reached a low plateau in 1980, where it remained until 2004 whence it resumed modest growth.

The incubation period of Palestinian research output (figure 2.5) during the years 1980 to 1990 was erratic as a result of the repressive conditions under which Palestinians live. After this difficult start, research in Palestine grew to exceed, or to be comparable with, the growth of the six Arab states in 2007–2010: Libya, Mauritania, Yemen, Bahrain, Sudan, Iraq.

Algeria (figure 2.7) did not show an early response to the increase in oil revenues in 1973. Its output increased between 1980 and 1989, then growth settled to a modest rate until after 2003 when it resumed rapid growth.

Tunisia, a non-oil-producing country, started its R&D growth in 1967 from a very low level, and it has sustained this growth ever since. Currently it is the second largest Arab research producer and is competing for this place with Saudi Arabia.

Generally, the economy has a direct impact on research output. However, Algeria, Libya, and Tunisia are exceptions. The poor performance of several oil-producing countries such as Iraq and Libya indicates that other factors are also important.

There are a number of additional interesting features (see ★Table A in ★Appendix 1), which are highlighted below:

1. Egypt, despite wars and the long military confrontation between 1967 and 1973, maintained a steady numerical growth. It generates the largest Arab research output. Saudi Arabia and/or Tunisia appear to be candidates for the position of leading research producer of the region. Egypt has an enormous reserve of underutilized human capital. It has yet to adopt effective policies to benefit from its science and technology capabilities and to develop and manage its human capital.

2. It is useful to recall that Egypt is a regional pioneer in the domain of higher education and science. This goes back to the era of Muhammad Ali at the beginning of the nineteenth century. Egypt had a university graduating 200 engineers a year in 1945 when British universities were graduating, for all of Britain, 800 engineers a year.[8] Cairo University sponsored research when no others in the region, except the Jewish universities in Palestine, did so. Despite this head start and the abundance of human capital, Egypt failed to take off. Incompetent policies and management aborted the process. We will see in chapter 8 that the factors that have prevented Egypt from benefiting from its rich supply of human capital still operate because of poor university-industry collaboration.

3. By contrast, Sudan's R&D, which was in third place after Egypt and Lebanon in 1967–1976, crumbled when the country suffered political unrest. A similar fate befell Lebanon, which was the second

Table 2.2 Neck and neck race of Egypt, Maghreb, and GCC

Area	2005	2006	2007	2008	2009	2010
Egypt	4,408	4,949	5,508	6,215	7,748	7,669
Maghreb	4,382	5,348	6,061	8,689	8,689	7,201
GCC	5,042	5,546	6,136	6,933	8,314	9,274

Source: Appendix 1

largest producer of R&D until 1975. R&D activity in Lebanon partially collapsed in 1975. Lebanon has made some recovery since then and is currently in 5th place, while Sudan was in 14th place among the Arab countries in 2007.

4. The GCC and the Maghreb countries had no significant presence in research until 1990, after which they exhibited a steady growth. Table 2.2 shows the combined output of the Maghreb and GCC compared with Egypt during the 2005–2010 period. The GCC has the highest output in four out of six years, the Maghreb was in first position during two years out of six, and Egypt was in second position during 2005 and 2010. The population of the Maghreb countries was 77.3 million, Egypt's population was 83 million, and the GCC had a population of 37.9 million in 2009. The GCC countries lead in per capita output during the entire period.

5. Egypt, Saudi Arabia, and Tunisia, the three leading Arab countries, are also competing for first and second position. The Saudi/Egypt ratios for 2003, 2007, and 2010 were 0.55, 0.48, and 0.68, respectively. The Tunisia/Egypt ratios for the same three years were 0.32, 051, and 0.53. The Tunisia/Saudi ratios for the same three years were 0.58, 1.05, and 0.78.

It is difficult not to sense the competition between the Arab countries. Competition is healthy and natural and has been noted in numerous other regions of the world and between universities in most industrial countries.

Arab R&D and Graduate Education

Graduate schools are key organizations in national development. They provide the opportunities for academic researchers to

- contribute to the shaping of national science policies,
- identify national priorities and needs,

- help develop collaborative relationships between the research community and the economy, and
- serve as intermediaries for the flow of knowledge.

In industrial countries, universities are no longer the major producers of research, although they remain leading centers for fundamental research and scholarship. At the present stage of Arab development, it is to be expected that most (about 40 to 90 percent) of the R&D output is from universities (including medical schools) and hospitals.

Arab higher education has not yet opted for research-based graduate schools.[9] Saudi Arabia, however, announced in 2008 its plans to establish a research-based graduate school. This will be the first full-fledged graduate school in the Arab world. When these plans fully materialize, they are expected to have a massive impact on R&D in the region. Naturally, the Saudi initiative may lead to other Arab countries adopting similar policies and to an intensification of competition.

For the past several years Saudi Arabia has been seeking to integrate its national R&D with its economy. This move may terminate the dominance of technological dependence (and its powerful expression in technology-free turnkey contracts),[10] which has been an obstacle to benefiting from available scientific and technological competences.

Changes in R&D Output among the Arab Countries

The relative standing of the Arab states over the past 40 years has undergone considerable changes. There are further major changes in the making, and it is likely that current trends will intensify in the immediate future.

In table 2.3, I have grouped the Arab countries to better illustrate these changes. The Maghreb (Algeria, Morocco, and Tunisia) and the GCC countries have been exhibiting similar behavior, and they have been grouped together to compare them with Egypt and Iraq, and Jordan, Lebanon, and Syria.

The GCC output equaled that of Egypt in 1988 and they became for one year the largest publishing group within the Arab world. The GCC countries maintained parity with Egypt until 2001. Since then, both Egypt and the GCC have lost some ground to the Maghreb, but the GCC countries have partially recaptured leadership during the 2005–2010 period. As discussed earlier, the GCC and the Maghreb are neck and neck.

On a per capita basis, the GCC countries have remained in the lead, followed by the Maghreb countries. Iraq, Syria, Libya, Sudan, and Yemen make no significant contribution to Arab R&D output, and there are no

Table 2.3   Trends in Arab research output, 1967–2010

	Egypt	GCC countries	Iraq	Maghreb countries	Jordan, Lebanon, Syria
% Population	25	9	9	31	9
Year					
1967	63	2	7	8	13
1968	60	3	6	10	14
1969	60	2	7	9	13
1970	59	2	6	11	13
1971	59	3	7	13	14
1972	59	3	6	12	13
1973	52	7	7	14	14
1974	54	6	6	10	17
1975	55	6	7	12	15
1976	55	9	7	12	9
1977	49	11	12	14	8
1978	47	15	11	14	7
1979	46	15	11	14	7
1980	46	17	10	15	7
1981	42	20	8	15	8
1982	41	23	7	13	9
1983	40	25	7	13	8
1984	42	27	6	13	7
1985	39	27	7	13	9
1986	38	30	7	12	8
1987	38	32	6	12	8
1988	35	36	6	13	8
1989	39	33	7	12	7
1990	37	36	5	12	7
1991	37	33	3	15	6
1992	35	32	2	17	7
1993	33	34	2	16	8
1994	33	34	2	16	9
1995	32	33	1	18	8
1996	33	38	1	19	10
1997	31	36	0.9	20	7
1998	30	35	0.8	22	10
1999	29	34	0.6	24	10
2000	29	33	0.6	24	
2001	30	32	0.6	24	
2002	30	31	1.1	25	
2003	29	32		25	
2004	28	31		27	
2005	27	31		27	11
2006	26	29		28	11
2007	26	29		29	
2008	25	27		31	
2009	26	28	1.7	29	11
2010	26	31		27	10

Source: Appendix 1

Note: The total of each row does not equal 100 percent since Libya, Mauritania, Somalia, Sudan, and Yemen are not included. These countries (with 17 percent of the population of the Arab world) contribute some 5 percent to Arab output.

signs that this will change in the foreseeable future. Needless to say, these countries could, given the appropriate policies, equal or outproduce the other regions.

Qatar and the UAE are currently increasing the numbers of expatriate professors. These undertake research in their mother universities and cite Qatar or the UAE as an affiliation.

This may, or may not, be meaningful or useful to these two countries.[11]

The sudden increase noted in the R&D output of Qatar and the UAE has this activity as its origin. Yet, the unexpected may happen.

The majority of the scientists staffing research laboratories in most Arab countries are nationals of those countries. The only region that recruits expatriates in substantial numbers is the GCC. The insecurity and impermanence of jobs in the GCC region limits the benefits that may be derived from the importation of scientists. A study of the successful American experience with emigrant scientists could provide useful insights to planners of science in GCC countries.

The model of the United States, which imports scientific human resources globally, is not relevant to Qatar and the UAE. The United States adopts comprehensively the emigrant, including accepting him or her as a citizen. This is not the case in Qatar or the UAE. Furthermore, scientists in the United States, whether foreign-born or US born, operate within well-defined national programs designed and managed by American scientists and organizations. These organizations base their programs on publicly debated studies. Funding is related to the priorities identified through public studies and debates. This is not the case in either Qatar or the UAE or any other Arab country. There are no scientific societies, no science policy research, and no public debates. It is obvious that this problem is deeply integrated with the political economies of these countries.

Sudan has considerable human resources, most of which has been drained or incapacitated by its political culture. It is difficult to speculate about Sudan's future. Yet, if Sudan's enormous resources are tapped intelligently, there is no end to what it can achieve.

R&D output in most Arab countries is produced by a small proportion of the academic staff. Probably no more than 10–15 percent of medical doctors, science professors, and professors of engineering make research contributions.

What do Arab Scientists Research?[12]

Tables 2.4 to 2.7 and ★Table 2.8 present the distribution of research output by subject areas. The data as compiled from SCOPUS implies

Table 2.4   Output in basic sciences, 2005

Country	Physics & Astronomy	Mathematics	Chemistry	Biochemistry & Biology	Total
Algeria	256	154	121	62	593
Bahrain	18	8		10	36
Egypt	582	270	799	353	2,004
Iraq	15	5	24	10	54
Jordan	114	104	100	129	447
Kuwait	25	38	52	85	200
Lebanon	63	42	42	202	349
Libya	12	3	12	11	38
Mauritania	3	5	1	0	9
Morocco	198	184	163	111	656
Oman	39	33	19	21	112
Palestine	20	11	20	8	59
Qatar	14	8	14	7	43
KSA	159	179	191	175	704
Sudan	3	0	4	18	25
Syria	37	1	16	22	76
Tunisia	221	139	147	195	702
UAE	56	81	38	86	261
Yemen	4	0	6	6	16
Total	**1,839**	**1,265**	**1,769**	**1,511**	**6,384**

Source: Scopus.

multiple counting of some of the papers.[13] ★Table 2.8 reflects the impact of multiple counting on the totals.

One can see from tables 2.4 to 2.7 and ★Table 2.8 that the bulk of the R&D work is in clinical medicine, agriculture, and engineering. The 6,384 papers published in 2005 listed under the basic sciences cover essentially six very large areas of science: astronomy, physics, mathematics, chemistry, biology, and biochemistry, produced mainly in ten different countries. The remaining 11 Arab countries contribute very little. The bulk of the papers are on traditional topics. Research in fields such as molecular biology, genetics, nanotechnology, new materials, advanced areas of plasma physics or elementary particles, and advanced areas of computer sciences exists but on a limited scale.

In 2005 there were 6,660 papers published in the medical sciences, 1,477 in the agricultural sciences, and 7,057 in the applied sciences. The ratio of applied science papers to basic science papers is equal to 3:5. Yet, despite this high level of concentration in the applied sciences, one does not find significant self-reliance.

Table 2.5 Output in medical sciences, 2005

Country	Dentistry	Medicine	Pharmacology Toxicology	Immunology	Neuro-Science	Health Profession	Nursing	Total
Algeria	0	42	14	10	4		4	70
Bahrain	0	118	5	7	5	4	0	143
Egypt	18	839	220	129	34	0	4	1,240
Iraq	0	77	0	6	0	5	4	92
Jordan	35	242	51	40	44	0	0	412
Kuwait	25	268	48	0	17	0	0	358
Lebanon	0	821	32	84	61	68	23	1,089
Libya	0	17	0	7	0	1	0	25
Mauritania	0	4	1	1	2	0	0	8
Morocco	0	286	32	39	29	0	0	386
Oman	0	128	7	0	9	0	0	144
Palestine	1	30	4	5	0	0	0	40
Qatar	2	113	8	4	5	0	0	132
KSA	35	850	112	59	50	17	0	1,123
Sudan	2	78	6	39	0	2	1	128
Syria	6	45	4	6	1	0	0	62
Tunisia	0	652	37	97	31	32	0	849
UAE	0	226	30	26	32	0	0	314
Yemen	0	35	5	3	1	1	0	45
Total	**124**	**4,871**	**616**	**562**	**325**	**130**	**32**	**6,660**

Source: Scopus.

The impact of the quality of Arab medical schools and schools of agriculture may be seen in the medical and agricultural sectors (discussed in chapter 3).

The total number of papers on earth sciences (geology, hydrology) was 649, on chemical engineering the number was 1,030, and on the science of the environment it was 778.

The acuteness of Arab water problems, the chemical engineering requirements of its petroleum and other chemical industries, the environmental problems arising from climate change, desertification, and pollution all require a much greater effort. Yet, available research capabilities are underutilized as a consequence of the heavy dependence on foreign consulting and contracting services.

Pharmaceutical companies in the region have developed capabilities for the production of generic drugs. Some of these firms have been exporting drugs to the European and US markets. In view of such success in an important industry, it would have been constructive to extend the capabilities of these companies. Such an objective would require considerable

Table 2.6   The output in agriculture, 2005

Country	Agricultural	Veterinary	Total
Algeria	67	3	70
Bahrain	12	0	12
Egypt	344	50	394
Iraq	11	6	17
Jordan	111	15	126
Kuwait	27	0	27
Lebanon	60	0	60
Libya	9	0	9
Mauritania	10	2	12
Morocco	135	16	151
Oman	47	7	54
Palestine	10	0	10
Qatar	7	0	7
KSA	75	20	95
Sudan	48	18	66
Syria	80	2	82
Tunisia	192	20	212
UAE	52	20	72
Yemen	1	0	1
Total	**1,298**	**179**	**1,477**

Source: Scopus

Table 2.7 The output in applied sciences, 2005

Country	Environmental Science	Earth & Planetary Science	Engineering	Chemical Engineering	Computer Science	Material Science	Total
Algeria	35	32	330	78	133	0	608
Bahrain	7	8	40	9	9	12	85
Egypt	188	173	820	300	133	560	2,174
Iraq	7	0	34	3	3	7	54
Jordan	80	56	211	88	73	80	588
Kuwait	43	0	162	68	0	0	273
Lebanon	51	24	198	31	0	37	341
Libya	7	6	28	21	3	7	72
Mauritania	2	6	0	0	1	0	9
Morocco	94	80	122	67	51	19	433
Oman	22	41	111	26	23	0	223
Palestine	21	9	25	8	6	0	69
Qatar	13	8	48	23	4	9	105
KSA	71	65	366	137	79	128	846
Sudan	5	6	0	0	1	0	12
Syria	21	23	13	9	2	0	68
Tunisia	64	63	270	99	98	0	594
UAE	43	41	258	62	77	0	481
Yemen	4	8	9	1	0	0	22
Total	778	649	3,045	1,030	696	859	7,057

Source: Scopus.

academic research support in pharmacology and related disciplines. The small research output of 616 publications from the entire Arab world in the pharma area is certainly too limited a research base for a modern pharmaceutical industry.

Since the late 1990s, increasing efforts were deployed in some Arab countries to link R&D to applications in industry; however, progress has been slow. The intentions are there, but the enabling environment is either weak or nonexistent. SABIC, the leading Saudi petrochemical firm, has been a diligent pursuant of local R&D to support its industrial expansion. Continued success in this effort could establish them as a role model in the region.

The R&D output in the applied sciences provides a starting point. Only five countries had an output above 500 publications in all the applied sciences in 2005: Algeria, 608; Egypt, 2,174; Jordan, 588; Saudi Arabia, 846; and Tunisia, 594. Nine had an output of less than 100. Half the output in the applied sciences was in civil and mechanical engineering. Yet the Arab world still imports these technologies, and they are far from making efforts for utilizing local capabilities or seeking self-sufficiency.

★Table 2.8 shows the totals of tables 2.4 to 2.7 and compares the resultant total 21,578 with the total number of 16,232 papers published in 2005. We note that the method SCOPUS utilized to organize the data by subject areas (owing to double counting) leads to an increase in paper count by a third.

Concluding Remarks

The research output of the entire Arab world is now comparable to that of an active small industrial country. However, the limited availability of scientific societies or of integrative science and technology infrastructure prevents the Arab countries from benefiting from regionally available capabilities.

CHAPTER 3

R&D AND ITS FUNCTIONS

Introduction

In this chapter we examine the functions and significance of R&D activity. We shall explore the relationships in Arab R&D activity to

1. identify priorities,
2. compare Arab R&D output with that of other developing and industrial countries, and
3. search for the turning point in the volume of R&D output in relation to economic takeoff in developing countries.

Judging by the performance of most countries during the late eighteenth and early nineteenth centuries, all that is needed for a start in science "is common sense." The initiation of development in a nation does not need advanced scientific capabilities. This is why the Japanese in 1860 could decide what to do, despite the fact that, at the time, they were not knowledgeable in any modern science.

At the initiation of the process of development, the most crucial requirement, dictated by common sense, is self-reliance. To understand the importance of self-reliance, no formal education is required. Without an unshakeable commitment to self-reliance, almost all other effort is wasted.

In today's globalized world, a critical problem that confronts a developing country is how to relate to the outside world in a self-reliant manner. Industrial countries have established and developed a vast array of organizations with considerable technological capabilities. These organizations can design and build an industrial city in a remote area in record time, or can repair the Hubble Telescope in outer space. Arab countries, who can afford these services, are generally tempted to let such overseas firms get on with the job of their development.

Naturally, if such capable firms are invited to parachute their skills into industrial cities, harbors, pipelines, railway systems, and airports, the "native" human resources will never have a chance to acquire similar capabilities. Furthermore, national economies will be unable to benefit from the associated multiplier factors of such a development.

Work is the fabric that holds societies together. Through working together, people get to know each other, learn to collaborate, build their institutions, and develop their culture. This is why all countries that are concerned with their socioeconomic and cultural development make the effort to mobilize their limited resources to participate, with those possessing the know-how, in progressively acquiring the capabilities to build their own countries.

There is a great deal to learn from major multinational firms when designing and constructing major projects. Self-reliant societies seek to relate to these powerhouses of technological and managerial capabilities in a manner that enables them to participate fully in the process of national construction. We observe that countries that have mastered efficient methods for acquiring know-how attain the standards of OECD countries and join the club.

It is counterproductive to deploy R&D resources to rediscover the wheel; it may often be cheaper, faster, and better to learn (from the published literature) how to construct and use it. Buying the wheel ready-made is economically advantageous. Creative energy should be deployed to research more relevant topics.

Arab countries, for a variety of political reasons, as well as because of large differences in their factor endowments, have generally preferred to seek the fast road of commissioning the masters of technology to undertake their major projects, with limited or no local participation.

This approach enables political leaders to act independently of their societies and thus to demonstrate their full independence: some leaders seem to believe that their dependence on foreign firms and governments is less demanding than dependence on their societies.

There have been some successful exceptions to this approach. Private engineering firms throughout the Arab world emerged and participated in important developmental activities. Some governments have adopted a technology-transfer model, such as that of the Syrian government with the erstwhile USSR in the construction of the Euphrates Dam. As a result, Syria gained a number of major contracting companies.[1]

The efforts deployed in the Arab world in the direction of the acquisition of technological capabilities have been far less than those made in other developing countries. The bottlenecks have originated in an inability to support collaborative pan-Arab policies. This is despite numerous attempts, at the highest levels, by various regional organizations to promote pan-Arab collaboration.

Developing labor skills and adopting quality control measures are neither difficult nor expensive, yet the Arab countries have lagged behind most other nations in this direction. As a result, labor productivity is poor, and the Arab countries resort to recruiting massively from abroad when their own labor remains largely unemployed.

Limited public debates on national and regional policies and the shortcomings in mobilizing the population contribute to this sad situation. A society and its political leadership clarify their functions and relationships through public debate in order to define challenges and priorities. As a collateral benefit, they learn to identify their comparative advantages and to focus attention on important practical issues.

Arab scientific and technological human resources are truly considerable, and these could be readily increased and strengthened. But these are not structured in effective professional societies and organizations capable of raising issues and finding answers. Opportunities for serious policy analysis in the Arab world are limited. The cultivated absence of reliable and up-to-date statistical data protects the patronage system and its dependants.

A recent study of the era of Fuad Chehab, president of the Republic of Lebanon (1958–1964), illustrates the resistance to even modest national reforms in at least one Arab country.[2] There is a shortage of literature on past attempts to reform government in the region.

Relationship of R&D to National Priorities and to the Sustenance of Higher Learning

In the industrial era, R&D has become the oxygen of sustainable development and national security. We shall examine below the relationship of R&D to the sectors of health and agriculture and its importance to the maintenance and development of Arab universities.

The relentless advances in science render any academic not engaged in research obsolete in a short time. Thus, for a university to be able to educate its students to current international standards, its faculty must be enabled to maintain itself through R&D.

I have chosen 17 research topics as indicators of relevant R&D activity. The measure of the commitment of Arab countries to these micro-objectives is determined by the amount of research undertaken on these topics in their universities. One could have chosen any other set of research topics as indicators of R&D activity and arrived at similar results.

Macro-National Objectives: Health and Agriculture

Health and agriculture are of considerable importance to all societies. It is natural that these two areas of science and technology were of concern to all Arab countries when they secured their independence. Arab performance in health and agriculture will be compared with that of China and India to obtain a measure of the degree of achievement.

Most Arab countries had been under colonial domination and could not undertake even modest improvements until they attained their independence. The approach of most Arab governments to both these priority fields was extensive but not comprehensive. Their efforts entailed establishing educational organizations, supporting some research, sending students abroad to continue their studies, and setting up medical schools, hospitals, and extension services.

Health

Life expectancy at birth is an indication of the quality of a country's health services. Life span in a country is the result of a combination of factors, the most important being

- clean water and sewage disposal (this is an input by civil engineering and socially responsible government), and
- good nutrition and adequate primary health care (a product of medical schools, medical research, and the adoption of appropriate health policies).

Advanced countries give high priority to R&D in health matters. This may be partly because politicians are generally older and are concerned with their own health, and thus are prone to support research funding for the medical sciences. In developing countries, the wealthy class and the politicians have access to health services in industrial countries.

*Table 3.1 shows the standing of the Arab countries in life expectancy in comparison with three developing countries (Brazil, China, and India) and three advanced countries (Israel, Switzerland, and Sweden).

The highest life expectancy (78.4 years) in 2007 was attained in the UAE; most of the rest of Arab countries had a score above 70 years. Only three had their life expectancy below 70 in 2008; these were Djibouti, Sudan, and Yemen. India, one of the three developing countries chosen for comparison, had a life expectancy of 64. All three advanced countries had a life expectancy above 80.

Clearly the Arab countries are doing credible work in the health domain, though there is scope for significant improvements. The problems that they confront have little to do with the education of medical doctors, since the Arab world is an important exporter of medical expertise to Europe and North America. Improving the present state of health has more to do with the availability of education to all, the management and quality of existing services, and their extension to rural and impoverished areas.

Agriculture

Agriculture contributes to the management of the environment and produces food. A good government is concerned with promoting agricultural productivity as well as the improvement of nutrition. Agriculture is important to the Arab world for five additional reasons:

- More than half of all Arab food supplies are imported.
- The Arab countries have fertile land that is either not utilized or is low in productivity.
- Water use in agriculture is of low efficiency and wasteful.
- Arab agriculture is a major employer: almost 30 percent of the labor force is still employed in agriculture, compared with less than 5 percent in industrial countries.
- Rapid population growth is creating increased demand for food supplies and leading to high levels of unemployment, which is contributing to increased poverty and accelerated emigration.

To the credit of the Arab governments (*Table 3.2), the progress made by Arab farmers between 1975 and 1985 and between 1995 and 1997 was greater than the absolute value added by Chinese and Indian farmers in 1995–1997. But they have failed to make use of their scientific capabilities to seek parity with Europe and the United States in agricultural productivity.

The Arab world has the internal market to absorb a doubling of agricultural production. Furthermore, both the human and natural resources (including water) and the capital required to transform the agricultural sector are either locally or regionally available. Organizational and institutional obstacles have so far held back progress in this sector.

Between 1979 and 1985 and between 1995 and 1997 Saudi Arabia registered a six-fold growth in value added per worker as a result of its investment in the sector. However, Singapore's value added in agriculture was nearly four times greater than that of Saudi Arabia in 1995–1997.

The fact that the value added per Arab farmer is about 5 percent of that of a farmer in the industrialized countries is a measure of the opportunities facing the Arab countries. Science and technology are available to Arab countries; the challenge is to apply them suitably.

In the 1990s, only five Arab countries were significant producers of agricultural output: Egypt, Saudi Arabia, Morocco, Algeria, and Syria. (World Bank data did not include any information on Iraq in the 1990s.)

The development of the agricultural sector requires significant mechanization and reduction of farm labor. The agricultural sector is not undergoing a sufficiently rapid transformation to achieve this, and there is a need to accelerate the process.

No significant industrialization has taken place in the Arab world in order to absorb the available farm labor. Furthermore, some 30 million expatriate workers were imported to provide construction and other services instead of retraining rural native labor.

The Arab agricultural sector suffers from being located in the most arid region of the world. Water resources and management are crucial to agricultural production. Arab scientists have been contributing to the knowledge of Arab water resources. *Table 3.3 shows data on value added with respect to water use in total agricultural production. It is clear from this that there are significant differences in the efficiency with which water is used in different Arab countries: compare the performance of Jordan and Syria with that of Lebanon.

The value added by a farmer (*Table 3.2) in Finland, France, the Netherlands, or Singapore is some 30 times that of the Arab world (except for Saudi Arabia).

*Table 3.3 shows key indicators of the performance of the Arab countries with respect to water use in agriculture and total agricultural production. No Arab country compares well with European countries, especially with the Netherlands, whether we are examining water use or agricultural value added.

Micro-Priorities and R&D Activity: Seventeen research topics were selected for study. The first eight areas consist of a set of useful topics and the rest reflect activities in new areas of science developed during the past 40 years.

The eight practical topics selected were in research on aquifers, water desalination, solar energy, HIV, corrosion, fuel cells, genetic diseases (of considerable importance because of the high frequency of marriages between first cousins), and climate change.

The nine topics that were examined for their research importance were nanotechnology, black holes, fractals, immune systems, nonlinear dynamics, dark matter, gene transfer, psychiatric genetics, and stem cells.

The SCOPUS research output of the Arab world for 2000 and 2005 was searched for publications[3] on the 17 topics listed in ★Table 3.4.

Research on Topics of Current Practical Importance

The study of aquifers is of critical importance to all Arab countries, since these studies provide the information about where there are substantial amounts of underground water and where water may be stored for long periods of time. It is a good sign that the number of Arab countries studying aquifers increased from three to ten during this period of five years between 2000 and 2005 and that the number of papers on the subject nearly doubled.

Corrosion is an important problem in the oil, gas, and water industries, and it costs large sums of money to combat. It is a good sign that there is an increase in interest in the subject. Such an interest should contribute to improved management of pipelines as well as water distribution systems where water leaks, in many countries, exceed 40 percent.

Fuel cells provide a method for generating electricity directly from burning fuel. Some specialists believe that fuel cells will provide a new compact and efficient method for generating electricity. There is mildly increasing interest in this field in the region; however, the current effort is not significant.

Interest in HIV research appears to be on a limited scale and is not expanding. HIV is a very dangerous disease. Let us hope that the Arab countries will not be afflicted with it; nevertheless, it is knowledge that should be acquired in case it is suddenly needed. The skills acquired in researching retroviruses will also be useful in treating diseases other than HIV.

In some Arab countries, 50 percent of all marriages are between first cousins. It is important to counsel young people about the dangers involved in this model. Here the level of interest in the subject is limited considering the scale of the phenomenon. Furthermore, research on genetic diseases is an important research area of molecular biology.

Surprisingly, there is very little interest in research in solar energy in the land of sunshine. Clearly this is not a good omen for the future, especially as the UAE is investing billions of dollars in a modern city (Masdar) designed and built by international contractors. The GCC countries are expected to invest some $200 billion over the coming two decades in devices to generate renewable energy.[4] It is difficult to see the benefits for the GCC from Masdar or from investments in renewable energy without increasing the scale of both serious local R&D in these fields and the support of local and regional consulting and contracting organizations specialized in these technologies. Clearly, efforts need to be undertaken on a regional scale before they can yield significant benefits.[5]

Water desalination is a strategic technology for all Arab countries. A manual search of the database showed that there was more interest in desalination than is reflected in ★Table 3.4.

Nevertheless, the extent of concern with this technology is not commensurate with the scale of the industry in the Arab countries. These countries are the largest consumers of water desalination technologies.

Some entries concerning research in climate change was not included in ★Table 3.4 because the main participants were not based in the Arab world. Furthermore, the number of authors was very large (probably of the order of 50). Clearly, there is little local contribution to this topic. Arab interest in climate change appears to be insignificant.

The remaining nine topics in ★Table 3.5, except for nanotechnology and graphene, are research fields from the 1950–1980 period. Graphene was dropped from the table for lack of activity. Research on the immune system has been growing in importance as doctors have been learning more about the numerous diseases afflicting it. All of these research fields are failing to attract research interests commensurate with their importance.

Performance of Arab Countries in the Priority Areas

The information recorded in ★Tables 3.4 and 3.5 is used to estimate the entries in ★Table 3.6. The purpose is to obtain information on the responsiveness of the different Arab countries to national priorities and to advances in science.

The UAE and Saudi Arabia, relative newcomers in research, are in the lead. Egypt performed poorly by being involved in only 3 out of 17 areas in 2000, but it improved by 2005 by becoming involved in 8 out of

17 areas. Saudi Arabia's standing declined from being in the lead in 2000 to being in third place in 2005. It increased, however, its diversification from six areas in 2000 to seven in 2005.

In *Tables 3.4 and 3.5 the number after the name of the country is the number of contributions that scientists in that country made in that year to the designated field. In *Table 3.6 the number after the country is the number of areas (out of 17) to which scientists in that country contributed.

In 2000, Saudi scientists made 37 contributions to 6 different areas. This was the largest contribution and the largest degree of research diversification within the region during 2000. In 2005, Saudi Arabia's scientists made 37 contributions to corrosion studies as well as a total of 47 contributions to 7 areas.

In 2005, scientists in Egypt and the UAE made 22 and 18 contributions to 10 and 8 areas, respectively; while scientists in Kuwait and Lebanon made 8 contributions each to 5 areas.

Kuwait, Lebanon, and Tunisia made 12, 11, and 4 contributions, respectively, to 4 (Lebanon) and 3 (Kuwait and Tunisia) areas. Morocco made 19 contributions, all to corrosion. All the other countries contributed either to one area or to two out of the chosen 17 topics. In other words, not a very edifying performance.

Moza al-Rabban decided to pursue another approach to determine the standing of the Arab countries in genetics, biochemistry, molecular biology, immunology, and related subjects. She searched ISI for the output of the Arab countries over the past decade (2001–2010) in these fields. At the same time, she sought only those who received a high level of citations. She was able to find 31 scientists located in the Arab countries who have published a substantial number of papers and received high levels of citations. The range of publications by different authors was between 4 and 125, which received between 261 and 1,532 citations.

The scientists were all Arab and were distributed amongst the Arab countries as follows: Saudi Arabia, eight (plus one shared with Lebanon); Lebanon, seven (one of whom is shared with Saudi Arabia); UAE and Tunisia, four scientists each; Egypt, three scientists; Algeria, Iraq, Jordan, Morocco, Oman, and Sudan, one each. More than a quarter of the scientists were women.

Among the seven scientists from Lebanon, four were based at USJ and three at AUB, of whom one was associated with a Saudi organization. Of the eight scientists in Saudi Arabia, five were located at the King Feisal Hospital, one at King Saud University, and one each at two army hospitals.

Syria had no scientists in that specialty, but Mohamad Khair Taha, a Syrian, had excelled at the Institut Pasteur in Paris. He is a leading authority with 53 contributions and 1,553 citations.[6]

It is noteworthy that many Arab countries have shown increasing, but modest, research activity in molecular biology over the period 2000–2010.

How Does Scientific Research Become Operationally Useful to a Country?

Numerous advantages accrue to a scientist and to his country from research activity. The most obvious is that the scientist becomes more competent in his discipline. University professors engaged in research will be able to graduate students who have received up-to-date education. There is not much value in graduating medical doctors and engineers unaware of what all have happened in their fields during the past decade.

Researchers provide channels through which international information may be sought. They will realize this advantage once they are affiliated to organizations "linked" to higher education and the economy, as discussed in greater detail in chapter 4.

In a region dominated by oil and gas, it should be advantageous to become self-reliant in the management and development of these assets. Furthermore, as the world economy moves away from the use of oil and gas as sources of energy, it is of vital importance to the countries in the region to develop alternative industrial uses for oil and gas—and there are many such uses.

Finally, scientists engaged in frontline research are able to alert their countries to the implications of advances in science, thus giving them time to plan and respond.

R&D in Small and Large Countries

Does the size of a country affect the quality of the science it produces? Do large countries have "better" science or just "more" science?

Empirically, one finds that the *quality* of scientific activity is not dependent on the size of a nation. A very large nation may have scientific activity below the quality of a small nation, and vice versa. Small nations such as Sweden and Switzerland have been able to attain a quality for their science on par with that of leading nations such as the United States. Parity in the quality of science is more important than parity in scale: it allows a small scientific community to exchange knowledge with any other nation, while quantity, without quality, does not provide a similar advantage.

Countries such as Sweden, Switzerland, Australia, France, and Israel have a smaller output than the United States, the UK, and Japan. Yet they have attained scientific parity with leading countries and can exchange knowledge with them without difficulty. A recent survey of the views of scientists and the public in the United States concerning its international standing in science found that only 49 percent of the scientists and 17 percent of the public believe that the United States is the dominant scientific power in the world.[7]

Some of the processes of scientific exchange are mechanical and are carried out via the Internet and the exchange of publications. However, "frontline" knowledge is transferred from one scientist to another, usually through personal contacts. This is where the parity in the quality of science is of vital importance: unless there is parity, the scientists will not be able to belong to the same invisible colleges and thus enjoy the advantages of informal and direct communication with leading scientists.

Countries need little besides high quality scientific capabilities to take off. China and India became nuclear powers and achieved many other scientific feats in the 1970s when their research output was fairly small. In both countries there was a firm national commitment to supporting and benefiting from their scientific capabilities.

As late as the 1990s, and *on a per capita* basis, the research output of the Arab world was "numerically" ahead of both China and India. But the Arab countries provide limited support to their scientific communities and do not pursue a policy of self-reliance. They did not achieve any significant scientific attainments by comparison with China and India, except in the fields of health and agriculture.

Until 1985, Brazil and South Korea had a smaller R&D per capita output than the Arab world (★Table 3.7). But South Korea, Brazil, and China charged ahead, and the Arab countries did not.

Once China, South Korea, and Brazil decided to move full steam ahead, their need for scientific capabilities increased dramatically and they acted accordingly. Thus, China increased its output between 1995 and 2000, 2000 and 2005, and 1995 and 2007 by factors of 2.7, 3.4, and 12, respectively. By contrast, the Arab world increased its output between 1995 and 2007 by only 2.3 times, while South Korea increased it by a factor of 8 during this same period.

In 2009, Manmohan Singh, the prime minister of India, announced "an increase in government investment in science and technology from the present 1 percent of GDP to 2 percent over the next year or two."

Furthermore, India is establishing a number of new organizations to support and develop national scientific capabilities.[8] China has been increasing its support of R&D at the rate of 20 percent annually for the past decade.

Formation of Regional and International Cooperative Research Organizations

Scientific research is competitive, and no scientist wishes to take second place; thus, the speed with which projects are completed is important. Countries with limited resources have to plan and organize their work to enable them to compete effectively with research groups in better-endowed countries.

Different approaches have been pursued to attain this objective, depending on the size of the facilities required and the nature of the work. A large country (such as the United States) would establish regional national laboratories (such as the Fermi Lab in Chicago and Brookhaven on Long Island) to serve all its interested scientists.

In countries with a shortage of scientists, such as Sweden and Japan, companies established research centers in foreign countries to benefit from the availability of human resources there. The United States has successfully learnt to solve its shortage of scientific expertise through attracting international talent; several European countries have lately decided to adopt a similar approach.

In research areas where massive amounts of funding are necessary and the facilities required are expensive, European governments learnt very early the importance of cooperation in order to share the cost of joint laboratories.

One brilliant and successful solution was the Conseil Européen pour la Recherche Nucléaire (CERN) in Geneva. CERN was established when European countries realized that none of them could undertake research in fundamental particle physics on their own. This centre recently launched the most expensive experiment in the history of science (with a cost in excess of $ 1 billion). CERN has been a brilliant success and has led to many collateral benefits.

There is now a wide variety of such cooperative research centers of different sizes in different fields, with varying numbers of partners. An interesting, well-established model is that of the Consultative Group on International Agricultural Research (CGIAR), which manages more than 21 international research centers in the field of agriculture spread around the world. One of them, the International Centre for Agricultural Research in the Dry Areas (ICARDA), is based near Aleppo in Syria.

The Arab countries experimented successfully with the Arab Centre for the Study of Arid Zones and Dry Lands (ACSAD) near Damascus, and the Gulf Organization for Industrial Chemicals (GOIC) in Doha, among others. They have yet to fully exploit these models.

Strong national research traditions facilitate collaboration among nations. This is especially true in the basic sciences, where the scientific standing of the participants is of paramount importance. By contrast, the purpose of applied research is to develop, adapt, and attain some specific objectives. The existence of well-defined objectives helps to focus the attention of the management of such cooperative operations.

These cooperative ventures have generally been very successful. This success should not surprise us, since scientists are selected on the basis of their competence rather than on their political, religious, national, or ethnic affiliations.

R&D Levels at Takeoff

In self-reliant countries, R&D activity, no matter how modest, has both a direct and indirect impact on economic planning and thinking. Local R&D provides the major connection that the country has with international science.

When the governments of South Korea, China, and India needed foreign advice and technical services, they sought it through national organizations in a mode that led to the acquisition of additional expertise as well as the strengthening of national scientific organizations. The turnkey contracts awarded to international firms with no strings attached regarding technology transfer and with no local participation, so popular in the Arab world, are unknown in these countries.

★Table 3.7 and table 3.8 show the changes in research output of various countries near takeoff. South Korea began its national effort toward modernization and self-reliance in the 1960s. Overcoming the consequences of the "civil war" between North and South Korea was a major burden. It was not until the 1970s that serious progress began to be registered by South Korea's modernization effort. At that time, higher education and R&D were still on a modest scale. The per capita research output per million in 1981 was half the value of the Arab output. But by 1980 South Korea was already in takeoff mode; by 1985 its output became

Table 3.8   Number of publications (per million inhabitants)

Country	1981	1985	1990	1995	2000	2005	2007
Arab world	11	15	25.6	26.7	30.6	42.2	44.7
China	1	3	7.9	14.0	36.7	121.9	154.4
India	17	15	14.9	14.1	23.1	33.4	41.1
Brazil	—	—	20.9	32.9	85.1	121.9	161.1
S. Korea	6	15	39.4	114.9	363.7	704.4	866.3
Nigeria	—	—	13.4	6.7	9.7	14.9	23.5

Sources: ISI and demographic data from UN sources.

equated with the Arab research output. After 1985 the gap with the Arab world steadily increased. By 2007 South Korea was outproducing the Arab world 20-fold.

If we compare China's performance with that of the Arab countries, we find that it overtook them around 1997. Obviously, China had passed ahead of the Arab world in the military industrial field much earlier.

From the time of its independence, India adopted self-reliant policies; nevertheless, it is still producing scientific publications at a lower level per capita than the Arab countries. It has, however, set in motion recently a number of measures that will increase its R&D output in the immediate future.

Some components of China's and India's systems of higher education are of better quality than those in the Arab world, and their R&D programs are far better integrated with their economies. Both are more active in frontline scientific fields than are the Arab countries.

Nigeria, like the Arab countries, started its own development several years after gaining independence; it is currently lagging behind the Arab world in development.

One can see from ★Table 3.7 that the per capita output of the Arab world is nearly stable at some 2 percent of that of the industrial countries. We can see from the experience of South Korea, Brazil, and China that countries that pursue a culture of self-reliance can move rapidly ahead. Such dynamics are not the result of accident, but rather of deliberate national effort.

By contrast, the Arab countries with a GNP greater than $1.5 trillion in 2007 invest only a few billion dollars annually on R&D (some 0.2 percent of GNP). Arab governments show limited interest in mobilizing and utilizing the scientific and technological capabilities that they possess (see table 3.9).

Table 3.9   Research output in the Arab world and
in industrial countries (per million inhabitants)

Country	1990	2000	2007
Arab world	25.6	30.6	44.7
Australia	739	1,280	2,244
Spain	114	698	1,026
Sweden	1,171	2,000	2,606
Switzerland	1,221	2,288	3,301
France	634	1,017	1,488
Israel	1,474	2,110	2,546

Source: ISI.

Is There Such a Thing as Arab Science?

For "Arab science" to exist, it would be necessary for scientists in the different Arab countries to exchange knowledge, collaborate, participate in the same scientific societies, and share common research centers. These activities do take place, but on a very limited scale. Thus, one is forced to conclude that there is a "limited" Arab science. Scientific activities can be found in 21 Arab states, but there is very limited communication and collaboration between their scientists. The available know-how is fragmented and there is limited diffusion.

The obstacles to the development of an Arab scientific community are many:

- absence of resources to fund cooperative and collaborative research among Arab scientists;
- absence of common facilities to enable cooperation between scientists;[9]
- absence of local scientific periodicals of world standing;
- very limited number of joint research centers and quality graduate schools;
- weak relationships between universities and the economy; and
- absence of significant scientific societies.

Some Arab scientists do make personal efforts to promote such cooperation, but the resources at their disposal are too small to make any difference.

The total Arab capability in science and technology is many times that of any one specific Arab country. Through cooperation, every Arab country can obtain access to the *total* scientific capabilities of the Arab world—which is larger than that of Israel and many small industrial countries. This would be an important "expansion" of competences without significant additional cost. Such collaboration could lead to scientific and financial benefits to all the Arab countries.

Concluding Remarks

It was shown in Chapters 2 and 3 that the Arab countries have sufficient scientific capabilities for "takeoff," just as Korea, China, and India had when they took off. In the areas of health, agriculture, and poverty alleviation, the Arab countries have done relatively well by third world standards. They, however, have the human capital and expertise to do much better than they have done to date.

We have seen from chapter 2 that the Arab countries have a substantial supply of highly qualified human capital in all fields, and that they are a major exporter of world-class talent. So the problems facing them have nothing to do with the availability of university graduates, quality, literacy, or illiteracy. It has to do with policy and the development of the appropriate enabling infrastructure.

Furthermore, in the well-established industries—such as the phosphates, oil and gas, and petrochemicals—there are no good reasons why the Arab countries remain technologically dependent. They have access to technology, and they have the resources, markets, and professional human capital. But they have yet to adopt the appropriate policies to promote national engineering, industrial, consulting, and contracting firms capable of providing services and products in situ.

The half-life of a scientist is at most five to seven years. That is, every seven years, half the population of inactive research scientists become obsolescent and are permanently "damaged." Thus, scientists who have not successfully undertaken any research for 15 years are unlikely to be able to do so in the future. Considerable investments in the education of promising persons are wasted through neglect.

In other words, the billions of dollars that the Arab world is "investing in higher education" is of little use unless there is a reasonably rapid solution to the lack of organizational structures that can draw benefits from these talents.[10]

The advantage of the brain drain is that it allows educated Arabs to lead a successful professional life, whereas many of those who stay home are condemned to professional suicide. However, as far as the Arab countries are concerned, emigrants face the same fate as those who die from obsolescence at home. Unlike Canada, China, India, Korea, and others, there are, so far, no serious efforts to benefit from Arab emigrants.

CHAPTER 4

SCIENCE, UNIVERSITIES, AND ENTERPRISE

Introduction

Science, universities, and enterprises are three entities that are central to all stages of development. In order to function effectively and productively and contribute to national well-being, these three have to be organically linked. In other words, each one of these entities on its own would be of limited value. It is through their cooperative functions that societies derive benefits from labor, educational systems, and science (local and universal). Enterprise incorporates labor in all of its forms: unskilled, skilled, and entrepreneurial.

Science, universities, and enterprise form a triad. The degree of organic integration of this triad is reflected in the quality and value of its material and immaterial outputs. The processes underlying the triad are governed by the national political economy.[1]

The three components of the triad become activated as soon as a country begins to acquire knowledge, foreign and national education, and the importation of equipment and capital goods and the services of foreign experts. For example, Egypt sought foreign education during the regime of Muhammad Ali.[2] Muhammad Ali undertook monumental public works.[3] Yet the methods employed illustrate the absence of serious efforts to organize and mechanize simple canal-clearing operations in order to improve labor efficiency and well-being. Many of the technological advances during the eighteenth and nineteenth centuries were, directly or indirectly, motivated by the pursuit of higher labor efficiency, but this does not appear to have been a matter of concern.

I have shown that in 1952 Egypt and China had an equal number of research personnel; the advanced academic degrees held by Egyptians were earned mostly in the UK.[4] At the time, Egypt had a higher per capita income than did China. China enabled its scientists to be productive, while Egypt failed to do so. These are illustrations of the fact that the "ingredients" for significant advances in the performance of the triad were available in Egypt, but the Egyptian triad did not function appropriately.[5]

Thus, Egypt, which imported locomotives at the same time as Belgium, did not attempt, like Belgium, to manufacture these engines, although this was within its reach at the time. Egypt still imports locomotives; while Belgium began to export them some eight years after their first machines were imported.

Another illustrative example from the perspective of science and technology is Jordan's 1986–1990 Development Plan. This plan illustrates the limitations of Arab planning. In this analysis, five aspects, all central to the triad, were emphasized. These were:

- the place of science in development planning;
- the incorporation of education and labor into planning;
- embodying national instruments of technology acquisition and accumulation in relation to foreign contract awards;
- outsourcing/externalization; and
- the integration of science into project negotiations.[6]

Yet, Jordan did not make appropriate provisions in its plans for any of these aspects, and it continues to neglect the enumerated vital activities that are within its reach.

The argument advanced here is that the obstacle to Arab development is related to the absence of organic relationships between these three critical entities. The continuation of this state of affairs derives from the governing political culture, limited regional collaboration, and the methods adopted by governments for securing international technological services.

The historical root causes of the unraveling and fragmentation of the Arab world probably began with the collapse of their global transport and trading system. Until 1498, this system provided the functional and integrative linkages that sustained the socioeconomic and cultural unity of the people of the Arab and Islamic worlds.

The destruction of this system, beginning with the arrival of the Portuguese in 1498 and ending with the establishment of the three East India Companies (Dutch, British, and French), brought about the end of Arab Asian trade. During this period (1498–1630), creativity in the Arab and Islamic world had already dried up, and the Arabs could not come up with countermeasures to retain some or all of their past economic activities or to invent new ways to earn a living.

Following this unmitigated disaster, the Arab world drifted downward under the protective mantle of the Ottoman Empire—the leading land power at the time. But eventually the Arabs woke up (c. 1798), with Napoleon's army breathing the Nile air. By then, the nascent industrial revolution was facilitating the global spread of European power. With the enormous knowledge gap that had developed during the previous several centuries, the Arab countries had regressed to the extent that they were culturally and politically unable to acquire the newly emerging technologies. Corruption, ignorance, and fragmentation induced by the long mamluk rule, as well as chaos and colonialism, reduced the region to its present state.[7]

The Three Entities and Their Characteristics

This chapter is devoted to a discussion of the internal functioning of the triad, rather than of science, universities, and enterprise. The motivating energy of a country's triad is derived from its creativity. Universities and enterprise are entities empowered by creativity. It is wonderful that some people love and devote their lives to science and enterprise. Their discoveries and knowledge enrich our lives and fuel the global economy. Without their creativity there would be no science and no application of knowledge via enterprise. Without their creativity there would have been no development anywhere at any time.

Despite the fact that scientists are highly motivated and are not demanding, society has still to provide them with basic support to enable them to realize their dreams (they needed libraries 2000 years ago—that is, access to past knowledge—today they need multibillion-dollar laboratories). The cost to society of their education is trivial compared to their contributions to civilization and the economy.

Alan Turing—one of many scientists who made his mark in history and who is the father of computer science—did it all on his own; without him the Allies would have had a much more difficult time defeating the Axis Powers. Yet the "cost of enabling" his creativity is almost zero relative to the enormous benefits that he and others like him generated during the Second World War and thereafter. *The acquisition of scientific capabilities by an individual is relatively easy. Making this capability available to society is triad dependent.*

Industrial societies evolved their management of the three entities in question over several centuries, and they succeeded in attaining a high level of effective integration of triad functions.

The fact that the sciences are taught and researched in universities makes universities important. But unless these centers of diffusion are well connected to potential users, universities cannot make any contributions. The vital connections linking universities to potential users are dependant on the political economy and are essentially beyond the control of university professors.

A modern society develops a wide range of centers of knowledge production, accumulation, and diffusion. These include professional societies, libraries and information services, museums, testing services, quality control and standards services, technical schools, do-it-yourself activities, agricultural extension programs, and many others.

All of these centers are interdependent and complementary. In a modern society, science is like a fluid that can get spread unobstructed throughout the pores of society and its organizations. The easier and simpler the access of labor and enterprises to centers of diffusion, the greater will be their output and their productivity.

Since science and technology are constantly changing, all workers need constant upgrading and training. Different sources of knowledge are accessed separately by each worker. In a properly functioning society each worker knows how to relate to the appropriate diffusion center.

The poor functioning of the triad in Arab countries has been well documented in the literature of the Middle East for almost the past two centuries. I have reviewed illustrative problems elsewhere,[8] and there are numerous reports and studies by various organizations on the subject. A report submitted to the Arab Republic of Egypt in 1995 provides illustrative details of the multitudes of these problems.[9]

Operational Aspects of the Triad

Universities have been in existence for a long time, so we know a great deal about what they do, what they need in order to function properly, and how much they cost.[10] As already noted in chapter 1, competent human capital is essential to enabling a society to be self-reliant and capable of producing the products and services it needs.

We also know a great deal about the activities that universities must undertake to keep their professors qualified to provide relevant and quality education. Universities need to be constantly evolving in relation to advances in the world of knowledge. Science has a universal and unique quality that makes it instantly available everywhere to anybody who possesses the ability to understand it and wishes to access it.

One should add that societies that are unable to stay in tune with the advances of science deteriorate and eventually collapse. We see around us countries such as Sudan, Somalia, Afghanistan, Pakistan, and Yemen that have crumbled, or are in the process of crumbling, before our eyes under the impact of change. They all have universities, but these universities failed to train and graduate the creative minds that could have saved them from their misery.

Fulfilling the expected functions of a university is simply impossible without research and scholarship. The more underdeveloped a society, the greater its need for creativity, scholarship, and genius. Creativity and genius are not more "expensive" than mediocrity. In fact, the opposite is true: the lost opportunities arising from mediocrity are far more costly than the cost of genius. The choice between creativity and mediocrity is a political decision and not a financial one. Hence the Arab countries continue to face the difficulties of being ruled by political cultures that maximize the number of Baumol's type of destructive entrepreneurs on the lookout for an opportunity to drain national treasuries.

We have seen in chapter 2 that Arab R&D is concentrated in scientific fields that are older than 30 years. The rate of scientific advance is very high, as judged by the number of new fields of science at any time. At any one moment it is estimated that a significant proportion of all scientific research activity is on topics that are less than six years old. This means that Arab higher education suffers from a large and expanding "science gap" with other countries.

This does not mean that young Arabs cannot go abroad and "catch up." They do go abroad, and they are normally successful in their endeavors. But when they graduate they cannot find suitable employment at home that would enable them to maintain their standing in science.

The facts are that between 1998 and 2008 the Arab countries increased their appropriations to ministries of higher education from $3.77 billion to $16.26 billion. Enrolment expanded from 2.45 million to 6.62 million students.[11] We do not know, of course, how the $16.26 billion were utilized and what proportion was "invested in buildings and land" rather than improving the quality and facilities of the faculties.

If the Arab countries were concerned with a productive output from investments in their universities, they would have slowed the increase in enrolment and used increasing appropriations to improve quality and the ability to benefit from available human capital—that is, improve the vital relationships that empower the triad.

If Arab governments had adopted appropriate policies to establish and develop their triads, their GNP would have increased substantially and thus enabled them to finance a more rapid expansion of enrolment and improved quality at all levels of education.

In other words, Arab governments could first have improved the quality and subsequently increased the availability of higher education, but at different rates. This was not undertaken. As a consequence, the problems facing the Arab labor market were aggravated: the newly added graduates lack the expertise needed to cope with the current crises.

Scientific activities undertaken in "good" universities normally benefit from the intellectual conditions that prevail in them. Here I have in mind the multidisciplinary climate that universities are expected to provide, as well as a high density of young and creative minds. It is well known that young people in the age group 20 to 30 are naturally more creative than older people. These two "assets" give the universities a qualitative edge in comparison with other centers of research.

Law and the Operational Aspects of the Triad

The processes underpinning the triad are essentially governed by legislation. Employment, manufacturing, exports, imports, contracting and subcontracting, and every other aspect of economic activity are governed by such legislation. It is well known that the tapestry of these laws is of great complexity, and thus great care has to be taken when drafting them to make them fair, equitable, understandable, useful, supportive of entrepreneurship, productive, antimonopolistic, appropriate, and socially acceptable.

For example, Henry and Springborg note that in Egypt the manner in which the law is made leaves much to be desired. The authors state:

> Virtually all legislation is produced in the government itself, with individual ministries assuming primary responsibility for designing the content of proposed bills. Public hearings do not constitute part of the drafting process and only rarely are public hearings used when legislation is being considered in the standing committees of parliament. Because many or most of the stakeholders who will be impacted by substantive law play little if any role in its formulation, and because of inadequate drafting procedures, numerous outright mistakes occur. Mahmoud Fahmy, Secretary General of the Maglis al Dawla (State Council) and architect, personally, of much of the legislation associated with economic reform, once observed that a key piece of legislation "violates the constitution because it introduces articles with no legal precedents; its articles furthermore contradict other existing laws."[12]

The other Arab countries follow, generally, in the footsteps of Egypt in legal matters.

Performance of Universities

The importance of research function in universities has steadily increased since the early nineteenth century. In industrial countries research has increasingly dominated the function of the leading universities.

Universities have been moving away from providing training for skills, since other organizations can do the same at much lower costs. For example, the US armed forces, rather than the universities and colleges, supply skilled technicians to the US economy. Community colleges, technical schools, and a variety of similar organizations provide the education for middle-level skills.

The same trend has been going on in Japan, where business and vocational schools have been booming. Lately, more Japanese have been attending technical high schools, colleges, and other training vocational schools due to the high cost of entry into universities.

University graduates constitute the backbone of the skilled labor force simply because they are the umbilical cord to the future by virtue of their ability to access advances in knowledge. In industrial societies today, 30–50 percent of the labor force has been through tertiary education and been exposed to the possibilities that may be engendered by creativity.

Creativity is a natural gift; some people possess more of it than others. Creative people need an appropriate environment to enable them to express their creativity. Creativity can be easily "turned off" by government control over university recruitment and activities, by the admission of poor-quality students, by high teaching loads, and lack of suitable educational and research facilities.

The Interface between the University and Employers

The educational system is not designed to train students for any specific job. The reason is obvious: no student knows the likely job opportunities of the future four years in advance. One of the indicators of the efficacy of an education system is the graduate's preparedness in learning new skills. The training to improve a person's usefulness to an organization is generally provided by the employer, since the employer is the only one who knows what is needed from an employee. It may take hours, days, weeks, or months to train a new employee, depending on the complexity of the job.

The GCC governments devote considerable resources to training their citizens to become employable in the private sector. The strategic error is that they do not incorporate training programs to suit the employer's activities. Here we see the paramount importance of the enterprise within the triad. Until the job is specified, it is difficult to define the skills required and to tailor training programs.

In the Arab world it is wrongly assumed that because new graduates cannot just walk into a job and perform well and because university graduates remain unemployed for years it means that the education is ineffective or inefficient. The graduates who emigrate do find jobs and often do brilliantly, because they get the necessary training.

The interface between Arab education and employment needs more attention. Systematic training, productivity measurement, and comprehensive labor statistics are rarely encountered in the Arab world. Yet these are of paramount importance to monitor the minutiae of triad processes with a view to optimizing the performance of the economy.

Science and the Interface between Employer and Products

Needless to say, good training is not sufficient for a firm to be successful in what it does. In order for an industrial firm to succeed in producing marketable products, it must adopt a competitive technology and a suitable management system. The science and technology needed, in most traditional branches of the economy, are generally available to competent and experienced engineers and industrialists. In general, these engineers should be able to cope with most problems that arise in the acquisition and application of technology. Unusual problems call for R&D.[13]

Fierce international competition has placed a high value on inventiveness and creativity. Obviously, some products need much higher levels of creativity than others. As the shift of manufacturing to China goes global, first the United States and now Europe have been compelled to move out of manufacturing and into invention and design, leaving the subsequent steps of production to China or other third world countries.[14]

Even food products today are subject to constant change and development under the pressure of dieting habits, changes in taste, cost of production, and changes in the availability of raw materials.

A host of factors are important to secure acceptable returns from economic activities. William Lewis has provided us with a magnificent account of the unexpected consequences of human behavior embodied in traditions and conventions.[15] Lewis shows that successful economic performance depends on the productivity of labor and of capital, plus the impact of a host of additional factors that influence the competitiveness of the firm. Only firms, governments, and societies aware of the complexities of these relationships and astute enough to manage them effectively will be able to cope with the challenges. All of these dimensions are of importance to the management of the triad.

Arab firms that used to assemble black-and-white TV sets failed to notice the shift to the use of color TV. They failed to adapt their technology suitably and thus went bankrupt. Unless a product is tolerably useful, people will not buy it.

When governments "protect" the output of poorly performing industries by restricting imports, the buyers refuse to buy such poor quality national products. What happens is that smuggling, in collaboration with government agencies, supplies imports to meet the demand. The massive damage inflicted on society by patronage, corruption, and whimsical political practices are well known, yet these are widely practiced.[16]

Industrialization in the Arab world faced difficult days because of its low effectiveness, whether it involved assembling TV sets, making cars, or deriving significant benefits from the region's bountiful natural resources.

Financing Education and the Triad

Private and public sectors in all industrial countries make substantial contributions to higher education. Otherwise, most students would not be able to afford the cost of quality education.

Naturally, economic organizations employ labor on the basis of their ability to operate the employers' science and technology. Thus, all three components of the triad are meant to be mutually reinforcing. Clearly, poor education and an absence of effective on-the-job training undermine triad relationships.

In the Arab world, these functional triad relationships are substandard, and thus the contributions that Arab university graduates and Arab labor make to the economy is severely limited.[17]

Two Major Causes of Arab Triad Paralysis

There appear to be two major causes contributing to the paralysis of the triad in Arab countries.

The first, which is of direct relevance to us here, is that science in the Arab world is injected via foreign-controlled turnkey contracts. This means that indigenous scientific capabilities are kept frozen. This approach to science essentially disrupts the natural role of the triad.

By contrast, the importation of new technologies through the medium of national consulting and contracting firms, employing national labor, contributes to the effective participation of these organizations in the process of knowledge transfer.

Acquiring knowledge through transfer does not reduce the importance of R&D, as scientific advances are constantly taking place. Needless to say, R&D is an integral part of the transfer of complex technologies.

The second cause is the financial system that allocates the means to execute a project. Henry and Springborg find that credit allocation is at the heart of the MENA patronage system, which is controlled by the national banks, and there is limited availability of information.[18] Short-term patronage in the early phases of the process of technical change *may* even accelerate the process of development, as we can see from Taiwan and South Korea, though it did not work as well in Indonesia and Latin America. Excessive patronage always seems to have a damaging effect. When patronage favors turnkey contracting with multinationals (or national firms) that employ foreign labor, the process of technology acquisition is turned off.

Technology-free turnkey contracts are a "greater evil" than patronage or corruption.

The Operational Aspect of the Triad

Industrial societies have evolved an elaborate and varied infrastructure that serves to integrate the three Triad entities. This infrastructure is subject to both formal and informal processes. The operational structure is dominated by three major concepts:

- self-organized criticality (SOC)
- nodal points
- connectivity to nodal points

The collaborative performance of science, universities, and enterprises depends on their freedom and ability to self-organize spontaneously. SOC is fundamental to scientific activity: a scientist must be able to spontaneously exchange and communicate with his peers. "Standing on the shoulders of giants," or the acquisition and accumulation of knowledge, is impossible without efficient associations, communication, and diffusion of information.

Economists have been speculating about the reasons why Arab economies have failed to benefit from massive investments (some $3 trillion or more during the 1970–2000 period). Resistance to SOC blocks the establishment of forward and backward linkages, which drive socioeconomic growth. The technology-free turnkey contract is the "terminator" of forward and backward linkages in the triad.

In the Iraq of the 1980s, government stopped publishing the annual national statistical handbook. This was supposedly to protect the country from spies.[19] Ministries were allowed to see their own data but not those of other ministries. Lebanese statistical services are no better, but for other reasons. It probably has to do with a desire to keep secret the iniquities in the distribution of public services within the country. The vacuous contents of UN statistical tables on the Arab countries are a further illustration of this state of affairs.

Organizations, societies, and associations constitute nodal points by virtue of being centers of organized collective activity. The denial of SOC in Arab countries inhibits many of these organizations from performing their normal tasks. Often organizations—such as associations of industries, bankers, labor unions, farmers' unions, contractors, municipal councils, and chambers of commerce—are hijacked by a small number of members who use them to serve their own personal ambitions rather than that of the collectivity.

The Formal Triad Operational Infrastructure

We have discussed some of the formal processes that are undertaken within the triad. Employment by firms, training of new recruits, cooperation among scientists employed in the various branches of the economy, and upgrading the technology used by firms are all routine triad activities.

These processes are as ancient as history. The advice of scientists on practical projects has been sought throughout the ages. Leonardo da Vinci was extensively consulted with respect to the largest civil engineering project in medieval Europe: Le Canal Des Deux Mers in southern France. Sadi Carnot made dramatic contributions to the understanding of the functioning of the steam engine, which led to higher operational efficiency and to the science of thermodynamics. Since 1800, the relationships among industrial countries have been deepened and have become more and more extensive through triad operations.

By contrast, excessive technological dependence of the Arab countries has led to limited development of their triad. Making universities more useful to the economy depends not only on their professors but also on the structure of the triad. Because of the severe underdevelopment of their triad, Arab governments cannot appreciate the value of quality education. *Their economies are disconnected from national universities.*

The Informal Triad Operational Infrastructure

In chapter 1 I discussed the importance of economic activities under-taken outside the market economy. The Tofflers defined these activities and estimated that they contribute to the world's economy as much as the market economy. If so, this do-it-yourself (DIY) activity is on a grand scale and contributes significantly to triad activities in industrial countries. These activities, being less organized and more entrepreneurial than those sponsored by companies and formal organizations, contribute to reducing barriers and to the emergence of chaordic relationships.[20]

DIY activity breaks down barriers in the technical flow of information between people: there is today a continuum—a barrier-free space—between amateurs and research workers.

DIY activity plays important educational and training roles in modern societies. DIY-active members in OECD countries have access to learning skills and knowledge other than those provided by the formal educational system. The sophistication of some of the DIY products—computers, airplanes, cars, houses, medical services, software—certainly enable DIY participants to acquire the capabilities necessary to invent and innovate. DIY products may ultimately be marketed commercially.

DIY activity is pursued in the Arab world on a much restricted scale and with limited activity in advanced technologies. Recent Qatari and UAE initiatives encourage their young to innovate.

Under conditions of rapid technology change in industrial countries, the labor involved in DIY activities is keenly aware of advances in science. This informal and important linkage, based within the labor sphere, is missing in the Arab countries. The aforementioned Qatari and Emirati activities in this direction address the needs of youth and not that of labor. This is not a criticism, but it emphasizes the limitations of current efforts.

The Internet has intensified DIY activities, as exemplified by LINUX (a software), Wikipedia (the free online encyclopedia), and others. In industrial countries, several such activities take place informally and spontaneously. These are all examples of SOC. There is an entire industry in the market economy devoted to the promotion of DIY activities. There are programs providing training in flower arrangement, fashion design, child rearing, health care, interior decoration, instruction in construction, and other such topics. Advances in medical testing technologies noted in chapter 1 will contribute to the advancement of DIY activities in the health care fields.

Different countries have responded to this development in different ways. For example, Sweden and Japan have developed non-diploma courses and training opportunities through municipal governments and large companies. "Citizens' schools" or "people's universities" were established in Sweden and "culture centers" in Japan. These informal learning institutions deal in an amazingly wide range of subjects for short to medium terms and with low tuition costs subsidized by the local governments or by private companies. Both these countries have adopted the concept of lifelong education system, and citizens can take up any subject in any field of learning at any time in their lives. The cost is reasonable and enrolment is easy. Furthermore, Japan has developed its vocational school services extensively.[21]

A recent book on the subject exemplifies the enormous expansion of these activities and their increasing influence on the market economy.[22]

The Informal/Formal Triad Operational Infrastructure

Professional associations, which span both formal and informal activities, provide some of the most effective and important triad relationships. The necessary condition for the emergence of such associations is the presence of a sufficient number of research scientists and freedom of association. Their existence is indicated by the regular holding of scientific meetings. Such associations normally involve their members in diverse activities that are all linked to the advancement of science in some specific areas.

It is also important that these associations are formed by individual scientists and not as unions or federations of national organizations, or as an extension of some political party or activity. The limited opportunities for political expression in the Arab world have led many technical organizations to become unduly concerned with political issues. Such involvement often leads to great difficulties: the activities of the organization are diverted to nonscientific ends, and the security services become excessively concerned and interfere in their functioning. Needless to say, politics and science do not make happy partners.

Clearly, funding the cost of travel and per diem of members to attend meetings is a major challenge in establishing scientific associations. In industrial countries, travel support is routinely provided by agencies that provide grant and sponsor research and/or employers. It is taken for granted that these activities are important to increase the output of scientists.

Associations and the Integration of
the Scientific Community

Members of scientific associations are normally employed throughout a national economy; they thus bring much diversified experiences to their societies. Furthermore, these associations serve as centers of diffusion of knowledge about current advances in every scientific field. Thus, associations are intensive nodes for the exchange of knowledge among participants who are members of the labor force and of national scientific communities.

Members of associations cooperate to adapt their respective sciences to respond to the needs of their various occupations. This includes the adaptation of educational systems to the changing demands of the labor market as well as to advances in science. Needless to say, members of such associations will be concerned with the social and public policy implications of advances in their scientific fields. Thus, they would be expected to advocate appropriate national policies and measures to respond to scientific advances.

It is sadly noted that it is rare for an Arab scientific organization to take a public stand on a scientific issue, or in favor of a science policy.

In industrial societies, professional associations provide simple and informal mechanisms for the exchange of experiences among peers working in completely different areas of the economy. These organizations also help to bridge the formal and informal divide within every profession and across professions.

Associations and Their Diversified Contributions

Professional associations that have among their members world-class scientists provide a critical connection to the international scientific community, which facilitates the flow of knowledge.

To summarize, professional societies serve to:

- integrate each specific discipline with its national environment;
- enhance the scientific competence of the members of each discipline;
- adapt formal educational programs to local needs through greater and better communication with the practitioners and teachers of science;
- facilitate communication with foreign-based researchers to promote the transfer of science and technology;
- adopt public positions on scientific issues of national importance;

- support and promote the development of scientific work in their field; and
- explain and promote public policies that may have developmental, health, or security implications.

The Triad and the Quality of Universities

Universities are simultaneously hothouses of scientific discovery and learning as well as major centers of knowledge diffusion. They are therefore critical components of the triad, for they supply the critical learned human capital capable of innovating and taking leading roles in society.

The top 100 universities in 2008 were in the following countries: United States, 54; Britain,11; Germany, 6; Canada, 4; Japan, 4; Sweden, 4; France, 3; Switzerland, 3; Australia, 3; Belgium, 2; Netherlands, 2; Denmark, 2; Israel, 1; Russia, 1.

The factors that determine the quality of a university are so well known that it is now standard practice to grade and rank universities globally. Recently, Chinese professors in Shanghai wanting to understand how China was doing in higher education developed a systematic approach to ranking the top 5,000 universities in the world.

In the first year of their program they found no Chinese university among the top 100 universities of the world. There were, however, 27 Chinese universities ranked between 100 and 500. There was not a single Arab university in the top 500. The top 20 consisted of the following: US universities, 17; British, 2; and Japanese, 1. The top 100 were dominated by 77 universities as follows: United states, 54; British, 11; Japanese, 6; German, 6; Canadian, 4; French, 4; Swiss, 3; Holland, 2; Australian, 2; and Israel, Denmark, Norway, Finland, and Russia, one each.

The scope of research activities at universities declines as one goes down the scale. There is a big gap in research output and standing between the top 10 universities and the next batch of 25, and so on. By the time one reaches number 200, the quality and scale of research is seen to have shrunk substantially. By level 400, we are no longer talking of universities in the sense of significant research organizations.

The Chinese researchers found 16 Arab universities ranked between 637 (King Fahd University of Petroleum and Minerals in Dahran) and 3,962 (Cadi Ayyad University in Morocco) among the 5,000 universities. The former ranked first and the latter ranked 16th among the Arab universities.

Interestingly, there were three Palestinian universities among these "top" 16 Arab universities. Birzeit University ranked third among the Arab universities and 1,382 worldwide. The Kuds University ranked eighth and the Islamic University of Gaza 15th among the Arab ones, and these two ranked 2,785 and 3,943, respectively, worldwide. It is significant that a destitute, occupied, and oppressed country ranked so well compared to sister countries with far better resources and living conditions.

The Shanghai group is continuing its annual exercise, and some universities have improved their standing after supplying more data on their activities. Thus, Cairo University in the later setting (2007) ranked 403.

Since 2006, numerous teams around the world have generated ranking tables. Details are available on the Internet.[23]

The Arab Response to the Poor Performance of Their Universities

It appears that there is widespread acknowledgement of the weakness of higher education in the Arab world. This has, very surprisingly, encouraged the founding of profit-making universities and additional foreign universities subsidized by Arab governments!

The Chinese sought to understand what makes a great university by studying 5,000 universities every year. Arab investors saw profit in the shortage of universities and opted to benefit commercially from this opportunity. Governments thought that by bringing in outposts of excellent Western universities they would overcome the problem of lack of quality in education. Nobody bothered to find out why the present system does not work.[24]

What is also surprising is the muted Arab reaction to the actions taken in the domain of higher education. Few scholars have taken notice of the consequences of widespread use of foreign and confessional universities in Lebanon. These organizations may have contributed to Lebanon's fragmentation and made the country more resistant to integration. As other Arab countries appear to be conforming to the Lebanese model, one would have expected some interest in the study of its consequences. But there have been no such research efforts to date.

Eminent scientific and scholarly societies normally take a position on major cultural issues. The absence of such voices reflects badly on the prevailing intellectual climate in the Arab world. The absence of significant scientific and scholarly societies in the Arab world is a reflection of the weakness of research activity and the constraints imposed on the free association of scientists, scholars, and professionals.

The Triad and the Output of the Education System

Since the early nineteenth century, industrial countries increased their investment in education, research, and innovation at all levels. These measures led to the rapid evolution of the triad in industrial countries.

These efforts, which began during the French Revolution, had a dramatic impact on the triad in European countries, with concomitant influences on the balance of power in the world. Thus, the establishment of advanced educational facilities, such as the École Polytechnique in France in 1794, by leaders of the French Revolution gave Napoleon a comparative advantage over Prussia and the rest of Europe.

The defeat of the Prussians at the battle of Jena in 1806 was a wake-up call for them. The Prussians investigated the causes of their defeat and ascertained that it was associated with the role of science in Napoleon's army.[25] They immediately adopted appropriate policies with respect to science and education. Germany went on to become a leading center for science and technology in Europe and invented the graduate school, which became a strategic engine for creativity and change.

These efforts intensified after the Second World War. Industrial nations were no longer satisfied with simply educating their people; they also began to pay increasing attention to the quality of this education.

The increase in military confrontations, commercial competition, and ideological struggles between different political systems all contributed to an increasing demand for human capital and the development of the national triads of industrial countries.

Upon gaining independence, all the Arab countries sought to overcome this educational deficit at a fast rate. The recent World Bank publication *The Road Not Traveled: Education Reform in the Middle East and North Africa* reviews the high rate of investment in education by Arab countries in comparison with other regions of the developing world. Despite some 50 years of such investment, the Arab region is still lagging behind other developing regions. The main deficit in these Arab efforts is that they pay inadequate attention to the importance of quality and creativity in education. It is surprising that while one military defeat was enough to help the Prussians see the cause of their weakness and to adopt the appropriate solutions, numerous defeats and massive economic losses have failed to induce a similar inquiry in the Arab world.

Over the past 30 years there have been numerous fruitless efforts to examine aspects of Arab education and the labor force. These efforts have been of very limited value because of the absence of relevant, detailed, up-to-date statistical information and imaginative inquiries.[26] There is very little empirical data on the quality of Arab education systems with emphasis on student performance in standardized tests, scientific research (with emphasis on relevance and quality), the labor market, labor productivity, and innovation. Needless to say, statistical information and in-depth studies on how Arab countries deal with technology are all in short supply. Such studies would have helped the public and governments to identify the problems plaguing their triads.

With few exceptions, Arab countries, of all political persuasions, have sought speedy acquisition of products rather than the accumulation of knowledge. This has meant that native labor and education as well as the triad have constantly been marginalized.

It is thus of importance that two new organizations, the Arab Thought Foundation in Saudi Arabia and the Sheikh Mohammed Bin Rashed Al Maktoum Foundation in Dubai, have adopted aspects of labor, education, knowledge, and research as subjects of their concern. The Arab Thought Foundation has already organized four events on the subject of Arab culture; science and technology was a prominent component of this culture. The Maktoum Foundation sponsored a series of studies on the knowledge society and it culminated in an annual report. Will these organizations be able to alter the current outlook in the Arab countries? So far they have showed limited interest in creativity, quality, efficiency, and productivity.

Some Comparisons

Why do Arab countries have one of the highest unemployment levels in the world and at the same time import millions of expatriates to do their work? How come both China and India, with no significant oil and gas resources, have acquired the technologies needed to explore for oil and gas and build refineries and petrochemical plants while the Arab countries, after a century of being important oil producers, are still technologically dependent in all priority areas?

China and India are now recognized as having well-functioning economic systems. Yet, on the basis of available statistics, the Arab countries were, until recently, doing better than either of them in terms of education on a per capita basis (table 4.1). This is true for education both at home and abroad.

Of course, both China and India are large countries, and each is politically united under one government. Could this be the reason for their success? A check of UNDP and World Bank statistics shows that small countries perform better than large ones. Seven of the ten leading

Table 4.1   Study abroad and at home for selected countries

Country	Study Abroad		Population	Study Abroad	Study at home	
	1999	1999 Corrected	(1997, m.)	Per million	Enrolment In Higher Education	Per million
Arab World	111,854	120,602	253.4	476	3,168,445	12,474
China	95,899	106,036	1,227.0	86	7,364,000	6,002
India	48,348	52,932	962.0	55	9,834,000	10,223

Source: Compiled from UNESCO statistics and others. The second column contains UNESCO data. The third column was obtained through the supplementing of UNESCO data with EU statistics (2004).

Table 4.2   Number of HSP in OECD countries, 1999

Country	Expatriates	HSP %	HSP, Number
Arab World	4,462,391	22	967,548
China	1,928,199	51.9	1,000,735
India	1,649,711	39.6	653,286

Source: Table II.A2.6, SOPEMI 2004, *Trends in International Migration Annual Report*, OECD, 2004.

countries in the world in socioeconomic performance are small, with Norway and Iceland in the first two positions. So size is not a sufficient explanation for the difference between Arabs, Chinese, and Indians in technological performance.

Furthermore, the Arab world has contributed as many high-level personnel (HSP) as China to the brain drain to OECD countries, and 30 percent more than contributed by India (table 4.2). Interestingly, the total number of emigrants (unskilled, dependants, and skilled) in 1999 (the last year for which data was available in 2004) from the Arab world to the OECD countries is greater than the total number of Chinese and Indian emigrants.

The Arabs lose four to five times as many HSP per capita as China or India. In other words, the latter two countries are able to retain more of their professionals than the Arabs are. This makes sense, since China devoted in 2009 some $155 billion towards R&D, or 35 times more than devoted by the Arab world on a per capita basis.

In other words, the three regions—the Arab world, China, and India—were roughly at the same level in terms of education and research when both China and India were rapidly progressing economically and technologically. Yet the Arab countries did not exhibit any signs of an equivalent rate of development, despite the enormous human and financial resources at their disposal.

If we look more closely at the relationship between the emigrants and their home countries, it will be seen that both China and India make considerable efforts to benefit from their emigrant human capital, while the Arab countries do not display more than a superficial interest in deriving some reflected glory from their successful emigrants.

Learning the necessary technologies is neither difficult nor costly. It only requires determination and a national policy of self-reliance. The simple and direct way in which the Chinese mechanized their agriculture is a marvelous display of the simplicity of acquiring technology.[27]

The Triad and the High University Enrolment in the Humanities

Communication among the labor force within the triad is obviously of paramount importance. It is obvious that communication depends on mastery of the mother tongue and communication skills. Both of these are supposed to be inculcated in students in high schools and first-year university. Teachers who have mastered their national language and are qualified in the humanities are all that is needed to inculcate such competence in their students.

The high proportion of students in the humanities in Arab universities often attracts comments and criticism. Serious discussions of the reasons behind this condition are rare.

The teaching of any scientific or applied subject calls for considerable facilities, unlike the teaching of the humanities. Most Arab governments are not prepared to provide the funds required to increase educational facilities in the applied scientific subjects. At the same time, universities are constantly pressured by governments to increase enrolment. The only accommodation that universities can make at low cost are in the humanities, which can be done by increasing the ratio of students to teachers and by reducing the quality and standards of the course. So what if graduates cannot write a sentence and do not read?

One should add here that the public seems to believe that quality of education in the humanities is of little relevance, while the man in the street realizes that a poor-quality engineer can cause buildings to collapse and that an incompetent medical doctor can dramatically increase mortality rates. But few seem to realize that poor education in the national language and culture may have even more dramatic consequences than collapsing buildings and inadequate health services.

Importance of the Humanities

The humanities are thought to provide cheap palliatives to satisfy public demand for pieces of paper certifying the "possession of a university degree." Nothing could be further from reality.

The humanities and social sciences are of vital importance to a developing country in two respects:

- to staff the preuniversity education system; and
- to enable society to develop its social, economic, and political culture to meet societal challenges.

With the high birthrate prevalent in the Arab world, two-thirds of the population is below the age of 25. This means that there is an enormous demand for teachers at all levels of education. The teaching of languages and culture is the main activity at primary and secondary schools.

Language learning is of supreme importance, not only for communication but also to train the mind in logical thinking. A thorough command of the mother tongue is essential to the learning of science and mathematics. Command in a foreign language is essential for benefiting from the world's treasure of knowledge. Most of the teachers in these disciplines will obviously be graduates in humanities.

Naturally, if the quality of education in the humanities in universities is poor, society is going to have poor-quality teachers in languages and basic cultural courses. This, of course, limits the potential of future generations in all vital areas of living.

Hence there is importance in improving the quality of education in the humanities. Fortunately, the cost of education per student in the humanities is much lower than that in medicine and engineering. Thus, improving quality in the humanities does not involve a great increase in expense. Yet the returns on the investment in the humanities will be considerably greater than that in the sciences and engineering.

Considering that a substantial proportion (probably in excess of 66 percent) of medical doctors educated in Arab universities emigrate, it should not be a significant loss if the education of doctors—and also of engineers—are curtailed sufficiently (no Arab employer will notice the difference if enrolment in medical schools and schools of engineering were reduced by 25 percent) to raise enough funds to transform the level of education in the humanities.

Such an action would improve higher education in all disciplines, and it might very well lead to a reduction in the brain drain of doctors and engineers. Better education in the social sciences would inform students and the population at large of the enormous cost of the brain drain and how to reduce it. Improved teaching in the social sciences might even improve the prevailing political culture.

Concluding Remarks

The acceleration of scientific and technological change continues. The combination of the following aspects will necessarily lead to novel global conditions:

- the global impact of advances in science;
- population decline in industrial countries;
- massive emigration from the third world; and
- the rise of China and India.

At the moment, some Arab countries are sleeping through these exciting times. Many important changes are taking place in the Arab world without any public debate

Arab governments sought, and still seek, to develop the three entities of the triad. Yet they do so without giving adequate attention to their organic relationships. This pattern of behavior is well established, as can be seen from the various studies of the political economies of the Arab countries. Patronage, cronyism, and constraints on freedom of association and expression are dominant factors within the Arab triads. Consequently, Arab countries will continue to miss the bountiful benefits that may be derived from available human capital. The Spring Revolution has yet to bear fruits.

The perpetuation of the patronage system is embodied in the styles of entrepreneurship promoted in the Arab world since the nineteenth century.[28] The impact of technology change on the region was especially destructive as a result of the dominance of commission-agent entrepreneurs who have controlled the flow of new technology products during the past two centuries.[29] Here I am referring to failure of the Arab countries to acquire the know-how underlying the technology of products sought.

CHAPTER 5

SCIENTIFIC COLLABORATION IN THE ARAB WORLD

Introduction

Science is a universal enterprise. Thus, communication, cooperation, and collaboration among its practitioners are fundamental and natural aspects of scientific and technological activity.

The subject of scientific collaboration has been receiving increasing attention in industrial countries. Godin and Ipperseil note that scientific collaboration was already responsible for 2 percent of scientific articles in 1760, growing to 7 percent during the nineteenth century and reaching 80 percent in the natural sciences today.[1]

The role, nature, participants, importance, effectiveness, and economics of collaboration are constantly under review in industrialized countries and aspiring developing countries. The subject is never far from the attention of scientists and policy analysts.[2]

In the first four chapters of this book I presented information on the development of the following:

- scientific and technical human resources;
- R&D activities;
- the evolution of R&D in different Arab countries;
- the relative standing and changes in standing of the Arab countries;
- the performance of the Arab world compared to leading third world countries.

For a society to benefit from science, it needs to provide an appropriate infrastructure to support the activity and to make adequate provisions to facilitate its application in order that they are able to respond to market demand. In this chapter I will discuss collaboration between scientists in different Arab countries. Chapter 6 will be devoted to international collaboration as a vital dimension of scientific research.

Collaboration naturally starts at home but does not end there. Arab-Arab cooperation is considered in this chapter. It is here considered as "in-country" because of many inter-Arab agreements that aim to bond these countries together. This is a modest expression of a feeling of belonging to one Arab nation among the people of the region.

Arab-Arab collaboration is of vital importance to benefit from a wider scientific base to solve local problems. A simple example will illustrate the importance of Arab-Arab collaboration. All Arab countries suffer from a variety of water shortages. The study of these problems involves numerous disciplines. Few Arab countries today possess the full array of expertise needed. Yet a survey of the ISI data base shows that more than 973 scientific publications have been published on aquifers and related topics by scientists in the Arab countries during the decade (2001–2010). This means that through Arab-Arab collaboration every Arab country could have ready access to comprehensive capabilities, including sufficient differences in opinion to secure heated debates.

Collaboration depends on freedom of association and the formation of scientific societies. The successful establishment of active scientific societies naturally depends on the level of scientific research within the country and the resources available to members to organize fruitful and frequent meetings.

I have already addressed the vital linkages researchers have with consulting, contracting, industrial, and other organizations whose function is to apply science.

As already noted earlier, there are many ways of applying science. A road, a structure, or an industry may be built in different ways. It is possible to utilize the services of international firms or develop national and regional capabilities to perform the same tasks. The latter process is initially more demanding but, as we have noted earlier in this book, it is economically and socially more fruitful to learn to perform these tasks using national resources. The Arab world provides a world-class internal market for the full range of technologies. Responding effectively to these demands would create massive employment (thus reducing the prevailing high level of the unemployment and poverty in the Arab world) and enhance the multiplier factor associated with Arab investments.

From the early days of independence Arab governments and society have recognized that cooperation within and between Arab countries is vital to their development and independence. But attempts made in the 1960s and 1970s to adopt significant joint effort in various technologies have failed, mainly due to lack of sufficient attention to the establishment of the necessary science and technology infrastructure and inadequate management.

From the available information, we are led to the inevitable conclusion that what is missing in the Arab countries is neither human capital in science and technology nor even international collaboration on the level of individual scientists. What are missing are decision makers who are aware of the complexity of the processes of development and are prepared to support the development of the required enabling infrastructure.[3]

The massive reliance on turnkey contracts without provision for extensive local participation is the sine qua non for marginalization and continuing technological dependence.

The Industrial Revolution and the Collaborative Processes

It is useful to reflect on the evolution of science and technology after the Industrial Revolution from the perspective of the organization of its functions and the nature of collaboration among its active agents. The organization of scientific and technological activities evolved in many different ways to respond to a variety of factors.

The Industrial Revolution increased

- the range of products that are manufactured,
- the scale of operations,
- the complexity of facilities utilized, and
- the rate of change of science and technology.

It has been noted by a number of authors that the new textile industries of the nineteenth century needed to be close to the manufacturers of their equipment to assure continuing operations through effective clustering. This was dependent on organic links between inventors, manufacturers, and users of innovative devices. Inevitably, the Arab countries too have to proceed through a similar route of clustering.

As technology matured during the nineteenth and twentieth centuries, there was a tendency for firms to grow vertically and thus absorb many of the functions that could be imported from, or undertaken by, other firms. Giant firms emerged that tended to incorporate most of the functions necessary for design and production. In this phase of development, collaboration among scientists and technologists was intrinsic to the firm.

Eventually, large firms tended to undergo a variety of developments toward outsourcing and/or internalization of a wide variety of functions. The engineering design and construction functions of plants and factories were outsourced early on. This process increased collaboration between technologists in different organizations, and often in different countries.

The process of outsourcing started earlier in the construction industry, where there is a natural division between the ultimate owner of a building, a canal, a road, or a railroad and its engineering design and construction personnel. Thus, all types of civil engineering and railway projects were internationalized early in the nineteenth century.

With the advent of electronics, computer, and biotechnology industries, the boundaries between research, invention, innovation, and manufacturing were diffused in a number of small and large firms.

The high rate of technology change and the associated high risks of these industries led to the growth of a large number of networked firms. Such clusters grew in different places, with the most famous being in the Silicon Valley.

Collaboration through Brain Drain

Several Western countries have at times during the past 500 years facilitated the emigration to their respective countries of persons with specific skills. In Elizabethan Britain the government encouraged Europeans skilled in textiles, glassmaking, and iron foundries to immigrate to England. During the past 30 years, considerable efforts were made by Western governments to encourage the emigration to their countries of persons skilled in computer science. This involved hundreds of thousands of engineers, scientists, and programmers.

All of these inputs of skills were absorbed by creative entrepreneurs who formed "clusters of firms" capable of translating these skills to services and products for which consumers were looking. These entrepreneurs themselves had one foot in science and technology and one foot in enterprise.

These illustrations indicate that "collaboration" encompasses nonscientists and involves governments in various supportive roles. Thus, a shortage of technical skills in Western countries caused them to make changes in emigration laws and regulations to facilitate a brain drain from other countries to bring in the necessary skills. These examples illustrate the flexible political environment needed to support scientific and technological development.

Once the dazzling accomplishments of Silicon Valley became known, most industrialized countries wanted to do whatever was necessary to encourage the formation of similar clusters in their own countries.

The Transition from Education to Collaboration

The acquisition of well-defined knowledge is outside the boundary of collaboration as discussed here, and falls squarely in the domain of education. Education is similar to the processes falling under the term technology transfer and acquisition. Most of these processes do not involve any significant amount of research. Collaboration in the sense used in this chapter must be research- based, and not education-based.

A patient may need a specific type of surgery. To undergo it, all that is required is to find a competent surgeon. The surgeon only needs the appropriate facilities for a short duration to perform an operation. In some medical centers these services may be provided remotely via robots and the Internet. Needless to say, most patients are not interested in acquiring surgical technologies, and are happy to secure a competent service.

When the number of patients in a community is large, the frequent flying in of doctors becomes expensive. In such a case, some national authority, or a private donor, may commission a hospital to acquire the know-how to undertake that type of operation routinely, rather than wait for a visiting surgeon. Thus, a local surgeon acquires the surgical technology, and the process is elevated to one of learning rather than a technology-free process.

There are today an enormous variety of international facilities to enable any hospital to achieve such an objective. These various channels are organized and subject to standards and certification. Tens of thousands of Arab doctors are pursuing such objectives in hundreds, if not thousands, of hospitals around the world. They are all engaged in acquiring expertise through training and sometimes through limited research collaboration.

Transfer of knowledge is complementary to R&D. Some persons believe that countries not in possession of known technologies should not import them, but rather they should develop them on their own. Such an attitude would be very damaging since the amount of knowledge that would need to be rediscovered is enormous, and would consume all the limited R&D capabilities of a developing country. It is far faster, and less expensive, to acquire knowledge in an organized manner and complement it with R&D to acquire new knowledge when necessary.

A standard example of this process takes place daily in China, Korea, and other countries. Recently, the transfer of wind turbine manufacturing to China has been reported in the *New York Times*. China set up a wind farm of Spanish design on condition that the Chinese will manufacture all the parts. The Chinese "enabling environment" facilitated the process of technology acquisition by providing all the needed facilities to achieve their objectives.[4]

Types of Collaboration

Collaborative activities pervade communities of researchers. The scale of cooperation varies a great deal, from collaboration involving a small number of scientists to a large number of them.

Such collective activities have been taking place at major national and international research centers. These activities may involve thousands of scientists. Naturally, all of these scientists are involved in hundreds of different groups, centers, and experiments.

Collaboration Involving Research Centers

An important type of collaboration is that between a scientist and a research center. Many research centers have been established to provide opportunities for scientists to use large and expensive facilities.

The standard method for establishing a research center begins with scientists who are looking for support to develop a facility to enable them to pursue a specific field of research. Thus, the research center is designed by scientists to fulfill their research wishes. It is not the result of a political or bureaucratic decision. Behind every successful research center there is a group of scientists.

Scientists may have semipermanent relationships with such centers. CERN, the Brookhaven National Laboratory (BNL), Fermi National Accelerator Laboratory (Fermilab) in Chicago, the ICTP in Trieste, the Consultative Group on International Agricultural Research of 15 affiliated agricultural research organizations spread throughout the world, and many others are illustrative examples of such centers.

The BNL was established in the 1950s on Long Island in New York State for the purpose of providing American scientists access to state-of-the-art facilities in nuclear physics. It rapidly became involved in other fields, and has remained a center for frontline science.

In 2004 the US Congress authorized the financing of an $85 million Center for Functional Nanomaterials at the BNL. There is little relationship between nanotechnology and nuclear physics. What brings them together is the quality and capability of the BNL to take charge of such a mission.

The International Centre for Scientific Research (CIRS), created in 1998, is designed to foster and promote all aspects of science and scientific research. It aims at the largest possible audience: specialists, researchers and students, as well as everyone interested in science.

In 1999 the CIRS created an Internet portal of scientific websites, which has since become a valuable worldwide reference source. The entire information offered on the CIRS websites is freely accessible. The CIRS is recognized as a professional organization.[5]

Transplanting a Research Facility to Create an International R&D Center in Jordan

The Synchrotron Light for Experimental Science and Its Applications in the Middle East (Sesame Centre) in Jordan was established by international organizations. The cornerstone of the center is the generous donation by Germany of a $60 million synchrotron when it was replaced by second-generation equipment. The center was created under the auspices of UNESCO. It benefits from the support of numerous distinguished scientific organizations. These played the role of a midwife in the birth of the center.

The center is located at Al-Balqa University in Jordan. It became operational in 2007 and is expected to provide excellent facilities for research on materials, molecular biology, surface and interface science, micro-electromechanical devices, X-ray imaging, and other fields. There is potential for a large number of different research teams to pursue separate research projects at the center. All of these are important research areas that can make significant contributions to the region.

There is a nominal international group responsible for the center: Bahrain, Cyprus, Egypt, Iran, Israel, Jordan, Pakistan, the Palestinian Authority, and Turkey. Other countries may join in the future. It is surprising that Iran would have been willing to participate in a project that involves Israelis. Roula Khalaf et al. speculate concerning Sesame and the assassination of two Iranian scientists in Iran.[6] Both of them were associated with the Sesame project: Massoud Ali Mohammadi and Majid Shahriyari. The article offers no information on a linkage between Sesame and the assassinations. It, however, raises questions about the wisdom and security implications of such a regional organization in the light of the long Israeli record of suspected assassinations of scientists in Egypt, Iraq, and Iran.

Extensive planning and training were undertaken to prepare for its launch. Scientists expecting to use the facilities have been involved in a number of programs taking place at similar centers abroad.

The key measure of the success of the administrators in setting up this center is the number of research papers published from the center two or three years after it started up. This is a reasonable assessment, since the scientists concerned have been involved at eminently qualified centers prior to joining here.

A search of ISI in December 2010 to determine the research output of the teams involved with the Sesame Centre revealed one presentation at a conference[7] and one regular paper.[8] Though the project took ten years in planning and implementation (at a nominal cost of some $100 million), it is surprising that the research output is so limited.

The main defect of the project is that it does not meet the standard method of setting up a research center. A research center is normally the result of the efforts of a group of research scientists who seek support for "their" project. Scientists setting up such a research center know what they want and have planned the experiments that they wish to carry out. This is the normal method for setting up research centers.

The administrator of the project could have searched for scientists from the concerned countries who are seeking to undertake the type of research that can be carried out at Sesame. Such scientists may have already become part of the brain drain, but they could be "retrieved" from the Diaspora. Aternatively, if this suggestion failed to deliver, the administrator could have awarded 20 doctoral fellowships and 20 post-doctorates (annually) to those willing to work at the center under a team of four or five leading scientists recruited for the center. The leading scientists could, if they so wish, remain permanently at the center. The young scientists trained at the center could eventually provide staff and/or be recruited by affiliated universities.

Atoms for Peace and Physics at AUB

In December 1953, President Dwight D. Eisenhower spoke at the UN concerning the adoption of an Atoms for Peace program as an instrument for development. An international conference on the subject was organized in Geneva in 1955 and there was hope that nuclear science will provide new avenues for development.

In 1958, Egypt, and Iraq, soon thereafter, secured from the USSR a 2MW light water research reactor (the ETRR-1, which went online in Egypt in July 1961).

The US government response to these developments was to donate a reactor to Iran and to offer another one to the AUB. At that time, I happened to be the acting chairman of the Physics Department. When I was informed of this offer, I turned it down. My argument was that such a reactor will not enable the Physics Department to build any useful research activity. Furthermore, there was nobody in the department who was interested in the project and there was no expectation that Lebanon will ever go nuclear.

The Physics Department then did not possess any equipment that could be used for undertaking research in Physics, yet we had definite plans to develop a research program in low temperature spectroscopy, low temperature physics, electron and nuclear spin resonance, and various areas of theoretical physics. My counterproposal was that they should donate the funds available for a reactor to purchase equipment that would be useful for our program. The objectives of the Atoms for Peace Program would be satisfied by such an action. However, this offer was turned down.

But soon after, the unexpected occurred. The Physics Department was visited by President Lee A. Du Bridge. Du Bridge was the president of Caltech. It turned out that he was invited by the US State Department to find out how effective was US science support to third world countries.

It was clear from the observations he had collected on his way that we both had similar views. I recounted the offer that we received and the counteroffer that we made. Shortly after Du Bridge's return to the United States, the State Department accepted our proposal in a modified form.

The Physics Department had to share the grant with the Medical School of AUB. The Medical School received a part of the funds to acquire a cobalt source for radiotherapy and equipment to support biochemical research.

The equipment was of immense medical, educational, and research use for at least two decades, and a substantial number of research papers were made possible by its use.

Obviously, the Sesame Centre is a much more ambitious and extensive project and has a greater scope for inducing changes on a regional level.

The Motivation for Arab–Arab Collaboration

Most of the Arab world is in an arid zone where water is scarce; this dictates a permanent interest in water resources, water use technologies, research on water use in agriculture, and in water management. Likewise, several Arab countries are major oil and gas producers; this provides common technological challenges and opportunities for sharing knowledge and experience.

Interestingly, at the beginning of the Arab conquests 14 centuries ago, Arab political leadership was very concerned with water technology and diffused throughout the Arab empire the water technologies developed by the Nabateans, Yemenis, Omanis, and Hadramutis for arid zone conditions. Today one finds very little expression of this great Arab sense of technological self-reliance and solidarity.

The economic usefulness of research in water, oil, gas, and agriculture to the region depends on the quality of extension services, the effectiveness of national planning, the scope and competence of financial services, and the involvement of national consulting and contracting firms in designing and implementing new projects in these industries. Unless such instruments are combined with an extensive fabric of collaborating research scientists, it is difficult to benefit from individual competences.

With a population of some 1.5 million engineers, the Arabs possess considerable human capital in these fields. The region also has a large number of schools of engineering in the major applied sciences. It has some of the world's largest oil and gas companies, the world's largest installations for desalinization, and a number of regional organizations in these fields. The combined number of consulting and contracting firms in the region is in the tens of thousands. The internal market for services in these technologies runs into hundreds of billions of dollars annually. It is thus surprising that these vast opportunities have not been exploited by appropriate public policies to enable, direct, and motivate the private and public sectors.

Consequently, instead of the Arab countries becoming world leaders in water, oil, and gas research, they are lagging behind, and remain totally dependent on external suppliers for know-how and for equipment and supplies. Surprisingly, even repair and maintenance of these installations is dependent on imports.

Agriculture, oil, and gas are not the only massive markets available to locally developed technologies. The Arab construction industry is world-class in its scale and demands.[9] There has been significant growth of local consulting and contracting firms, but they do not yet dominate the national markets. They are also still dependent on the import of foreign labor—even though national labor is unemployed and plentiful. Furthermore, the Japanese have shown how companies can train illiterate labor (in the United States, Europe, Asia, and Latin America) to work in complex industrial plants and to reach a high level of productivity.

When it comes to construction materials, some 80 percent of these are still imported. These are products of basic technologies; because they are heavy, their transport cost is high and thus there is a competitive advantage in manufacturing them near to the market.

Enterprising countries such as South Korea, China, Brazil, and others note the opportunities provided by the dependent Arab markets and develop their capabilities to compete and acquire contracts in the Arab world.

The Metrics of Collaboration in Research

One common method of estimating the extent of collaboration among research scientists is to analyze the affiliations of coauthors of scientific publications. The affiliated organizations may be located in the same city, in different cities, in the same country, in different types of organizations, or in different countries.

The affiliations of the authors of a scientific paper determine the category of collaboration: local, Arab–Arab, Arab–OECD, and so on. However, in order to find out the exact nature of a joint publication, it is necessary to examine more closely the nature of the "cooperative relationship." This type of analysis has to be undertaken in every research center because detailed and personal information on the collaborators is not included in the text of a publication. To date, no such analysis on publications from the Arab world has been undertaken.

Data

The data presented in the tables for 1990 and 1995 are derived from ISI. The data used in the tables for 2000 and 2005 are derived from SCOPUS. The data utilized in discussing interorganizational collaboration in four Arab countries (Kuwait, Lebanon, Tunisia, and the UAE) have been obtained from SCOPUS by downloading an affiliation country search for all their research organizations. The data downloaded include all the research papers noted in the SCOPUS database for that country up to that date. The SCOPUS database apparently was still being developed, and thus the data for earlier years were less complete than for more recent years. The data downloaded cannot be compared with the output for a single year. The search for Lebanon was conducted in April 2009, and for the rest it was in May 2009.

Arab–Arab Collaboration

We have noted that the Arab countries share a wide range of common scientific and technical problems. Thus there should, in principle, be considerable incentives for cooperation among their scientists. The purpose of such collaboration would be to adapt knowledge to local use as well as to enable each society to benefit from the scientific capabilities of sister Arab countries in a manner most suitable to its socioeconomic and cultural requirements.

Table 5.1 is a summary of scientific publications that resulted from collaboration during a specific year between scientists affiliated with two or more Arab countries over the period 1990–2005. We note that collaboration varied numerically over these 15 years; there were 249 papers in 1990, 663 in 1995, 339 in 2000, and 905 in 2005.[10] The share of collaborative papers out of the total output of Arab publications was 5 percent in both 1990 and 2005.

Though the proportion of Arab–Arab collaboration has remained at 5 percent, the increase in total R&D output has resulted in an expansion of the activity. As an illustration, let us consider the case of Algeria. Algeria had only two collaborative Arab–Arab publications in 2000; this was 0.42 percent of the 481 publications by Algerians during that year. One was a paper in applied mathematics involving four authors from Tunisia and Algeria. The second was in dermatology and involved six authors from Tunisia and Algeria.

However, five years later, in 2005, there were 36 collaborative research papers registering 3.25 percent of the year's output of 1,108 publications.[11]

Of these 36 papers, there were Algerians working: 16 in Saudi Arabia, 4 in UAE, 4 in Tunisia, and 2 in Omani organizations. The remaining papers involved more than two countries. For example, there were 3 papers involving Egyptians, but two out of the three papers involving Egyptians also involved a French person, a Turk, and an Austrian. Two papers involved Moroccan organizations, one of which also involved French organizations. The remainder of the papers involved Bahraini, Lebanese, and other organizations.

A third of the papers were in solid state physics; six in material science and/or theoretical chemistry, one in robotics, one in optics, and one in fuzzy sets; two in aeronautics; five in applied mathematics; one in medical science; and one on health and the environment.

In short, the 36 papers were in serious pure and applied sciences. Two-thirds of the total reflects migration of Algerian scientists to the

Table 5.1 Collaboration of Arab-Arab scientists

Country	1990			1995			2000			2005		
	Total	AC	% AC Vs Total	Total	AC	% AC Vs Total	Total	AC	% AC Vs total	Total	AC	% AC Vs total
Algeria	172	4	2.00	328	3	1.00	481	2	0.42	1,108	36	3.25
Bahrain	59	3	5.00	106	3	3.00	94	2	2.13	227	0	0.00
Egypt	1,677	100	6.00	1,999	123	6.15	2,956	97	3.28	4,387	251	5.72
Iraq	256	1	0.00	114	12	11.00	94	1	1.06	183	8	4.37
Jordan	236	13	5.00	266	18	7.00	662	28	4.23	996	81	8.13
Kuwait	487	14	3.00	290	26	9.00	583	13	2.23	806	49	6.08
Lebanon	41	3	7.00	73	1	1.00	508	8	1.57	828	40	4.83
Libya	58	3	5.00	58	7	12.00	67	3	4.48	111	9	8.11
Mauritania	0	0	0.00	0	2	0.00	13	0	0.00	30	1	3.33
Morocco	240	0	0.00	536	22	4.00	1,167	8	0.69	1,269	12	0.95
Oman	48	5	1.00	83	24	29.00	262	15	5.73	471	27	5.73
Palestine	0	0	0.00	0	0	0.00	57	2	3.51	144	8	5.56
Qatar	48	8	17.00	59	9	15.00	61	9	14.75	251	24	9.56
KSA	1,031	65	6.00	1,240	161	13.00	1,857	61	3.28	1,999	210	10.51
Somalia	17	0	0.00	6	0	0.00	0	0	0.00	0	0	0.00
Sudan	101	7	7.00	112	45	40.00	99	9	9.09	169	14	8.28
Syria	61	0	7.00	134	44	33.00	137	9	6.57	229	12	5.24
Tunisia	268	0	0.00	342	122	36.00	734	13	1.77	1,831	27	1.47
UAE	51	15	2.90	137	26	20.00	421	55	13.06	989	85	8.59
Yemen	31	8	2.60	30	15	50.00	42	4	9.52	71	11	15.49
Total	**4,882**	**249**	**5.90**	**5,913**	**663**	**11.00**	**10,295**	**339**	**3.29**	**16,099**	**905**	**5.62**

Source: ISI for years 1990 and 1995; and Scopus for 2000 and 2005.

Note: AC—Arab Countries.w

GCC. The papers involving Tunisia, Morocco, Lebanon, and Egypt (the remaining 39 percent) involved collaboration and possibly (for a third of these) were a product of study/research abroad. These papers also involved researchers from a third or even a fourth country. In other words, Algerians have embarked after 2000 on an exploratory process of developing relationships with Arab and other countries. This evolution of the Algerian situation reflected a broadening and diversification of national expertise.

The move of Algerians to the Gulf region is a new development. Algerians had not previously explored the possibilities of academic employment in the GCC countries. The Maghreb is underrepresented among the Arab GCC expatriates.

Scientists in Algeria, Morocco, and Tunisia published a total of 1,264 papers in 1995; of these, some 804 were coauthored with scientists outside their own countries. Only 11 of the 804 publications involved scientists from two Maghreb countries. Of these 11 publications, only one paper was conducted exclusively by Maghreb scientists. Regional collaboration in the Maghreb was thus exceedingly rare before 2005.

During the period 2000 and 2005 a transition took place to a higher level of regional collaboration.

Scientists in GCC countries published 1,722 papers in 1990 and 2,716 in 1995, of which 95 and 223, respectively, were the result of Arab-Arab collaboration. In 1990, collaboration within the GCC was 2.7 percent of all coauthored papers; this increased to 6 percent in 1995.[12]

In 2000, GCC countries had a total of 154 collaborative papers with other Arab countries, out of 3,115 papers. By 2005 these numbers increased to 395 collaborative papers out of 4,743. In other words, they increased the proportion of Arab-Arab papers from 4.9 percent to 8.3 percent. Of the 395 collaborative papers, 88 were generated within the GCC (*Table 5.2). Hence net Arab-Arab collaboration excluding GCC collaboration was 6.5 percent.

The leading collaborating country in the GCC is Saudi Arabia, followed by the UAE and Kuwait. Oman and Qatar contribute 10 percent of the Saudi output.

There are a number of collaborative articles involving a large number of authors and organizations. For example, one paper is concerned with a workshop organized by a group from Canada, Spain, Armenia, and others; but only meteorological services from GCC and non-GCC Arab countries were listed as cooperating.[13] This data was not included in table 5.1.

The leading countries in Arab–Arab collaboration are those that employ substantial numbers of Arab expatriate professors and professionals, such as Oman, Saudi Arabia, Kuwait, UAE, and Libya, as well as the Arab countries that provide the bulk of these expatriates: Egypt, Jordan, and—increasingly—the Maghreb countries.

In 1995, Qatar University had 23 university professors who indicated, on their publications, an affiliation with Qatar University and with an Egyptian University. Cairo University appears to have had a dominant influence over the Qatari academic market: in 1995 Cairo University filled 10 out of the 23 positions occupied by Egyptians. NCR, Tanta, and Zagazig universities appear to be part of the quota of Cairo University. The rest (numbering nine, that is, some 40 percent of the Egyptian professors) came from the following universities: Alexandria, 3; Ain Shams, 3; Suez Canal, 1; and Mansoura, 2.

In the case of Syria, some of the Arab–Arab cooperation is to be ascribed to the contributions of ICARDA, the international research center specializing in arid land. ICARDA sponsors joint research projects in the region and worldwide.

The data also shows that there was genuine collaborative research undertaken between three hospitals in Qatar, Kuwait, and the UAE. This project was concerned with the impact of fasting during Ramadan on persons with cardiac and diabetic conditions.

Pan-Arab Science versus National Science

One can say, with confidence, that collaboration in R&D within the Arab world to date has received limited attention. One would have expected that old professions such as the medical sciences and health services, agriculture, civil engineering, and the construction industry would exhibit collaboration; but in fact in none of these fields, except in the medical sciences, can one find much evidence of it. It is likely that there is collaboration at a level that does not end in research publications.

In the absence of studies on this subject, I interviewed a small number of researchers in the medical field to obtain a measure of the extent of collaboration

- through joint conferences;
- in the exchange of speakers and scientists between medical schools; and
- in the study of common diseases.

I learnt that the extent of such collaboration is on a small scale. Even the extent of participation in each other's medical conferences was limited.

Collaborative activities generated by the engineering unions are also on a limited scale. Years of discussion, by the Federation of Arab Engineering Unions, about adopting common codes failed to achieve this goal.

Similarly, the Union of Arab Engineers and the Union of Arab Contractors have not sought to develop standardized construction components or construction methods and materials, or to advocate the enforcement of quality control or improve the training of Arab labor employed in construction. The adoption of such measures would have enhanced employment in the Arab world, reduced the cost of construction, promoted quality control, improved safety at work, and increased the productivity, competitiveness, and profitability of the sector and of Arab labor.

There is limited cooperation in the basic sciences. One of the earliest conferences sponsored by the League of Arab States was on scientific research in 1952. ALECSO, a regional organization, was established by the League to promote Arab–Arab cooperation in culture, education, and the sciences. It currently (2010) makes limited contributions to scientific collaboration in the region.

Despite the limited regional scientific activity, the feelings of Arab scientists are such that the emergence of pan-Arab science is only a matter of time. The forces driving such an emergence, in the view of many Arab scientists, are compelling. The expectation is that the pressures engendered by the loss of opportunities incurred by each Arab country as a result of their fragmented and noncollaborative approach will drive them toward adopting a more collaborative posture. Naturally, the growth in R&D activities will facilitate this process.

Poor Integration of R&D with National and Regional Economies

The ability to apply scientific capabilities to the solution of developmental problems depends on stable links between researchers, consulting firms, and industrial firms, as well as with government planning agencies. Through such links the know-how generated in research laboratories could find its way into applications and contribute to the solution of developmental problems.

Waleed El-Shobakky, writing about the wave of cosmetic science parks established in the Arab countries in the previous decade, says that "there were more expectations than outcomes."[14] The proper way to connect science and technology to the economy is through self-reliant and effective involvement of national consulting, contracting, and industrial firms in the planning and execution of projects under way in the Arab world. At the moment, the considerable academic resources of Arab universities play a limited (if any) role in the process of planning and development.

The heavy utilization of technology-free turnkey approach makes it more difficult for Arab scientific manpower to contribute to national economies. Government officials and other observers of the Arab R&D scene have generally blamed the scientists for living in an ivory tower. These observers fail to recognize the marginalization of Arab scientific resources by the adopted technology policies.

Arab scientific and technological capabilities are most prominently utilized in the agricultural, medical, and civil engineering sectors. However, the contributions made to date are a fraction of what they could contribute if these capabilities were established within an effective triad (see chapter 4) and supported by effective national science and technology systems. Unless R&D contributes to the growth of Arab GNP there will be little political motivation to increase support for Arab science.

Collaboration between Arab states in the domain of science and technology will follow, and not precede, the incorporation of national science and technology in their national economies. Until Arab governments develop the necessary infrastructure to benefit from national capabilities they will find it difficult to collaborate with scientists in other Arab countries.

The Importance of Multi-Sector Collaboration

Every society adopts its own approaches to planning for, and the implementation of, new technologies. I have discussed elsewhere the central roles of collaborative activities in the diversification of the economy in developing countries. It is clear from the study of international experience that collaboration within a country and with foreign sources of knowledge is central to successful and speedy development.[15] These two forms of collaboration are mutually reinforcing and complementary. The interaction of critical internal and external collaboration contributes to the sharpening of the intellect of scientists and renders them more effective. Transparent and open debates in well-managed scientific societies are critical to a developing country.

Countries such as the Republic of Korea acquire and adapt technology as an integral part of simultaneous internal and external collaboration in the design and execution of their major developmental and industrial programs. Such programs entail the adoption of measures that involve the education system, the testing services, the adoption of appropriate standards, and effective methods of contracting that facilitate and promote the transfer of technology to national firms. Such practices have been adopted in the Arab world in limited cases.[16]

Successful technological optimization and development often involves collaboration of a variety of stakeholders. The ability of a community to standardize its products can reduce their cost, improve quality, and reduce the time required for production. For example, engineers and industrialists in the United States saw at an early stage the value of standardizing house designs and the corresponding specifications of the materials required. This has improved the quality of housing and reduced the cost of construction. Naturally, this has also increased the productivity of the workers and engineers and their income.

This approach increased American prosperity and efficiency, since people could build higher-quality homes at lower cost. Such a creative and collaborative activity cannot be performed without collective social–economic thinking and without a popular understanding of the importance and nature of technology, standards, specifications, quality control, and modes of production.

Americans have a plentiful supply of wood, so many of their houses are built from this material. However, once they moved to building skyscrapers, they adopted a similar standardized approach, but now using steel. In the Arab world, engineers still specify windows and doors, wall panels, and tiles of any size they please. This increases unit cost, since it is more expensive to meet a wide range of specifications. In other words, architects do not design space to be multiples of standardized elements.

Though aluminum and plastic products, which are locally produced in the Arab world, have now replaced wood in many of the basic components of modern buildings, Arab countries still import massive amounts of wood for construction. The glass and aluminum used in construction are also mostly imported, although the Arab countries export the raw materials for their production. They are only slowly exploiting their comparative advantages.

In short, the level of sophistication of the scientific and engineering professions is critical to the adoption of effective and useful policies capable of harnessing the power and benefits of collaboration within a country. The limited state of such collaboration is a reflection of limited sophistication. Quality scientific societies normally promote creativity and the optimal solution of problems.

Extensive data is needed to measure, assess, and promote collaboration. The lack of statistical data on

* contracts that involve technology acquisition;
* employment by occupation, skill, and education;
* labor productivity by sector and activity;
* the activities of Arab scientists and engineers; and
* the weakness (and often absence) of relevant scientific societies

has kept these vital dimensions of the economy in the dark.

Concluding Remarks

Arab–Arab collaboration in R&D is happening on a limited scale, despite the existence of good reasons for promoting such activities. The Arab countries have not, so far, established a sufficient number of joint regional centers to mobilize their scarce resources to address common problems in agriculture, construction, water, oil, gas, and in other areas of strategic importance.

Needless to say, the weaknesses and small number of scientific societies in the Arab world limits Arab-Arab collaboration.

CHAPTER 6

INTERNATIONAL COLLABORATION OF ARAB SCIENTISTS

Introduction

International collaborations in many frontier scientific research areas are driven by the increasing complexity of scientific problems that call for a greater number of participants, the need for more intensive deliberations among scientists, and considerable investments in expensive research facilities.

Another drive toward collaboration originates in the simultaneously collaborative and competitive nature of science. In small scientific communities where all members know each other personally and where many are students of a few older professors, it becomes difficult to disagree and to compete. Collaborating with distant and "foreign" scientists helps to enable young scientists to acquire a more normal concept of the scientific enterprise. The alternative is decline.

The worldwide expansion in collaboration among scientists has led to acceleration in the rate of scientific research. This increase in rate and intensity of research is putting greater stress on the competitiveness of scientists. Third world scientists, not incorporated in international collaborative processes, are placed at a great disadvantage.

Studies of, and concern with, international collaboration has increased over the past few decades. For example, the high cost of research for new drugs (currently about $1 billion per new drug) has increased the concern of the pharmaceutical industry, despite the huge profits generated by successful discoveries. Many companies are seeking a variety of new patterns of national and international collaboration to reduce their risks by sharing the cost of R&D.[1]

During the past few decades several governments have increased their support for collaborative opportunities of their scientists. The European Community devotes considerable resources to these objectives. The EU sought to increase collaboration within the European region and also internationally, without neglecting the development of collaboration with third world countries. American organizations and the US government have been pursuing such international collaborative objectives since the end of the Second World War.

The maturity of national scientific communities determines the possibilities and nature of collaborative patterns of scientists. The development of collaborative activities depends on meetings between scientists in formal and informal gatherings where they get to know each other to discover common areas of interest and the feasibility of collaboration. The existence of innovative scientific societies and communities is critical to the facilitation of these processes. Scientists in third world countries are handicapped because they are neither sufficiently affiliated with relevant invisible colleges nor generally well funded to participate in such activities.

There are differences in the purposes of collaboration in the basic and applied sciences. Collaboration in the basic sciences contributes to the advancement of science, the sustenance of the scientists, and the enhancement of the quality of higher education. Scientists undertaking research are better qualified to alert and prepare their countries for technical change brought about by advances in science.

By contrast, collaborative research in the applied sciences and technologies has immediate applications and economic implications. Collaboration related to industrial processes poses its own constraints. In advanced industrial countries there are strict laws against monopolistic behavior, which affects the possibility of some types of collaboration among industrial firms. Special legislation is sometimes required to permit such collaboration. These problems do not arise in the Arab world, partly because of the limited extent of such collaboration and the extensive dependence on the importation of technology.

Types and Forms of Collaboration

Governments in industrial countries have been attentive to the promotion of various patterns of collaboration. Naturally, the mechanisms for cooperation vary, depending on whether the cooperating parties are individuals, small and medium enterprises, or large firms.

Scientists in industrial countries, despite the fact that they enjoy world-class scientific facilities and conditions, find benefits in collaborating with each other. According to a study undertaken for the Office of Science and Innovation of the United Kingdom, "Collaboration is encouraged at a policy level because it provides access to a wider range of facilities and resources. It enables researchers to participate in networks of cutting-edge and innovative activity. For researchers, collaboration provides opportunities to move further and faster by working with other leading people in their field."[2]

For scientists in third world countries with limited facilities and opportunities for scientific contacts, collaboration is even of greater importance than it is in industrial countries. However, opportunities for these scientists to cooperate are generally much more limited and often constrained by dependence on donor countries.

The fundamental purpose of frontline scientific research is discovery. There is considerable competition in R&D work, especially when the research could lead to economically useful results. In sports, the player who arrives second or third receives a silver or a bronze medal. In science, the full reward goes to the first scientist who makes the discovery.

There are advances going on in all areas of the economy, from agriculture, to water resources, construction, and oil and gas. However, the areas of R&D that are fast moving are in ICT, biotechnology, and in new materials leading to nanotechnologies and their associated applications. Hence the growing habit in industrial countries of utilizing their university professors and researchers as consultants has reduced the distance between all parties and disciplines involved in invention and production.

A close and effective communication of third world scientists with the international community is essential in enabling them to learn of progress made in their fields and of successes and failures. These communication channels enable scientists to avoid repeating experiments that have proved useless, to modify approaches that were tried and failed, and to explore new strategies in their research.

The only way scientists can learn of ongoing work in such detail is through participating in specialized conferences and by visiting other scientists in their laboratories.

The motivation of late professor Abdus Salam to establish the International Centre of Theoretical Physics (ICTP) in Trieste was to provide third world scientists working in elementary particle physics with a "home base" where they could meet with world-class scientists in order to overcome their isolation. The center that he spent much of his life promoting still exists, thanks to the support of the Italian government. This center has been of great benefit to many young scientists, and it is a tribute to its sponsors.

The increasing importance of collaboration among scientists is indicated by the trend toward increasing dominance of teams in the production of knowledge in all fields. This trend is supported by extensive recent studies.[3]

Collaboration with International Organizations

International organizations such as FAO, UNESCO, WHO, ILO, CGIAR, and others sponsor multinational research projects. The participation of Arab countries in these research programs appear to be limited, and declining. In 1990 the total was 140 publications, or 3 percent of the Arab output, increasing to 225 in 1995, or 4 percent of Arab research output, and then declining to 45 in 2000, or 1 percent of the output; it then increased marginally to 50 publications in 2005.

Egypt was the leading Arab participant in this activity, accounting for about a third of the Arab total in 1990, 22 percent in 1995, 14 percent in 2000, and 22 percent in 2005 (★Table 6.1).

Arab collaboration with international organizations declined despite a three-fold expansion of research activity in the Arab world over the 15-year period.

Collaboration with OECD Countries

Table 6.2 shows the changes in the level of collaboration of scientists in the Arab world with OECD scientists over the 1990–2005 period. We note that the number of collaborative articles increased from 1,064 in 1990 to 4,385 in 2005. The proportion of the share of OECD collaborative papers in total Arab output varied from 22 percent in 1990, to 24 percent in 1995, 23 percent in 2000, and 27 percent in 2005. The research output increased by 21 percent during the 1990–1995 period, 59 percent during 1995–2000, and 54 percent during 2000–2005.

Saudi Arabia showed remarkable growth in total output after 1995. The rate of Saudi cooperation with the OECD countries remained at the same level: 15 percent (1990), 13 percent (1995), 14 percent (2000), and 14 percent (2005).

The levels of cooperation of Egypt with OECD countries were 268 (1990), 367 (1995), 559 (2000), and 944 (2005). In the case of Saudi Arabia the corresponding numbers were 150 (1990), 161 (1995), 254 (2000), and 283 (2005).

Table 6.2 Collaboration of Arab and OECD scientists

Country	1990			1995			2000			2005		
	Total	OECD	% OECD Vs Total	Total	OECD	% OECD Vs Total	Total	OECD	% OECD Vs Total	Total	OECD	% OECD Vs Total
Algeria	172	120	70.00	328	187	57.00	481	149	31.00	1,108	434	39.00
Bahrain	59	13	22.00	106	11	10.00	94	14	15.00	227	20	9.00
Egypt	1,677	268	15.00	1,999	367	18.6	2,956	559	18.91	4,387	944	21.52
Iraq	256	38	15.00	114	20	18.00	94	8	9.00	183	40	22.00
Jordan	236	42	18.00	266	58	22.00	662	150	23.00	996	260	26.10
Kuwait	487	95	18.00	290	56	19.00	583	89	15.00	806	158	20.00
Lebanon	41	17	41.00	73	27	37.00	508	153	30.11	828	314	38.00
Libya	58	11	13.00	58	18	31.00	67	13	19.00	111	38	34.00
Mauritania	0	0	0.00	0	0	0.00	13	8	62.00	30	13	43.00
Morocco	240	132	55.00	536	241	45.00	1,167	465	40.00	1,269	603	48.00
Oman	48	19	40.00	83	22	27.00	262	51	19.00	471	103	22.00
Palestine	0	0	0	0	0	0	57	16	28.00	144	36	25.00
Qatar	48	8	17.00	59	9	15.00	61	8	13.00	251	49	20.00
KSA	1,031	150	15.00	1,240	161	13.00	1,857	254	14.00	1,999	283	14.00
Somalia	17	13	75.00	0	5	0.00	0	0	0.00	0	0	0.00
Sudan	101	39	39.00	112	45	40.00	99	27	27.00	169	39	23.00
Syria	61	10	16.40	134	44	33.00	137	42	31.00	229	88	38.00
Tunisia	268	69	25.00	342	122	36.00	734	221	30.00	1,831	634	35.00
UAE	51	17	33.00	137	25	13.00	421	96	23.00	989	317	32.00
Yemen	31	3	10.00	30	15	50.00	42	11	26.00	71	12	17.00
Total	**4,882**	**1,064**	**22.00**	**5,907**	**1,433**	**24.00**	**10,295**	**2,334**	**23.00**	**16,099**	**4,385**	**27.30**

Source: ISI for years 1990 and 1995; Scopus for years 2000 and 2005.

Jordan's cooperative activities with OECD countries were maintained at nearly the same level during these 15 years: 18 percent, 22 percent, 23 percent, and 26 percent. The rate of international coauthorship in the Mashreq countries is close to the worldwide average of 25 percent of output.

The countries that exhibited the largest scientific cooperation with OECD countries were Algeria, Egypt, Lebanon, Morocco, Tunisia, and the UAE. Arab scientific workers cooperate equally with European and North American scientists. It is notable that Egyptian collaboration with Japan in 2005 was 10 percent of its level of collaboration with the OECD countries. Egypt may have increased further its level of collaboration with Japan since then.

The level of collaboration of the four Maghreb countries with OECD countries for the years 1990, 1995, 2000, and 2005 was as follows. Morocco's collaboration varied from 132 (55 percent), to 241 (45 percent), 465 (40 percent), and 603 (48 percent). Morocco shows the same steady expansion of cooperation with OECD countries as Tunisia; this increase was also combined with steady expansion of overall research activity in the country.

Algerian collaborations with OECD countries were 120 (70 percent), 187 (57 percent), 149 (31 percent), and 434 (39 percent). There was an increase in terms of the number of joint publications, but their share of total national output declined because total research production increased at a faster rate.

Tunisian collaboration increased from 69 (26 percent) in 1990, to 122 (36 percent) in 1995, then to 221 (30 percent) in 2000, and 634 (35 percent) in 2005. The number of joint papers steadily increased, though the proportion of total output that was the result of collaboration was nearly constant since total research production also increased.

Libya increased the number of collaborative papers with OECD scientists from 11 (19 percent), to 18 (31 percent), then 13 (19 percent), and to 38 (34 percent). The small scale of research activity in Libya combined with the erratic level of collaboration makes it difficult to see a trend. Libya's scientific output is exceptionally low compared with its GNP and the performance of its Maghreb neighbors.

Collaboration with Countries Other than OECD Countries

Scientists in Arab countries also collaborate with non-Arab countries[4] that are not within the OECD (*Table 6.3). This type of collaboration was insignificant before 2000. Arab collaboration with non-Arab and non-OECD organizations was 4 percent of output in 2000 and 6 percent in 2005. We note from *Table 6.3 that in 2005 the Arab countries recorded 842 publications coauthored with such countries out of a total output of 16,304 papers. By comparison there were 4,469 papers coauthored with OECD scientists, only 50 with international organizations, and 877 with Arab scientists in the Arab countries. Thus this category of collaboration, though small, is comparable with other categories. Marginal Arab countries, such as Mauritania and Sudan, had 47 percent and 14 percent of their research output, respectively, in this category of cooperation in 2005.

Collaboration through Conferences

A different form of cooperation takes place in conferences. A large number of international conferences (*Table 6.4) are held annually where scientists meet, make friends, and exchange information. In 1995, for example, there were, worldwide, about 18,000 international scientific meetings whose proceedings were published. It is certain that the number of annual conferences increased during the succeeding years, but it was not possible to fund the research required to find out how much.

Arab scientists contributed a total of 3,056 papers to the conferences held during the period 1991–1997, or an average of 510 papers per year, which is roughly 10 percent of total Arab output. The second column in *Table 6.4 gives the number of scientists from each country that presented a paper at these conferences.

The last column shows the number of international scientific conferences held in Arab countries during the period 1991–1997, which is a total of 38; this works out to some seven conferences a year. Certainly a poor record.[5]

Comparative International Collaboration

Table 6.5 shows the level of collaboration of leading industrial countries, China, and India. The data covers two periods of five years each. During the first and second periods, the average numbers of collaborative papers published by China per million inhabitants[6] per year were 4.30 and 9.10, respectively.

By comparison, and in the same units, the numbers of collaborative papers coauthored by Arab and OECD scientists were 3.8 (1990), 4.94 (1995), 11.98 (2000), and 23.97 (2005). It is clear from table 6.2 that the

Table 6.5   Total research output and collaboration

Country	1996–2000				2001–2005			
	Output (000s)	Output % of world	Collab. (000s)	Collab. % of Output	Output (000s)	Output % of world	Collab. (000s)	Collab. % of Output
UK	338.4	9	97.6	29	358.7	9	144.5	40
USA	1,262.3	35	244.9	19	1,352.4	34	334.7	25
Canada	167.2	6	55.4	33	184.4	5	75.7	41
France	229.8	9	82.1	36	244.8	6	107.7	44
Germany	310.0	8	106.8	34	340.9	8	146.6	43
Japan	329.4	9	54.3	16	360.9	9	77.2	21
Australia	100.5	3	30.7	31	117.0	3	48.5	40
China	101.6	3	25.8	25	210.1	5	54.5	26
India	76.2	2	Na		98.9	2		
World	**3,602.6**				**4,019.4**			

Source: Adams et al., *Patterns of International Collaboration*, Table 1, 10.

proportion of collaborative papers by Arab scientists with OECD countries over the period 1990–2005 showed considerable growth and was comparable with that of China on a per capita basis.

Collaboration between scientists in industrial countries is higher than that for China: the equivalent data for the UK was 325.3 for first period and 481.7 for the second. Clearly the gap between developed and developing countries (China and the Arab countries) has been narrowing.

If we were to inquire into the usefulness of the collaboration to the parties concerned, we would need additional data not presently available. One can safely conclude that individual Arab scientists are able to collaborate internationally at rates comparable to China. Unfortunately, no data for India's collaboration was provided.

R&D Activity in Four Selected Countries

I will discuss below the similarities and differences in the R&D collaborative performance of Lebanon, Kuwait, the UAE, and Tunisia. The data discussed include all the publications recorded in the SCOPUS database in 2009 (see earlier comments for more details).[7] ★Table 6.6 summarizes the abbreviations used in the following tables.

The total research output of these four countries in 2007 was 5,977 (see ★Table A, ★Appendix 1), which corresponds to 29 percent of total Arab output. Their total population of 22 million is 6.6 percent of that of the Arab world. This was 272 publications per million inhabitants—some seven times the average output per capita for the Arab world.

Tunisia ranked in 2007 as the second largest producer of research after Egypt. Tunisia produced 50 percent of the research output of Egypt, whose population was 7.7 times larger than that of Tunisia. Lebanon ranks fourth along with Jordan, while the UAE ranks eighth and Kuwait ranks ninth. In other words, these four countries occupy a notable research ranking within the Arab world.[8]

The data to be reviewed below focuses on the degree of diffusion of R&D capability within the four countries, as well as on the degree of diversity of the R&D pursued. These positive patterns are interpreted as indicative of an increasing level of innovation and increasing capacity to integrate scientific and technological potentialities with entrepreneurship.

Lebanon

There were 15 major publishing organizations, including the American University Hospital (AUH), as distinct from the American University of Beirut (AUB), functioning in Lebanon that published more than 15 papers during this period. Among these 15 publishing organizations there are 9 universities and five hospitals (★Table 6.7). Information is provided below concerning data on small organizations not included in the table.

The leading R&D organization in Lebanon is AUB (including AUH), contributing 42 percent of the output, followed by the Lebanese American University (LAU) with 12 percent. Université St Joseph (USJ), the second oldest university in Lebanon, contributes 9 percent of output (a third of AUB's output, without AUH). The Beirut Arab University contributes 3 percent of Lebanon's output. The Lebanese University, the largest in the country by student enrolment, contributes 5 percent of R&D output.

AUB published 4,425 papers (authored by 2,927 different persons) according to the SCOPUS download. These authors collaborated with 1,986 organizations to publish these papers. In some cases there was strong collaboration: for example, 389 (20 percent of affiliations) of the papers were jointly published with AUH. This was the strongest affiliation of AUB. The second strongest was with LAU, with 92 (4.6 percent) joint papers.

Since every organization that affiliates with another in Lebanon is counted, there is a considerable number of double and triple counting. Thus the total number of 7,120 included in ★Table 6.7 reflects the extent of collaboration. Naturally, the foreign collaborating organizations do not lead to double counting.

There were some 35 small organizations that published, over the years, about a dozen papers each—some published more and some published less. The bulk of these 35 organizations were active in the medical field. A few examples are presented here to illustrate the organizations that were left out from ★Table 6.7.

Including them here illustrates a Lebanese streak to support collaboration; Lebanese organizations always search for fresh ideas and contacts with the outside world. The four countries included here share this streak.

Aboujaoude Hospital, as SCOPUS states, published seven documents, which had seven authors. The publications noted some 24 affiliations distributed partly in the Middle East (6 affiliations) and in Europe and the United States. The details provided are incomplete as to the location of some of the affiliates.

The Abyad Medical Center in Tripoli, Lebanon, published 13 papers in medicine, three in biochemistry, two in social sciences, one in agriculture and biological sciences, and one in health professions. The center's publications had affiliations with seven organizations: five in Lebanon that engaged with old age; and two abroad.

The Lebanese Agricultural Research Institute published 41 papers by 40 authors and collaborated with 26 organizations: 26 papers had some collaboration with LU, AUB, and USJ; the rest collaborated with Aleppo University and ICARDA of Syria, with Tunisian organizations, and with research organizations in Italy and France.

Khatib and Alami Consolidated Engineering Co. published eight documents. Its authors collaborated mostly with AUB and LU faculty and three foreign organizations.

Dar Al-Handasah Consultants had 12 publications in various areas of engineering. Of these collaborations, 60 percent were with AUB professors. In total they collaborated with ten different organizations. AUB was their leading partner.

One notes from the available information that there are no industrial or public sector organizations in Lebanon that have made significant R&D contributions during this period, aside from the Ministry of Agriculture and CNRS, which contributed 4 percent of research output.

The four hospitals—Hotel Dieu, Rizk, Makassed, and St George—together contributed 14 percent of research output, which is comparable to that of the older and larger AUH, which contributed 15 percent of output.

The extent of R&D collaboration of Lebanon with other Arab countries is 5 percent of the Lebanese output. The two largest research organizations (AUB and AUH) contribute 22 percent of the research papers falling under the category of Arab–Arab collaboration. AUB and AUH are responsible for 42 percent of Lebanon's research output.

In Lebanon, 40 percent of publications are from work undertaken fully in the country. The combined number of papers resulting from international collaboration with Europe and the United States accounts for 54 percent of total output. Lebanon's collaboration with third world countries, China, Japan, Latin America, and international organizations is on an insignificant scale.

One would have expected that the well-established medical industry in Lebanon—involving several medical schools and numerous hospitals—would have led to the development of advanced public health policies and established local research centers, and attracted international ones, in the pharmacological sciences—which in turn might have led to the establishment of manufacturing industries of medical supplies and equipment. Interestingly, no such developments took place.

Despite the high share of research in clinical medicine throughout the Arab world, no industries have grown out of their activities. For example, one does not find significant industries associated with the production of medical equipment, hospital management services, consulting services in hospital design, and construction or pharmaceutical production. AUB and other medical schools have evolved an education program that is oriented toward hospital-based medicine; a high proportion (probably of the order of 66 percent) of their graduates gravitate to the United States and Europe.

AUB and AUH had 1,160 papers with North American organizations compared with 432 papers with Europe. This yields a ratio of 2.7 (North America) to 1(Europe). But the output of Lebanon as a whole is slightly more inclined toward Europe: 1,857 (with North American collaborators) compared to 2,017 (with European collaborators). This yields a ratio of 0.92 (North America) to 1 (Europe).

We note the degree of collaboration with third world countries as well as China and Japan to be negligible. Interestingly, there is a small level of collaboration with Australia; this may be the result of long established Lebanese emigration to that country.

Kuwait

The total SCOPUS research download for Kuwait was 4,514 papers. Of these, 50 percent were the result of local research; 789 papers (18 percent) were a product of collaboration with North America; 602 papers (13 percent) were a product of Arab-Arab collaboration and an equal number of collaboration with European scientists. There were 1.4 papers that resulted from collaboration with North America and 1 with Europe. Some 6 percent of the papers were a product of collaboration with third world scientists.

Kuwait has three universities with very unequal research output. The University of Kuwait's (2,085 publications) share of total output was 46 percent, while College of Technology Studies (96 papers) has a share of national output of 2 percent, and the Gulf University for Science and Technology (51 papers) has an output of 1 percent.

Kuwait had 13 publishing hospitals with an output of 1,505 papers and a Ministry of Health publishing 314 papers; 87 percent of the hospitals' publications are local, while 37 percent of the publications of the Ministry of Health were the result of collaboration. By comparison, there were 5 hospitals in Lebanon publishing 2,022 papers and 17 hospitals in the UAE with an output of 1,340 papers.

Kuwait incorporated science and technology into the economy. For example, Kuwait had four medical research centers (★Table 6.8) in the fields of genetics, Arab medical literature, drug control, and health sciences. These were not very active in publishing: they had 231 publications, which was 5 percent of the total output. These centers supported collaboration with other scientists in the Arab world and elsewhere.

Kuwait has also more than ten research centers (★Table 6.9) located in the ministries. Compare this with Lebanon, which supports only the CNRS and the Research Center in Agriculture. The Kuwaiti research centers published 328 papers, 7 percent of total output. Kuwait has a substantial applied R&D center, the Kuwait Institute for Scientific Research (KISR), of long standing. Surprisingly, SCOPUS does not record any publications from KISR. Yet, KISR is an important applied science research organization. Between 1986 and 2007 KISR published, according to ISI, 31 and 64 papers.

KISR was established in 1967 and was upgraded in 1973 under a strong leadership. By 1989 it was already publishing 50 papers a year. It maintained this level of output until 1990. KISR was looted during the Iraqi invasion and had to restart after the country was freed from its occupation. It appears that by 2007 it resumed its vigor and was publishing 64 publications per year.

KISR pioneered a direct interest in the local economy. For example, it realized at an early date that the rising demand for air-conditioning during the summer months would put great burden on electric power generation. It developed construction codes with the objective of reducing heat leaks in residential buildings during the summer months. Electric power demand during the summer is a major and costly problem that plagues all GCC countries.

The early efforts to bring science and technology into the economy failed to be adopted fully. This led to a setback and a reduction in the support to the expansion of the national scientific base. Of course, Egypt had pursued that route long before any other Arab country. Yet Egypt failed to obtain sufficient returns from its efforts, resulting in a loss of interest.

The UAE

The UAE has 16 organizations offering higher education. The research output of these educational organizations was 4,659 papers.

The faculty of health and medicine of the UAE University alone published 1,561 papers; and the UAE University published 1,420 papers (making a combined total of 2,981 papers), compared to Kuwait University's output of 2,082 papers.

Publications for the other major universities in the UAE were as follows: the American University of Sharjah, 542 papers (309 of which were a product of collaboration with North American scientists); the University of Sharjah, 420 publications; and the Zayed University, 256 papers.

Ajman University of Science and Technology published 82 papers, of which 52 were the product of Arab-Arab collaboration. There were seven academic organizations publishing less than 50 papers each, and four publishing between 50 and 99 papers each.

The 16 organizations offering programs in higher education vary considerably in type and size; from the fully fledged UAE University at al-Ain to smaller and specialized colleges such as Etisalat University College, or the Dubai Pharmacy College.

The high rate of injection of new faculty members leads to an increase of the "output" of the country. As was mentioned earlier, some of these papers may have nothing to do with the UAE, because the research was undertaken by scientists in their previous occupations who just cite the UAE as their current address. Of the 4,659 publications by UAE academic organizations, only 944 papers were the result of local research, 1,158 were a product of "collaboration" with North American scientists, and 1,085 were a product of "collaboration" with European scientists. One also notes that collaboration with third world countries (217 papers), Japan and China (93 papers), is relatively substantial.

The research qualifications of the faculty, though earned abroad, naturally adds quality to the academic program.

It is noteworthy that the local research production from the academic organizations of the UAE was only 20 percent of the output, compared with 50 percent in Kuwait and 40 percent in Lebanon. This may be an indication that much of the research work was undertaken before the faculty member joined a UAE organization.

The Faculty of Health and Medicine published 1,561 papers, of which 495 were the product of local work, 219 the result of collaboration with North American scientists, 350 the product of Arab-Arab collaboration, and 402 the result of European collaboration. The Gulf Medical College published 72 papers.

There are 17 publishing hospitals in the UAE that contributed 1,340 papers: 50 percent of the research output was the result of local research; 13 percent, the result of collaboration with other Arab countries; 15 percent, with North America; and 17 percent, the result of collaboration with European scientists.

The UAE has 14 research centers in a number of locally relevant applied fields (★Table 6.10). Here we find research activity on oil operations, electric power, veterinary sciences, aluminum, petroleum, roads, pharmaceuticals, forensic sciences, and environmental research. The total research activity is still limited, but this effort displays a national interest in the pursuit of R&D in many walks of life.

Eleven UAE ministries and companies sponsor research activity resulting in publications. ★Table 6.11 shows that ministries and companies are active in this direction. ★Tables 6.10 and 6.11 indicate that the R&D output totals 1,134 papers, compared to 469 from similar activities in Kuwait (★Tables 6.8 and 6.9).

Tunisia

The total number of publications downloaded for Tunisia in 2009 was 20,501, of which 10,120 resulted from work done in Tunisia; the rest resulted from collaboration with external organizations. The Tunisian output should be compared with 7,120 for Lebanon, 4,514 for Kuwait, and 7,153 for UAE. Tunisia is a latecomer compared to Lebanon. Whereas Lebanon held the second place in Arab research output before 1975, Tunisia had reached eighth place in 1976. Between 1976 and 2007 Tunisia steadily progressed up the ranking among the Arab countries: fifth in 1990, fourth in 2002, and second in 2007.

There are more than 100 organizations that publish in Tunisia. Of these, 34 are in higher education contributing 10,289 papers. Of these publications, 4,091 were the result of research performed in Tunisia; the rest were published through collaborative activity. Interestingly, publications in the medical sciences totaled only 2,298 papers (or 23 percent) of total output, compared to higher levels in other Arab countries. However, in 2005 (see chapter 2) Tunisian researchers published 849 papers in the medical sciences, that is, 48 percent of the total research output of 1,783. The "total download" from Scopus is not a correct representation of annual current output.[9]

Tunisia stands out in comparison with other Arab countries in the large number (40) of nonacademic research centers that it has established; these published 8,006 publications, of which 4,689 were undertaken in the country.

The output of these research centers is nearly equal to the output of the system of higher education. It is notable that this output is substantially greater than that of Kuwait (469) and the UAE (1,134) covering similar types of activities.

Collaboration with European scientists (mostly French) totaled 2,596 papers, while collaboration with North American scientists totaled 321—a ratio of 8:1. Tunisia has benefited from EU programs of scientific collaboration with third world countries. The considerable community of Tunisians in France has also helped to cement collaborative activities.

The tendency to establish specialized R&D centers on their own rather than under a broader appellation provides greater flexibility and allows for more personal ingenuity and less hierarchy. For example, L'Institut de l'Olivier could have been under the ministry of agriculture; the same goes for L'Institut National de Nutrition, l'Institut National de Recherche en Génie Rural, Eau et Forêts, and so on.

Interestingly, Tunisia has a small but higher level of cooperation with Japan and China than most (except Egypt) other Arab countries. Out of 20,501 publications, 106 are in collaboration with these two countries.

Nine ministries contributed 5,050 publications, of which only 194 are of local origin and the rest the result of collaborative activity with foreign organizations. In other words, research output from ministries is nearly 50 percent of that performed in the organizations of higher education.

Comparisons of Lebanon, Tunisia, Kuwait, and the UAE

It is interesting to note the differences and similarities among these four countries in the distribution of their R&D activities, the different patterns of collaboration with foreign countries, the degree to which they have established research centers to deal with specific applied problems, and the degree to which R&D activities diffused out of their universities.

The most notable features are the changes in the composition of R&D in the countries. With Lebanon, we find a traditional attitude of neglect. Kuwait showed serious interest in the applications of science from the 1960s to the 1980s. But somehow this pioneering attitude cooled down after 1990. The UAE is an enthusiastic latecomer. We have seen that UAE is promoting academic, medical, and applied R&D. Tunisia, however, has demonstrated very serious commitment to R&D by the considerable range of activities it has deployed. I will highlight in chapter 7 the implications of Tunisian R&D activities to its economic development.

Whereas Lebanon shows no R&D activity by any ministry (except the Ministry of Agriculture), Kuwait has more than ten centers of research at ministries, as well as independent research centers. Lebanon could only claim 252 publications from the National Centre for Scientific Research organizations, compared with 9,006 in Tunisia.

The UAE has 14 research centers that published 762 papers. In other words, the UAE research centers outproduce those of Lebanon. Even Sudan outclasses Lebanon: Sudan's 14 research centers published 656 papers, of which 257 research papers are local in origin. Kuwait has five research centers, which published 231 papers, of which 91 are local in origin.

All of these countries are in midcourse and it will take a few more years before the seriousness of their efforts can be demonstrated. Egypt had undertaken similar measures many years ago. It had nine such centers already in the 1950s. However, it adopted policies resulting in bureaucratic obstacles that prevented it from benefiting from its investments.

Another feature to note is the high rate of R&D growth in GCC countries and Tunisia compared with Lebanon, Egypt, and other traditional centers of research in the region. The ability of a newcomer like Tunisia not only to move to second place but also to adopt a wide range of effective measures to make significant progress is impressive.

Unfortunately, we have no measure of quality, productivity, or relevance in any Arab country; it is not possible to discuss this important topic before adequate data becomes available. It appears from current trends that serious developments may be expected during the next decade.

Concluding Remarks

It was shown in this chapter that there are growing differences amongst Arab countries in the deployment of their R&D expertise in their national economy as well as in the degree of collaboration with scientists in industrial countries. Algeria, Lebanon, Morocco, and Tunisia are leading the Arab countries in collaboration with OECD scientists. The rest are at a much lower level of collaboration. However, what matters is the degree of collaboration between R&D and the national economy.

It was shown that international collaboration of scientists, on a per capita basis, in the Arab world and China are comparable. However, Chinese and other Tiger scientists are integrated into

—a national scientific community, and

—a national economy through national technology policies and an effective national science and technology system.

No Arab country has adopted similar measures.

CHAPTER 7

SEEDING THE ARAB WORLD

Introduction

The concern with economic growth, employment, and improving the well-being of society is now widespread. Governments pursue their objectives in different ways and achieve different degrees of success. We have already noted the importance of the political economy to such processes.

The efforts pursued by governments and individuals hinge on the possession of knowledge and the conditions of its deployment and the effectiveness of its use.

As is clear from the accounts presented in this book, the Arab countries encounter difficulties in providing suitable employment to their labor force because of the technology policies that they pursue. The socioeconomic returns from massive Arab investments in higher education are reduced by their adoption of inappropriate technology policies. Consequently, they are unable to create employment, and this results in a massive brain drain that deprives them of the expected benefits from their investments in their educational systems.

Elsewhere, and over the past 50 years, developmental issues have attracted the attention of economists, planners, politicians, and policy analysts, resulting in a rich quantum of literature. The subject is complex and constantly changing under the impact of advances in technology and international competition.

Analytical studies of these conditions call for a considerable range of timely, accurate, and relevant statistics. Social scientists in industrial countries have benefited from an enormous range of data generated by their national statistical services. Scholars in industrial countries possess an amazing grasp of the factors that govern socioeconomic change, though they still face serious problems.[1]

The Arab countries suffer from a considerable shortage of accurate, timely, and relevant data. Attempts to apply methods developed for industrial countries rich in data to developing countries with limited (or no) data are absurd.

The lack of adequate statistical information hinders Arab planners and decision makers from becoming sufficiently aware of the low productivity of their economic systems and of their human capital.

There are many attempts to stretch the applicability of available analytical tools to understand prevailing conditions in Arab countries. To date, the limitations imposed by shortages of relevant data have limited the benefits of such exercises.

Statistics, Definitions, and Limits

It is useful to state a few words about the value and limits of some of the statements made concerning the Arab countries. One can, for example, obtain meaningful results when the indicator in question calls for simple and available data. The UNDP human development index (HDI), which is based on lifespan, educational enrolment, and per capita income, is generally reasonably meaningful, simply because the numbers utilized are simple to assess and their range of errors is acceptable for deriving order of magnitude indicators.

Perhaps the most difficult item in this indicator is educational enrolment. Here the quality of education would have been expected to pose serious difficulties. We know that there are enormous differences in the quality of education provided by the 200 countries that make up the international community.

It appears, however, that this has no impact on HDI! Enrolment in both high quality and poor quality education is assessed to be equivalent. The other two factors (lifespan and per capita income) may have been assumed to reflect sufficiently the quality of education.

This is strange, and one would expect that in extreme cases there should be consequences that are not borne out by common sense. We can see that in the rating of GCC countries, they all rate an HDI higher than other countries that common sense tells us are more developed and thus should be ahead of them. This is, of course, not the fault of the GCC countries that they have near 100 percent school enrolment for their children and very high per capita income because of natural causes: the geology and strategic location of their countries.

So when one looks at the standing of countries according to HDI, one finds surprises that can be figured out using common sense.

HDI is a crude indicator. It helps to alert policy makers about the standing of their countries. Obviously, the HDI of a country should prod its leaders to search for ways to advance it. Unfortunately, the HDI index does not tell us anything meaningful concerning the way to proceed to improve the standing of a country.

When one tries to make sense of more comprehensive approaches, such as the World Bank Knowledge Assessment Methodology (KAM),[2] the situation is more complex. The KAM approach is more elaborate; it attempts to include a wide range of factors in assessing the state of knowledge in a country.

In physics it is meaningless to apply the concept of temperature to a body that is not in thermal equilibrium. Similarly, in social sciences it is meaningless to investigate economic relationships when there is no correlation between income distribution and economic activity.

Thus, any meaningful knowledge index should include the sources of knowledge that generate the GNP in question. Countries that depend so extensively on technology-free turnkey contracts do not tap their national capabilities.

Arab technological dependence reduces the multiplier factors associated with investments to a low figure, and often may be negative. In industrial countries governments pay attention to the technological and employment contents of contracts that their private and public sectors undertake. This is not the case in Arab countries.

European countries purchasing warplanes from the United States arrange to export an equivalent amount of products and services to balance their loss of employment of skilled labor by the import of US weapons. This type of process aims to offset some of the consequences of the purchase. Offset programs undertaken with Arab countries are amusing in their technological and employment implications for the recipient country.

The above considerations are merely the tip of the iceberg. Many of the factors that seem to be relevant to KAM are meaningless with respect to many developing countries. For example, KAM includes a factor called governance. We are told that governance has seven subsidiary components, called regulatory quality, the rule of law, government effectiveness, voice and accountability, political stability, control of corruption, and press freedom.[3]

These subsidiary components are interesting and important, but they would be difficult to assess in a developing country with limited statistical information. For example, "regulatory quality" is defined (by KAM) as "[measuring] the incidence of market-unfriendly policies such as price controls or inadequate bank supervision, as well as perceptions of the burdens imposed by excessive regulation in areas such as foreign trade and business development."

Entries in the KAM tables for Arab countries concerning the subject of innovation systems are either 0.00 or n/a. There are no statistical data on innovation published by Arab countries.

The numerical entries in some of the tables refer to trade and foreign direct investment (FDI), which seem to be the magic tools of development.

KAM innovation categories also include the number of scientific publications and human capital resources. In this study it is felt that the absence of an enabling environment—that is, the absence of an S&T system and of relevant technology policies to direct economic activities toward acquisition and adaptation—incapacitates national human capital. In other words, countries may have potentialities but no capabilities.

It is therefore not useful to have a million engineers and 20,000 research publications annually if the country does not pursue appropriate technology policies.

Knowledge and Takeoff

It is difficult, if not impossible, to apply models that have been developed for Western market economies—forgetting the models that they pursued at their takeoff—to evaluate the likelihood of selected Arab countries to take off.

It is reasonable to assume that any serious economic development is powered by knowledge acquired by entrepreneurs. It is also reasonable to expect that freedom of association and the availability of resources are instrumental in such processes.

Significant technological activities would involve substantial numbers of professionals. These professionals need to be embedded in a scientific community.

Entrepreneurs can be from the private or public sector. In fact, the "advances" taking place in the Arab world are generally driven by public sector entrepreneurs. The construction of the Aswan High Dam in Egypt and the Euphrates Dam in Syria are clearly public sector innovations, and both had extensive impact on their countries because technology acquisition was associated with their implementation. Similarly, the nationalization of the Suez Canal was an important entrepreneurial act.

The Arab Addiction to Technological Dependence

The Arab countries have been soliciting and receiving the advisory services of leading governments, international organizations, and companies for some 50 years, and yet they have not been able to advance as significantly as South Korea or China.

Readers are probably aware of the considerable number of foreign universities currently being established in Arab countries. In November 2009 the US secretary of state, Hillary Clinton, announced the naming of "three prominent scientists as special envoys to assess the potential for scientific partnerships with Muslim majority countries."[4]

Are all of these efforts going to make a difference to the Arab world? Will parachuting science have a different outcome from the recent "investment" (by Arabs) of US $5–6 trillions in their countries?

The Diversity of Ways that Rent Impacts on Innovative Processes

Murphy et al. have attracted attention to the diversity of ways that rent-seeking affects an economy. They first demonstrate that rent-seeking is devastating to economic growth. But then they show that corruption in public organizations is especially devastating to innovators.

The authors conclude that

> public rent-seeking is either redistribution from the private sector to the state, such as taxation, or alternatively from the private sector to the government bureaucrats who affect the fortunes of the private sector. The latter kind of public rent-seeking takes the form of lobbying, corruption, and so on...Private rent-seekers go after existing stocks of wealth, such as land, output, capital, and so on. Bandits steal crops, lawyers sue deep-pocket corporations, and armies invade rich countries. In contrast, public rent-seeking attacks innovation, since innovators need government-supplied goods, such as permits, licenses, import quotas, and so on, much more so than established producers.[5]

Rent-seeking is rampant throughout the Arab world. However, the power of the bureaucrats to extract rent and the power of the citizen (or innovator) to negotiate and reduce demand vary considerably from country to country. Four countries—Lebanon, Tunisia, the UAE, and Kuwait—may, because of their size and the substantial number of innovators, have established a more satisfactory relationship between themselves and rent-seeking bureaucrats.

Naturally, the relative balance of power between bureaucrats and innovators in the effectively centralized states is much more in favor of the bureaucrat. In fact, the innovator is seriously impaired, and unless he yields enough of his project he has limited hope of achieving anything.

A Nondependent Approach

It is clear that several Arab countries appear to be expanding their R&D output, and many of them are beyond the critical level of 25 publications per million inhabitants per year in quality and refereed international periodicals. Some Arab countries are showing an increasing level of entrepreneurship. Could these measures lead to a breakthrough?

I searched for a combination of Arab countries

- that appear to be "making a significant effort" in the knowledge domain as indicated by the recent rapid change in their R&D output;
- whose public organizations appear to be R&D active;
- whose populations enjoy freedom of association;
- whose populations enjoy considerable international linkages;
- that possess large Diasporas that place their entrepreneurs in a global setting;
- whose populations possess a large number of linkages with each other;
- whose entrepreneurs have demonstrated a capacity to establish numerous, successful, and competitive entrepreneurial activities;
- that possess, or have access to, financial resources;
- that possess financial and legal institutions to manage their financial resources; and
- that have established track records for using these financial resources and knowledge capabilities in novel ways.

No Arab country fits the above check list. Yet, Saudi Arabia, Egypt, Iraq, Algeria, Morocco, and Syria come to mind as likely candidates for such a transition. These countries possess enormous potentialities and human capital. They are, however, held back by entrenched rent and ossified political economies. It is possible that these countries may be able to generate the political will to overcome inherited problems. However, there are no signs at the moment that such a move is imminent.

The Arab world today is like supercooled water that is prevented from undergoing a phase transition to ice. Seeding supercooled water may be induced by a dust particle or a microcrystal of ice. In the real world seeding entails a substantial number of persons, with the appropriate skills and resources, collaborating successfully to transform their socioeconomic reality. Countries where rent is least dominant and where innovative collaboration among different parties is intensive and facilitated are likely to generate such an event.

Can Kuwait, Lebanon, Tunisia, and the UAE Provide the Environment for Change?

It is speculated here that these four countries possess many of the ingredients needed to generate a breed of entrepreneurs capable of overcoming political boundaries.

It was shown in chapter 6 that Kuwait, Tunisia, and the UAE have distinguished themselves in the extent of collaboration between researchers at ministries and independent research centers. This activity is still in its initial stages. Lebanon has favored entrepreneurial activities inspired by encounters of professionals at its universities. But the Lebanese government, unlike the three others, does not support significant research at its ministries and independent research centers.

It was also noted that the universities in these four countries published 68 percent (Lebanon), 50 percent (Kuwait), 67 percent (UAE), and 50 percent (Tunisia) of each country's R&D output. The average rate for all four countries is that universities published 56 percent of R&D output, whereas the share of universities' output in the Arab world as a whole is above 70 percent. This is interpreted here to imply that R&D activity, especially in Kuwait, UAE, and Tunisia, is diffusing outside academia and may have a chance to influence the national economy. All four countries occupy a high research ranking within the Arab world.

When, after the Second World War, US military organizations expanded their R&D activities rapidly, they quickly discovered that their major departments needed to possess mini R&D functions in order to relate to national R&D activity.

The USSR, which had enormous R&D capabilities, discovered that centralization and bureaucracy prevented the economy from benefiting from its research. It attempted to bridge the gap between the centralized R&D activity and those that needed the output; however, the process was too slow and failed to benefit from its resources. It is clear that it is not enough to undertake R&D. There must also exist an enabling environment that facilitates the diffusion and application of knowledge.

Lebanon displays a very weak link between R&D and the economy because the public sector has shown no interest in supporting R&D in the country. There are cosmetic public sector activities, but these do not significantly change things at the national level.

Each of these four countries has a comparatively liberal atmosphere that enables their populations to live relatively free lives; to travel freely, unconstrained by government control; and to exercise the right of free association. Furthermore, their relatively small size gives them flexibility and a capacity to adapt more promptly to international change than the larger Arab countries.

I have noted earlier that a national science and technology infrastructure is critical for deriving benefits from R&D and from international collaboration. The Arab countries, including those under discussion, lack scientific societies and an enabling S&T system. Scientific societies are also vital to subjecting knowledge prior to its adoption to national scientific and social evaluation.

Innovative Entrepreneurship[6]

The level of entrepreneurial activity in Lebanon and Tunisia indicates that both countries have been moving through the early phase of a transition to knowledge-based societies.

Lebanon provides an interesting example of such a pattern of behavior. During the past 50 years entrepreneurial activity was initiated in Lebanon by university professors or graduates. For example, the "original" consulting firm, Dar al-Handasah, was founded by five Arab professors at the AUB.[7] Dar al-Handasah broke up in successive steps to spawn two other consulting firms, all of which are still operating (in 2010) and successful. These firms now employ more than 4,000 engineers plus numerous other knowledge workers. These three consulting firms provide consulting services predominantly in civil engineering. They compete and operate internationally. There are, currently, many similar organizations in Lebanon and elsewhere in the Arab world.

The universities in Lebanon (and possibly in Tunisia, UAE, and Kuwait) provide centers where competences collect, interact, and innovate entrepreneurially rather than collaborate in R&D. In many areas of engineering much of the creative output is embodied in buildings, infrastructures, industries, and so on. The process leading to such output integrates basic scientific and economic principles with economic, business, social, and cultural features.

The Consolidated Contracting Company (CCC), a large contracting company with global reach, was founded by three graduates from AUB in early 1952. With 140,000 employees on its payroll today, it is the largest (or one of the largest) contracting company in the Middle East. According to its website the total revenue managed by CCC was of the order of $5.5 billion in 2007.

There are today a number of Arab contracting companies with annual turnover running in excess of $1 billion. These firms are distributed over most of the GCC countries, Egypt, Algeria, Syria, Lebanon, Morocco, and Tunisia.

Thus, consulting and contracting firms have been founded by energetic and competent professionals throughout the Arab world. Nevertheless, there are many areas of consulting and contracting where Arab services are not yet available.

Chicken farming companies in Lebanon also originated with the initiative of graduates from the AUB School of Agriculture. This innovation spread like wildfire throughout the region.

Little is known about the original sparks that ignited the development of the Lebanese jewelry, fashion, and media industries, though it may have been the skilled and innovative Armenian community in Lebanon that sparked some of these developments. These firms design and manufacture fashion products, market them internationally, and are successful in a highly competitive global market. The entrepreneurs of these industries may have gained their expertise at home or by working abroad.

The Abella brothers launched a large-scale catering industry in the 1950s. This expanded globally and was followed by similar firms, especially in Saudi Arabia.

Banking has been an important entrepreneurial field throughout the region, starting with Tal'at Harb's Bank Misr in Egypt. Cement plants, quarries, a range of industries, transport companies, hotels, and so on have been established successfully in all these four countries and also in other Arab countries.

One of the assets of Dubai is Jebel Ali Free Zone, famous and much sought after by international firms as a site for manufacturing because of the high quality of its services; it is not only world-class but also a setter of global standards in harbor container terminal and industrial zone management.

Similarly, a range of small-scale pharmaceutical industries are equally notable in many Arab countries.

Other businesses were established in management, accounting, auditing, labor training, in the medical field, airlines, and so on.

Similar illustrative entrepreneurial examples can be cited for other Arab countries. For example, the Zamil brothers in Saudi Arabia established an important industrial empire. Sabic is no less brilliant an example.

There are also considerable efforts in the information technology field, with the notable example of Murex, a world-class company in advanced financial software established by three Lebanese brothers, based in France. Murex has been trying to develop a strong base in Lebanon, but this has been obstructed by the absence of appropriate legislation on double taxation.

Similarly, Knowledge View, established by an Iraqi computer scientist in the UK, has successfully developed and is marketing software for Arabic and English publishing. It has been successful in both the OECD and the Arab markets.

All of these activities are science-based and can serve as building blocks of a modern economy. The challenge facing Arab countries is how to enable the formation of a much greater number of such organizations and to enable them to compete successfully both at home and in the international marketplace.

Diaspora and Linkages

Both Lebanon and Tunisia have large, educated, internationally based, entrepreneurial, and successful Diasporas, which interact with other entrepreneurs throughout the Arab world and internationally. These entrepreneurs are not only aware of but also involved in scientific, technological, and business advances taking place worldwide.

GCC entrepreneurs have a global presence. There are substantial populations from GCC countries that live abroad, in locations of high business activity, almost on a continuous basis. There are infinite possibilities for substantial interactions among these different Diasporas and population groups.

Kuwait and the UAE possess extensive management capabilities in handling very large projects; their governments have also had to develop their financial sectors to manage large financial resources. Emirati and Kuwaiti entrepreneurs have been very active, at home and abroad in real estate, establishing hotel chains, a variety of large-scale industries, supermarkets, and other businesses.

The Tunisian government adopted quality control principles in its manufacturing industries more than a decade ago. This activity, also supported by the EU, aimed to promote Tunisian exports. Thus we find that Tunisian researchers (Chaffai and Guermazi) at the University of Sfax collaborated with a French researcher to investigate total factor productivity (TFP) in Tunisian industries. This type of investigation is crucial for the shaping of future public sector behavior.[8] To date, interest in this type of research is still on a small scale, and it is non-existent in most Arab countries.

Needless to say, all GCC countries have adopted high quality standards in their activities and industries, and thus they are prepared, at this level, for global markets.

Many entrepreneurs, especially from Lebanon and Tunisia, are already successfully competing in OECD countries. Thus, given imaginative political leadership in these countries it should be possible to accelerate the evolution of current trends.

Lebanese firms seldom benefit from public services or public support to facilitate their activities. Whether it is CCC, Khatib and Alami, a jeweller marketing in Geneva, a garment maker marketing in California, or a wine maker exporting wine to France, all these firms are competing in the international market and have to meet international norms. And they do succeed. Every Lebanese firm is born as an exporter.

The four countries contribute a complementary set of inputs necessary to initiate large-scale projects. What is suggested here is that these four countries provide a chaordic base for entrepreneurial activity that also welcomes entrepreneurs from other countries.[9]

Entrepreneurship and Science

It is interesting to note that Arab governments and the League of Arab States were concerned with science, technology, and pan-Arab economic activities before the late 1970s. Initial setbacks have cooled this early fervor.

The most notable effort was that of the Economic Department of the League of Arab States during the period extending from mid-1950s to mid-1970s under the leadership of Hasan Zalzalah. The Economic Department organized a number of activities to promote such an interest and to contribute to a series of Arab Summit meetings. These summits were concerned with the establishment of a series of pan-Arab companies.

Most of these projects have failed to take off. Inadequate planning may have caused their failure. Needless to say, the basic planning and legal framework for the emergence of these pan-Arab projects may still be worth resuscitating.

The Federated Arab Chamber of Commerce, Industry, and Trade, when under the management of the late Burhan Dajani, sought to establish a relationship between the world of technology and that of Arab business investors.[10] These efforts were focused on individual investments and have yielded some results.

The young Arab Science and Technology Foundation (ASTF), under the energetic leadership of its director, Abdallah al-Najjar, has been actively promoting a linkage between the scientific and business communities on a pan-Arab basis.

There are also initiatives taken by Arab scientists and engineers in the Diaspora to promote new investments and projects. There is little doubt that there is considerable effort going on, all seeking to promote entrepreneurial projects.

However, there is as yet no detailed and fundamental collective Arab effort to facilitate the establishment of national S&T systems to sustain these efforts, to comprehend the complexity of the measures required to reduce transaction cost and to promote both forward and backward linkages within the national and regional Arab economies.

To date, these activities have been undertaken without much attention to their economic advantage to the region. Obviously, it is the government that should provide appropriate incentives to encourage entrepreneurs to adopt policies that facilitate joint Arab cooperation, since this the only way that firms can compete by making use of their comparative advantages.

Water as a Likely Factor in Seeding the Arab World

I will chose the issue of water as a precipitator of the seeding process. One would expect that as water shortages become more pronounced there will be more serious concern about this issue throughout the region.

The Arab world affliction with aridity is well known. In 2007 a group of concerned public leaders established the Arab Forum for Environment and Development (AFED). The 12 founding members were partly (55 percent) persons with expertise in the concerned issues, such as Dr. Tolba, and partly eminent political figures and businessmen. The 11 persons who were added to the Board of Trustees in 2008 were mostly businessmen, with the exception of one eminent expert. Almost a third of the trustees were Lebanese and some 40 percent were from GCC countries—Omanis were surprisingly absent. There were four non-GCC countries involved: Lebanon, Egypt, Jordan, and Sudan.

AFED has not yet included among its trustees representatives of research, legal, and financial organizations or notable engineering and contracting firms. The trajectory that AFED will trace to develop an Arab water industry is not clear yet. One would imagine that the next step will be to mobilize the Arab public.

Lebanon is an eminent candidate for mobilization. Some 30 percent of its population has received the benefits of higher education, yet there is no mass public concern in matters of water and sewerage.

The shortage of appropriate scientific and technological associations delays the formation of bridges between the various parties that need to be involved in solving complex problems. The slowness with which the Arab countries respond to challenges in the water sphere is a measure of the lacunae of the scientific and sociopolitical infrastructure. Water is a higher necessity than oil and gas, or phosphates or the construction industry. All of these are enormous areas of technological activities of vital importance to the Arab countries, but they all have been lacking adequate attention. Yet, all have the capacity to seed the Arab world.

Knowledge Clusters and Development

Knowledge clusters often give rise to important inventions. These clusters may also be a source of "improved" traditional technologies and facilitate technology acquisition and transfer. Traditional technologies can serve as sources of innovation and development. Agriculture in the Arab world can still be improved considerably by better utilization of current advances.

Thus, the clusters that may evolve in the region could be based on advances in science as well as on upgraded traditional technologies, such as

- consulting and contracting industries, where the Lebanese already have a successful model;
- construction materials;
- health services;
- water-related industries;
- fashion and jewelry;
- agriculture and food production;
- phosphate-based industries; and
- oil and gas industries, and others.

There is an enormous demand for each of these technologies in the region. All of them are undergoing rapid change in industrial countries. Imagine meeting the food requirements of the expanding populations of the Arab world (the number of Arabs will double to 700 million or more during the next 30 years). The Lebanese have numerous world-class advantages in all of these areas, and they could play a leadership role in coalescing entrepreneurs with a global reach.

It is assumed that universities in all of these four countries will "evolve" innovation clusters as well as provide catalytic functions to bring together scientists, innovators, and entrepreneurs. The political leadership may recognize the benefits of the available opportunities and adopt constructive policies through the adoption of self-reliant technology policies.

The innovative business model adopted by Sheikh Mohammad bin Rashid al-Maktoum for Dubai may play a role in the crystallization of current assets into dramatic new pursuits.

The UAE government is financing and hosting a solar city with zero carbon production, and the UAE will also host the new UN Agency for Renewable Energy. The government is simultaneously preparing for its youth to assume important positions in these programs. There are colleges and universities throughout the Emirates that address issues of labor.

Kuwaitis, like the Emiratis, are global investors, and are part of the global economy and society. Each Gulf country has its own characteristics, but they also have much in common.

On the negative side, there are no signs that the four governments have adopted policies commensurate with the scale of the challenges or with the need to create effective bridges between the Arab countries to enable them to combine their capabilities in a profitable manner.

For example, the programs associated with Masdar and renewable energy in the GCC are very thin and limited. The UAE could use its interest in renewable energy as a focal point for private sector pan-Arab economic cooperation to drive the development of Arab industries in the area of renewable energy. They can attain their objectives through systematic collaboration among entrepreneurs by inducing profitable investments in this emerging area. The development of every Arab country is dependent on the development of sister countries.

By comparison with Masdar, which employs an insignificant number of "natives," jobs in the US renewable energy market have been increasing during the past decade at a high rate. There are now 770,000 jobs in renewable energy, compared with 1.27 million in oil and gas. Despite the small contribution to total US energy supplies provided by renewable energy, it already accounts for some 61 percent of those employed in oil and gas.[11]

Concluding Remarks

Four major factors are here assumed to contribute to the likelihood of the four countries merging their assets to develop a regional knowledge-based economy. This process is assumed to be private sector inspired, but enabled by the public sector.

The first factor arises from the current growth of R&D activities in these four countries. It is, alas, unlikely that the Lebanese government will evolve a national interest in this direction in the near future.

The second factor arises from the high level of innovative and complementary private sector entrepreneurship in all four countries.

The third is the highly developed Arab Diasporas and the successful export services generated by Lebanese entrepreneurs.

The fourth is the emergence of cluster formation in the UAE, Kuwait, and Tunisia. These may accelerate public sector involvement in the promotion of innovation and entrepreneurship.

The probability of the emergence of knowledge-based private and public sector economies in these four countries is significant because there is already a substantial infrastructure to support such a development. A substantial number of companies already exist that possess the means to pioneer in that direction.

Naturally, in the likely event that the political leadership[12] of any of these four countries supports such a development, the process could be accelerated and its probability of success significantly enhanced.

CHAPTER 8

SCIENCE AND NATIONAL SECURITY

Introduction

The history of the Arab world during the past thousand years has been dominated by issues of security. Until 1498 the Arab countries were attacked from many different directions and did suffer defeats, but these defeats were often followed by victory. After 1498 the story is one of constant defeats. It would be natural for national security to become an issue of primordial importance to Arabs. Security is not simply a military issue.

The history of security is dominated by science. The critical role of technology in warfare and in the economy has been known ever since man first chiselled a stone to use as an axe. However, beginning with Francis Bacon, the French Revolution, and the first Industrial Revolution, there was a more deliberate and dedicated effort to establish explicit systems to promote technological innovations and their adaptation for war and peace.[1] It is surprising that the extensive public concern of NATO countries with issues of national security has not elicited adequate responses within the Arab world.

In the United States and the Soviet Union the race in technology was very much a matter of national security. Eugene Sokolnikoff has provided a lucid and critical account of the relationship between science, technology, national security, and international relations.[2]

The power of scientific research is demonstrated starkly in the containment of potentially horrific epidemics. During the fourteenth century the Black Death caused the death of a third of the human race. At the time, science could not contribute to containing the epidemic.

Today the HIV epidemic and others have all been contained by the power of science. Yet, our science was unable to limit the consequences of the recent earthquake and tsunami in Japan.

Needless to say, all economic development and all improvement in health, including the prolongation of the average lifespan from 33 years until the eighteenth century to the current 85 year, are products of science. Countries that do not have access to the relevant sciences do not enjoy these advantages and live at various levels of ill health.

National security is a term that encompasses all the activities that a society has to undertake to ensure its health and well-being. This, of course, includes the ability to defend its borders, to prevent and contain criminal behavior, and to enable its citizens to live in freedom from fear irrespective of the origin of threats to their safety. A responsible society would be also concerned with

- climate change and its likely impact on the livelihood of its, and other, populations;
- the mismanagement of DNA information of its citizens;
- the likelihood of a collision between Earth and a comet; and so on.

Many threats to human life are global in origin, and no single country can contain them alone—thus the importance of international law and international collaboration.

R&D is essential to the identification of threats to national security as well as to the acquisition of capabilities to respond to them. The need for security is universal.

The decline and collapse of the Arab economic system in the sixteenth century has much to do with the inability of the Arabs to cope with the changes in science and technology that were occurring at the time. Three major technological advances sealed the fate of the Arab world for 500 years:

1. The inability of the Arabs to respond to advances in European naval technology during the fifteenth and sixteenth centuries. The invention of transoceanic ships was instrumental in the destruction of Arab-Asian trade and Arab trade and transport monopoly.
2. The failure to respond to the establishment of the East India Companies, which made possible the evolution of trading firms with sufficient capital to dominate international trade to the exclusion of Arab traders.

3. The inability to retain a substantial share of the lucrative coffee market after Western scientists and colonialists successfully transplanted coffee from Yemen to Brazil and elsewhere.

The technological basis of these reversals and the impact on the national security of the Islamic world were demonstrated in the naval battles between the Egyptians and the Portuguese at Diu in 1498 and 1513 and the decisive defeat of the combined Arab/Ottoman navy at Lepanto in 1571. These two defeats had a technological basis: the Diu defeat was the result of superior Portuguese ship design that gave them the capacity to carry numerous heavy guns; the Lepanto defeat was a consequence of the extensive adoption of handheld firearms by European soldiers.[3]

Arab/Ottoman national security declined in the centuries after Lepanto. By the time Napoleon invaded Egypt, Ottoman power had evaporated. By 1800 the Ottoman Empire was maintained by European rivalries rather than its ability to defend its territory.

Ottoman and Arab rulers appear to have been incapable of arresting the decline in their ability to defend themselves. With so much paralysis in the seat of power, the colonization of the Arab countries was inevitable. The valiant jihads displayed from Algeria to the Gulf during these centuries had a limited impact on the progress of occupation, because of the resulting technological gap.

Other examples of the impact of technology change abound: the undermining of the Arab textile industry at the beginning of the industrial revolution; the development of sources of mechanical energy to replace human and animal muscle; the enormous developments in agronomic practices that revolutionized food production; the failure of the Arab countries to be leaders in the development of their oil and gas resources; and others.

All these advances favored those countries that had the capacity to understand and manage the emerging sciences and penalized those that lacked this capacity.

The process of decline began, at first very slowly, with the policy of Al-Mu'tassim, who replaced Arab soldiers with mamluks (on a large scale around 837) and moved his court to Samarra to live with his mamluks. This was concurrent with the slowing down of the cultural and scientific advancement of the Arab world.

The caliph al-Mutawakkil (847–863) was assassinated by mamluk troops in 863; this event was followed by the Samarran troops laying siege to Baghdad in 867. The Abbasid court returned from Samarra to

Baghdad in 892. But the mamlukization of Arab political culture was already irreversible.

Decline and Disasters of Various Sorts

The onset of decline was the consequence of different factors that have not been adequately studied. The lack of political stability and security was probably at the center of these processes. Rulers of the Arab countries were unable to evolve a political culture that sustained stability. No doubt there were spectacularly successful moments in this period of history.

Rulers of the Arab countries between 890 and 1498 were unable to establish and manage a process of political and economic reform and development. This happened despite the presence of numerous eminent thinkers, philosophers, and scientists. Arab political leaders then, as now, had access to learned persons, but something did not click.

There were numerous external attacks on the Arab state from all directions. Yet "the state" endured for many centuries. Thus rulers had the opportunity to consolidate Arab control of the region despite many Crusades, Mongolian invasions, as well as the Black Death. There were also natural disasters arising from earthquakes, droughts and famines, floods, and multiple epidemics. There were also countless local civil wars and internecine struggles within ruling families and between neighboring states.

Attempts at Recovery

During the entire nineteenth century Egypt was in the lead in its exposure to the appliances of science and technology and to European learning. The rulers of Egypt employed large numbers (tens of thousands) of Europeans as technicians, military personnel, and consultants; they also imported the new technologies, ranging from steam engines to railways and the telegraph. They sent substantial numbers of students to study in Europe (in fact, more than the Japanese did 50 years later).

However, as a result of the nature of political rule in Egypt at the time, the notion of self-reliance was neither sought nor did it materialize. It had to await the emergence of the Egyptian national movement. But even then there was no adoption by the Egyptian political culture of this fundamental principle, despite its mass appeal.

The delay in pursuing such an objective was a massive setback to both Egypt and the region. Egypt failed to benefit from the period when it was relatively free, had a small population, and enjoyed a high level of prosperity arising from its cotton produce and its strategic location.

The Arab world has not been a fertile ground for the sciences for many centuries. The political and cultural degradations that took place in the region during the early centuries of the millennium were probably the major influence. This is a period of Arab history that has still to be investigated.

Arab National Security

The Arabs brought to the world they conquered an improved and extensive trading and transport system. Arab traders also provided local products with global markets. This increased local prosperity. The trading system was generally nonmonopolistic and was inspired by the rule of law. Furthermore, the Arab economy was neither centralized nor ethnically based. It was a private enterprise, generally open to all ethnic groups.

Arabs brought new crops from distant countries and created large markets for some products such as sugar and paper. During the early phases of the *futuhat*, alert and self-reliant Arabs observed their environment acutely and learnt new technologies. They thus learnt from Chinese troops how to make paper and explosives and many more skills.

Their pursuit of development and self-advancement led them to seek access to the then existing sources of knowledge. Enormous efforts were devoted to water supply, research, translation, and learning.

If the concepts of *umma*, *ijtihad*, and *shura* had been successfully developed during this early period, the Arabs would have evolved a democratic and modern state. These factors could have deepened social relations underpinning a productive multiethnic population. Such a development would have provided a secure base for a stable society. The Arabs failed to exhibit sufficient *ijtihad* toward such a goal or to establish a unified *umma* ruled by *shura* and justice. As a result the empire was vulnerable to both internal and external threats.

It is useful to examine the stages of the technological dismantling of the Arab nation during the past five centuries. There were three distinct phases in this process; each phase is linked to some technological development.

Arab National Security 1498–1630

The national security of the Arab world has been steadily degraded since 1498, when technological parity with Europe was overturned by

Portuguese advances in ship design. A small Portuguese armada then perpetrated flagrant acts of piracy on defenseless and peaceful Arab commercial shipping and paved the way for the entry of more powerful nations.

The Portuguese were not powerful enough to terminate the Arab-Asian trade. This was accomplished by the combined British, French, and Dutch with their invention of the East India Companies.

The Arab countries were initially saved from imminent European colonization by Ottoman military power. The Ottomans were then the world superpower on land. They first extended technical assistance to the mamluks in Egypt to improve the coastal defense of the Arabian Peninsula. This Ottoman contribution played a decisive role in the defense of Jeddah in 1517 against the Portuguese attempt to land in Arabia. This initial Ottoman contribution was followed by their invasion of the region and the partial control of the corrupt and incompetent mamluk rule of Egypt.

The Arab system of land and sea transport provided powerful integrative economic forces that held the Arab world together. These forces provided socioeconomic benefits arising from the massive circulation of people, goods, information, and services. This high level of circulation was made possible with indigenous technologies. The dependence of Arab transport on the camel achieved socioeconomic cohesiveness between the nomad and the city. It was a stable and self-reliant economy with a high multiplier factor.

The highly developed Arab transport system enabled them to build and service large urban areas. The prosperity generated by industry, agriculture, and trade covered the cost of maintaining these large cities.

Trade on the local, regional, and international levels helped to articulate a large and far-flung multiethnic community. One finds considerable economic specialization within this domain, the adoption of outsourcing practices combined with a nonbureaucratic and nonmonopolistic service sector. The highly decentralized private nature and flexibility of the trade and transport systems made it possible to circumvent venal and greedy military rulers who sought to exploit traders.

The progressive takeover of Asian trade by Europeans by 1630 led to its rapid dismantling. Ipso facto, this eliminated the economic basis for inter-Arab integrity.[4]

Arab National Security 1630–1800

Between 1630 and 1800 there followed a rapid reduction in inter-Arab commercial and cultural exchanges. Even the *hajj* between the Maghreb and the Holy Places of Islam shifted away from the land routes, either across North Africa or across Niger, Chad, and Sudan, to French ships linking Moroccan and Egyptian ports. This inevitably eliminated a powerful locomotive of the Saharan economy, since trade activity generally accompanied the *hajj* caravans.

Similarly, the successful transplantation of Yemeni coffee to the colonies of the British, French, and Dutch as well as to Brazil in British-owned plantations led to the loss of a very lucrative produce. The loss of the coffee monopoly primarily affected Yemen and Egypt (which marketed half the coffee output of Yemen).

The protection of the region by the Ottomans lasted until 1798 when the French occupied Egypt. This event revealed the weakness of Ottoman power. The removal of French troops was made feasible by British naval power.

The progressive decline of Ottoman military power during the seventeenth and eighteenth centuries was accompanied by further economic and cultural decline and a continuing failure to remain abreast of military technology. The Ottomans were far removed from the new sciences brought about by the European Renaissance and the Industrial Revolution.

Arab National Security 1800–1950

The explosive growth in science and technology after 1800 has had a dramatic and negative impact on the national security of the Arab countries.

Rapid developments in the European agricultural sciences combined with the mechanization of agricultural operations terminated the prominence of developing countries, until the end of the nineteenth century, in the production of cereals and other produce. Advances in organic chemistry eliminated international markets for natural dyes.

The relentless and spectacular discoveries in the chemical sciences added

- a wide profusion of synthetic dyes,
- a large variety of synthetic fibers,
- new leather substitutes, and
- new materials for all types of use.

Similarly, advances in physics, mathematics, various fields of engineering, geology, and biology added an endless series of new inventions, devices, machinery, new means of transport, and industrial processes. As a consequence of these advances the economies of industrial societies were progressively dematerialized;[5] the decline in the terms of trade of natural resources and agricultural produce was a natural outcome of these dramatic changes.

The Arab countries became a market for these new products and advances. The textile industries of the region were decimated. Arab governments opted for a technologically dependent role and could not benefit from the contributions that their assets could make.

The history of the Suez Canal is an illustration of how a national asset, in a technologically underdeveloped country, becomes a liability. The Pharaohs had constructed a canal linking the Red Sea to the Mediterranean. Yet, from the beginning of the Islamic era, Arab political leadership was opposed to the construction of a canal connecting the two seas. Arab rulers were conscious of the weakness of Arab naval power and of the vital importance of the Red Sea to the protection of access to Jeddah and thus to the two Holy Cities of Mecca and Medina. Muhammad Ali himself continued this policy of refusing to accede to the construction of a canal. But his successors were less concerned with the strategic importance of such a decision and provided the authorization despite the objection of the Porte.

From Pharaonic times Egyptian agriculture depended on the capability of excavating and dredging large systems of canals. The volume of excavations involved in constructing the Suez Canal over a relatively short time was enormous; this led to the mechanization of dredging and earth removal, now made possible by the application of fossil energy. Acquiring this technology should have been considered to be of strategic importance at this time, especially as its cost was lower than that of corvée labor, and Egypt was short of manpower at the time.

Egypt's political leaders at the time seem to have been oblivious to these positive implications to the country of the technology used to construct the Suez Canal. The project does not appear to have made an impact on Egyptian canal dredging.

The contractual conditions for the construction of the canal, as well as the lack of Egyptian interest in promoting technology acquisition and subcontracting, made investment in the Suez Canal a disastrous one. It served as a major instrument for undermining national and regional security by colonial powers.

The above brief historical sketches illustrate the complex interactions between science, technology, the economy, political decisions, international relations, and national security.

Divergent Technological Development

By 1498 the technology gap between the Arab world and the West was sufficiently large to start the dismantling of the economy and unity of the Arab nation. By 1800 all the traditional technologies in use had lost market share in the new world economy.

During the period 1498–1800 there was considerable divergence in the technological development of both regions. Napoleon's invasion of Egypt turned a new page in the confrontation. Napoleon transformed the struggle from the dismantling of international Arab economic activities to comprehensive direct colonization.

During the nineteenth century European economic influence began to affect the internal economy of the region on the level of each individual community. During the period 1800–1950 there were feeble movements toward education and the importation of new technologies. However, there was no convincing and successful effort devoted to the acquisition of the new knowledge.

Muhammad Ali in Egypt appears to have made substantial efforts. But this regime was fundamentally a mamluk-style political system. Ethnic discrimination against the native Egyptians by the ruling Albanians, combined with a scientifically illiterate ruling elite, vitiated the efforts made. Despite the presence of some high quality consultants, greed, corruption, inefficiency, and foreign interferences all combined to undermine the positive efforts that were made. The net outcome was the British occupation of Egypt, followed by British occupation of Sudan. Naturally, Sudan was colonized with Egyptian resources.

The considerable centralization of power in the hands of leaders with limited scientific education; the very poor level of public education in the sciences throughout the Arab world; nonexistent public libraries; the absence of credible scientific societies; the absence of free, serious, and structured public debates on critical issues confronting the Arab states all contributed to maintaining the status quo.

Defence Capability and the Economy

The cost of military hardware and maintenance of a standing army is high. Only wealthy countries can afford such a waste of economic resources. Most modern governments have opted for alliances, such as NATO, to reduce the cost of national defense. Other countries, such as Japan, have found a solution in remaining "defenseless" and adapting to living under the US military umbrella. Switzerland has adopted yet another format for securing its security, but with little military expenditure and using a civilian army. Hizb-Allah is the closest Arab model to that of Switzerland. Costa Rica found its fortune in eliminating its army. Clearly, there are many inexpensive ways of defending oneself, as the Vietnamese and Hizb-Allah have demonstrated.

Until recently there were only two superpowers in the world, because they were the only two countries that could sustain the levels of military expenditure required by modern warfare. The collapse of the USSR was brought about by the excessively high cost of military expenditure relative to its weak civilian economy, demonstrating that a science and technology base alone is not sufficient to safeguard national security.

Individually the Arab countries are too poor to sustain modern military establishments. They have adopted technology policies that depend on importing, at high cost, inappropriate military hardware from allies of their only enemy. Furthermore, they do not invest sufficiently in training to make good use of what they purchase. They have failed to develop an effective collective defense system.

But even if all the Arab countries were united, their GNP of some $1,500 billion (estimated for 2009) cannot support a modern military establishment. If they wish to maintain their traditional interest in a standing army, they need to increase their GNP and to learn to manufacture weapons adapted to their needs and budget. Alternatively, they need to adopt relevant and appropriate people-based defense strategies that fit their budget. But a people's army demands a different political culture than the prevailing one.

Delays by the Arab countries in realizing their economic and cultural potentialities undermine their ability to cope with their national security.

Unless a country possesses an industrial base, it cannot convert knowledge into the products that it needs for its defense. A people's army does not obviate the importance of science and technology. A strong civilian economy is essential to achieve such conversions. Such an economy has to be based on a strong commitment to science and technology.

The civilian economy is responsible for

- generating the taxes to finance and sustain national security;
- maintaining the socioeconomic well-being of society; and
- providing the industrial capabilities that may be converted, in time of war, to research and for manufacturing the required weapons.

Destabilizing, degrading, restricting, imposing embargos, attacking, occupying, promoting subversion and dissent between Arab states, planting rumors and distrust against individual Arab groups, and destroying eco-nomic assets are all means for undermining the capabilities of the Arab states to develop viable economies and relations with each other. All of these measures have been used by ex-colonial and neocolonial powers against Arab states (especially Egypt (1956–1976), Iraq (1980–2011), and Palestine (1920–2011)).

These foreign interventions contribute to undermining and distract-ing the Arab political systems from their national pursuits. The major sources of weakness of the Arab countries continue to be

- lack of national technology policies,
- disunity and lack of mutual trust, and
- an absence of accurate statistical information on their activities that would enable them to see the facts and plan more effectively for their future.

This ignorance of the facts militates against pursuing sound management and planning practices.

Despite the paramount importance of science, and the fact that the military establishment and the economy both depend on it, little progress has been made in establishing a satisfactory science and technology sys-tem in any Arab country.

Education and National Security

Muhammad Ali in Egypt and the Porte in Istanbul realized the military and economic importance of education. However, their antiquated politi-cal culture did not allow them to understand the revolutionary nature of the type of education needed by a post-Renaissance and post-Industrial Revolution culture.

Two centuries later, no Arab country recognizes the full implications of modern science and culture to the educational system. These impli-cations have a direct bearing on the political culture. Their impact on social values, academic standards, social mobility, and personal freedom are dramatic and constantly intensifying. The stultifying conservatism of Arab societies is in stark contrast to what is going on in the rest of the world. The challenge facing every society is to reinvent its traditions and values to suit emerging social-economic-cultural conditions. Little of this reinvention is taking place in the Arab countries.

In fact, these challenges are universal: spectacular changes are con-stantly induced by scientific and cultural change. These are forcing all countries and their educational institutions to be permanently on the alert to adapt, evolve, and change.

There is a considerable brain drain among Arab university graduates. In advanced fields of specialization, and especially in PhD-level manpower, the brain drain is probably of the order of 80 percent of each year's output.

The problems facing the Arab world stem far less from the large numbers of illiterates than from national technology policies, poor political leadership, poor quality of education—especially in languages, humanities, mathematics, and the sciences—and the absence of training to improve the productivity of their unskilled and skilled labor.

Prospects of Arab National Security in the Early Twenty-First Century

The only way to safeguard national security in the globalized modern world is by achieving and maintaining parity with other countries in competitiveness, science, technology, and creativity. Countries that do not achieve this parity will expose themselves to perpetual underdevelopment. The capacity to undertake R&D is what enables a community to secure and sustain its international standing in a world that is constantly advancing.

What has been taking place among industrial countries is the export of unemployment to countries with lower levels of investment in human resources. Thus, in order for South Korea, Taiwan, and Singapore to move ahead, they had to establish some of the world's most advanced systems of education: the students of these countries occupy high places internationally. The same applies to the productivity of their labor forces. The United States, to maintain its leadership position, sustains the highest level of labor productivity and so far has the world's largest R&D budget. China is now in second place in this regard. Japan has fallen to third place. The expectation is that R&D output from China will be in first position by 2020.

The competition is not determined by the number of scientific papers. Besides the quality of the publications, there is the issue of possessing the capability of converting science into useful inventions and being able to manufacture and market salable products. Only time will tell how China will perform in these different areas. China is certainly trying to attain its objectives on a scale and at a speed never attempted before.

By contrast, the poor educational level of the Arab labor force is inadequate for international competitiveness. According to a World Bank study, the average duration of schooling in the Middle East and North Africa (in 1992) was 3.6 years; in Latin America it was 4.9 years; in China it was 5.2 years, in East Asia, 6.5 years; and in former Council for Mutual Economic Assistance (CMEA) countries it was 8.2 years. By contrast, it was 9.6 years in the OECD. The forecast for 2010 was in the range of 4.5 to 5.5 years for the MENA region, in comparison with 5.4 to 6.1 in China, 7.3 to 7.9 in East Asia, and 5.5 to 6.1 in Latin America.[6]

Unemployment in the Arab countries has been on the increase. According to the *World Bank Development Report*, unemployment in Algeria and Jordan is about 20 percent; while that in Egypt and Morocco is about 14 percent.[7] Newspaper reports purport that these estimates have been exceeded. Unfortunately, accurate statistics on Arab employment and labor productivity are scarce, inaccurate, and generally out of date.

Competitiveness and Sovereignty

An interesting picture is painted by the World Economic Forum (WEF) annual statistics.[8] In the following, I will discuss the WEF data for 1997, 2007, and 2009–2010 to highlight some of the changes taking place in the Arab world.

Of the Arab states, only Egypt and Jordan were included among the 53 countries surveyed in the 1998 report. It was, of course, courageous of both countries to seek inclusion at that time. The leading three competitive countries in 1998 were the same in 1997: Singapore (1), Hong Kong (2), and the United States (3). Jordan improved its standing from no. 43 in 1997 to no. 29 in 1998; while Egypt went down from no. 28 to no. 38.

Iceland (population 300,000, whose main exports were based on fishing before securing a foothold in the dematerialized economy) ranked no. 30. It has a per capita income of $27,118 (some 50 percent greater than that of the UAE at the time, which had then the largest per capita income in the Arab world).

Iceland had 288 PCs per 1,000 inhabitants, and invested $98.6 per capita in telecommunication services annually. By comparison, Egypt and Jordan had 5.4 and 9.3 PCs per 1,000 inhabitants, respectively; they invested $5.2 and $3.1 per capita annually in telecommunication services, respectively. The annual per capita investment of leading countries in telecommunication systems were the United States ($896), Hong Kong ($310.3), Switzerland ($257.5), and South Korea ($97.4).

According to the same report, Egypt and Jordan rank between 41 and 50 (out of 53) in the categories of openness, finance, government bureaucracy, infrastructure, technology, and management. Clearly, the two leading Arab countries rank poorly among the leaders of the globalized world economy. China, the Ukraine, Russia, India, and Zimbabwe rank even lower. However, China, India, and Russia were moving rapidly ahead and overcoming their difficulties.

The Global Competitiveness Report (GCR) of 2006–2007 included 125 countries. Egypt and Jordan were now joined by seven other Arab countries. These were Algeria, Bahrain, Kuwait, Morocco, Qatar, Tunisia, and UAE. The 2006–2007 GCR compiled a great deal more data than earlier ones. ★Table 8.1 shows a selection of countries to compare with the nine Arab countries along with their rankings.[9]

The ranking of Jordan went down to 52 from 28 in 1998; while Egypt went down from 38 to 63. Interestingly, Tunisia secured rank 30 out of 125 while UAE and Kuwait secured ranks 32 and 44. In chapter 7 it was argued that Tunisia, Lebanon, UAE, and Kuwait possess some characteristics that *may* provide the spark that mobilizes Arab capabilities. The rankings of Tunisia, UAE, and Kuwait confirm expectations.

★Table 8.1 shows the rating for University/Industry collaboration for these countries. We note that for industrial countries the ratings of this index are all above 5 except for Hong Kong and Iceland. The more advanced the country, the higher the level of collaboration. Of the Arab countries, Tunisia has a rating of 3.7, which is below China with 3.9.

It was shown in chapter 7 that Kuwait, Tunisia, and the UAE exhibit a pattern of collaboration substantially different from that of all the other Arab states: they show a pattern of undertaking publicly funded R&D in ministries and in centers of applied research. It was argued that these beginnings may auger well and could lead to genuine collaboration between universities, research, enterprise, and industry. This is reflected in the GCR's figure of University/Industry R&D Collaboration.

Though Egypt supported substantial research activities in the applied sciences since the 1950s, the score of 2.6 for University/Industry R&D collaboration reflects a comparatively poor level of collaboration. Egypt's massive bureaucracies and rigidities undermine its many positive intentions.

One must still take the numerical assessments of University/Industry R&D collaboration with a grain of salt; there are as yet insufficient studies on this very important issue. The GCI estimates may be close to the mark for industrial countries where more detailed and reliable data is available.

Research organizations in Egypt can work to streamline their relationships with industry and adopt more direct and efficient processes.

The upper part of *Table 8.1 shows eight of the leading industrial countries. Switzerland is in the top position. Switzerland, a small country of some 5 million inhabitants, excels in everything it does, whether it is tourism, banking, industry, research, or health. The United States has fallen from top ranking in 2000 to no. 6 in 2006.

Among the top 29 countries, one finds 24 from Europe, America (United States and Canada), Japan, Australia, and New Zealand. The remaining five consist of Singapore, Hong Kong, South Korea (24), Malaysia (26), and Chile (27). The score of Malaysia is 5.11, compared to 4.71 for Tunisia. Tunisia has to make a massive effort to close the gap with the next level and reach a score for University/Industry R&D collaboration above 5.0 if it is to join the Tiger category.

South Korea has been very consistent in its efforts since the 1980s to move forward, and it is still at rank 24 with a score of 5.13. In 2006–2007 all the Arab countries were behind Tunisia.

The last two columns in the table give the number of PCs per capita and the use of the Internet. It is clear that these activities have a limited bearing on the GCI score or the GCI ranking. This is despite the evident intensive use of the Internet and PCs by leading industrial countries.

India and China have a score below Tunisia but above Algeria. But both countries exhibit a higher level of University/Industry collaboration than the Arab countries, except for Tunisia. The scores for China and India hide the great size of their economy and of their science base. The average for these two giants falls within the range of the nine Arab countries. However, these countries already possess very advanced research centers and industries not at all available in the Arab countries. The international competitiveness of both China and India is not determined by their "average competencies" but rather by their advanced capabilities.

The scores utilized by numerous organizations to compare countries all have their shortcomings and must be used with care. The score for Tunisia does not make it an industrial country. All it means is that if it continues in this direction with the same, or greater, level of effort it may either remain in place or move slowly up the table. Once Tunisia reaches level 25 and above, and maintains its position, we will know that it has made the transition to an industrial state. *Table 8.2 presents data from the issue of the GCI for 2009–2010 Report. The number of Arab states covered by GCI in 2009 increased from 9 to 13. Whereas Tunisia was leading the Arab countries in 2007 it is now lead by Qatar, UAE, Saudi Arabia, Bahrain, and Kuwait. Only Oman, amongst the GCC countries, is preceded by Tunisia.

The dramatic changes in the assessments of some of the GCC countries are not credible. The new universities recently introduced in Qatar and the UAE could not have made the improvements implied by the changes in the positions of these two countries between 2006 and 2009. Yet the rating of Saudi Arabia at 28 is more reasonable, since this has been a result of considerable effort during the past several years.

CHAPTER 9

SCIENCE AND POVERTY

Introduction

The key to overcoming poverty is understanding its origins and what sustains it. The Arab world imports some 30 million workers and employs several million others abroad to manufacture the products and agricultural produce they import. It is strange that such a region suffers from massive unemployment at home and loses millions of its highly educated who have joined the brain drain.

There are more than 50 million poor people in the Arab world. They need help to get out of their poverty trap despite their illiteracy. A good portion of the jobs undertaken by expatriate labor do not require school education. The skills are simple to impart by short-term training.

William Lewis, as a result of his extensive and comparative studies of economic systems around the world, comes to the conclusion that

> the importance of education of the workforce has been taken way too far. In other words, education is not the way out of [the] poverty trap. A high education level is no guarantee of high productivity. The truth of the matter is that regardless of institutional education level, workers around the world can be adequately trained on the job for high productivity.[1]

A major cause of the persistence of poverty in a society is the lack of sustained interest in the poor. The Arab countries are probably among the best in the attention that they have devoted to this issue. However, a great deal more can be achieved in a short time.

Comparative statistics show that the proportion of the population living under the poverty line of $1 per day in the Arab world compares well with other developing countries. Arab resources are such that there is no reason why anybody should be living below $2 per day.

The Achievements of the Chinese and Vietnamese

After the Chinese Communist revolution, the government was able to mobilize the population to attend to the basics of clean and healthy living. Many other countries at a higher level of income have not yet attained the same low rates of infant mortality and clean living as China has. Clearly then it is not all dependent on dollars and cents. There are cultural and political aspects that are primordial.

China was able, with very limited resources, to adapt its traditional medicine to address its challenges when it had no resources to adopt modern medicine. China obliterated flies without polluting the environment, provided simple housing by adapting and organizing its traditional construction technology and enabling the poor to build their own homes, and absorbed modern farming equipment by simple step-by-step learning and training.

Vietnam, with a per capita income of $200 (in 2000), was able to reduce infant mortality to European standards; it also provided homes for all, increased literacy rates to 90 percent, and ensured public places were clean.

The achievements of microfinance in many developing countries has demonstrated that the poor are smart, hard working, and, if given a small chance, are able to respond positively and creatively to opportunities.

Various measures taken around the world show that poverty is a readily solvable problem if the focus is on the poor and aid goes directly to them in a sustainable manner.

The Impoverishment of the Arab World

The economic decline of the Arab countries after 1498 led to the impoverishment of its population (see chapter 8). Between 1498 and 1798 Ottoman power was adequate to protect the region from Western colonization. However, Ottoman governance failed to deal with the economic decline that set in as a result of the losses of the sources of Arab prosperity.

Napoleon's invasion of Egypt demonstrated the power vacuum that prevailed in the region. This vacuum, once recognized, was exploited by Western powers, resulting in occupation and colonization of the entire Arab world, apart from Arabia and North Yemen.

By 1800 the population of the Arab world appears to have declined to some 30 million. Thus, at the onset of industrialization the region was underpopulated, defenseless, poor, and oblivious to the dramatic scientific changes taking place around it.

After 1800, Egypt experienced some prosperity and development. The Ottomans installed railway systems here and there in the Middle East, but it was, despite some efforts to the contrary, all in a technology-dependent mode. In time, these efforts paved the way for British and French occupation. More the "progress" that was made through technological dependence, more the foreign control.

The most important development in the Arab world during the 1800–1950 period is that practically all technological change that took place was planned and executed by foreign agencies. In other words, all imports of new technologies were undertaken without serious effort to enable the population to acquire the know-how. Acquiring know-how is essential to job creation, development, and economic growth.

Needless to say, the Arab world was not the only region of the world that was experiencing these technological conditions. Some of the other countries in a similar situation made greater effort to secure control of the processes of acquiring and applying new technologies.

The story of colonialism and exploitation is sufficiently well known and need not be reviewed here. Most Arab countries suffered. Colonialism, combined with a massive technology gap, had devastating effects.

During the colonial period the processes of planning and decision-making were controlled by foreign powers. These activities were carried out partly or wholly in the metropolis of the dominant foreign power (London, Paris, Rome).

Thus, whether it was constructing dams, irrigation systems, water works, sewage disposal, electric power stations, harbors, telephone exchanges, or railway systems, they were designed, contracted, installed, and often operated by foreign companies and or governments.

The net result is that at the time of independence the Arab political leaders could not plan for any technical activity that could be carried out by natives, even though there were already a number of qualified persons in Egypt; and this was much less in some of the other countries.

European governments, international agencies, and the increasing number of Western consulting and contracting firms were the main agents of technical change. The problem was not the use of these sources of know-how but rather the inadequate measures adopted to acquire know-how from these sources by nascent national organizations.

Despite the rapidly increasing number of Arab medical doctors, engineers, and agriculturists there was limited effort to accelerate the development of local consulting and contracting capabilities. It was during the Second World War years (1939–1945) that Western military needs forced imperial powers to employ local labor and engineers. By then, small-scale contracting firms began to develop in Iraq, Palestine, Lebanon, and Syria. Egypt had an earlier start in this domain.

During the colonial period there was no rapid population growth in the Arab world. The population grew from an estimated 30 million in 1800 to only 50 million by 1950, because mortality rates continued to be high due to poor education, sanitation, and health care. It was only with independence that there was improvement in health, decline in infant mortality, expansion of educational facilities, and improvement in urbanization and housing.

Early Attempts to Resist and Recover

Local political elites accepted this high degree of technological dependence as a corollary to the "technology gap." Yet this need not have been the case. It is a fact that European countries were able to learn from British efforts at the beginning of the Industrial Revolution despite Britain's attempts to make this difficult or nearly impossible. In fact, Britain attempted, during the first part of the nineteenth century, to restrict the outflow of British technicians and the export of capital goods to continental Europe. The British parliament rescinded these restrictive laws only in 1843 when it was shown that these restrictions were ineffective in preventing other European countries from securing access to British innovations. Also, during the nineteenth century Japan found the means to pursue a technologically self-reliant policy.

Muhammad Ali's Egypt had extensive access to European science and technology. However, the centralized economy failed to pursue technological self-reliance. Muhammad Ali sought control and "ownership" of the Egyptian economy rather than self-reliance.

Nevertheless, the seeds planted during the early nineteenth century led to the national revolution in 1919, Bank Misr, and attempts at industrialization. The government of Egypt established the Fouad I National Research Council by decree in 1939.[2] These efforts were handicapped by the Second World War, and there was no further chance to move forward until the 1952 revolution.

Science, Technology, and the Creation of Poverty

It is generally accepted that advances in technology destroy the employment of those who earn their living by using displaced technologies. Obviously, when cars were invented they displaced animals and carts. When oil and gas became a major source of energy it displaced wood and coal.

What is often neglected is how the technological dismantling of developing countries has destroyed employment and the economy. Prior to 1630, Arabs were major players in world trade. They manufactured the tools of transport, used the camel, and designed the ship; they also navigated through intercontinental spaces of land and sea to transport their products.

In the long intercontinental journeys that the merchants undertook, they benefited from large *khans* (inns) provided in the various cities on their routes. These inns provided ample safe storage facilities for their cargoes. The cities where they rested bought some of their products, sold them supplies needed for their journeys, and provided them guides with local knowledge. Some cities used these trading systems to export their products.

Large proportions of the rural and urban populations were employed in these activities. The system of transport and trade was a major employer. Alas, there are no estimates of the numbers employed in this way.

Once the European transport and trading systems replaced the Arab systems, neither camels nor land voyages were needed, and all the employment these activities generated disappeared. Loss of employment resulted in poverty. Historians note that there were nomadic invasions of agricultural areas as a result of the spread of unemployment among nomads, who lost their livelihoods derived from raising camels and guiding caravans.

The European system of international trade was organized on the basis of delivering the goods to seaports that dotted the Arab world. At first, caravans transported the products inland; but by the mid-1850s railway systems began to be imported and progressively replaced local means of transport. The Arabs did not seek, like the Europeans, to learn how to manufacture locomotives; they preferred to buy them on a turnkey basis. European operators came along with the imported machines, and European contractors were employed to construct the railways.

The technology of constructing railways and making locomotives is not terribly difficult, and the countries in the region could, with some effort, have learnt how to do it. All they had to do was follow the example of the Belgians. The Belgians bought two locomotives, one of which was used and the other was taken apart and copied. In a short time they were exporting locomotives.

We learn from the diary of Yusef Hekkekian, adviser to Muhammad Ali, that he trained (during the 1830s) about a hundred Egyptian technicians (his diary includes their names) to design and construct steam engines in Cairo. But he failed to obtain the financial support to manufacture steam engines and agricultural tools.

Naturally, Egypt imported the coal for the railways that the British had constructed. It took a century for Egypt to convert its railways from the use of imported coal to locally produced oil. British wartime constraints forced the Egyptian railway system to shift to oil to reduce demand on maritime transport, as the transport of coal from Britain could no longer be justified. Oil was less expensive, locally available, and more efficient, since one ton of oil has double the calorific value of one ton of coal. But the British managers of the Egyptian railway system did not see fit that Egypt should benefit from a local natural resource.

The moral of the story is that poverty is a by-product of prevailing technology policies. Technology dependence not only causes unemployment and poverty but also leads to the wrong choices of technologies for use. Clearly, one needs appropriate technology policies not only to survive but also to advance. In the absence of sound policies, communities will decline and unemployment—and, of course, poverty—will rise. Poverty is a reflection of the inadequacy of past technology policies. Poverty is thus man-made.

Building the Machinery of National Governments

A fragmented Arab world was emerging in 1950 from decades of colonial rule. It was confronted with spectacular technological advances and yet it had lost its economic base. The diversity of the material and population resources of the Arab countries, combined with the successful policies of divide and rule adopted by colonial powers, guaranteed that no Arab country emerged that knew how to collaborate with another Arab country. Since these countries were isolated from each other for more than a century, they neither worked nor traded together. A country is unified by the "world of work." The more people work together, the more they become integrated into one society.

For a long time the populations of the Arab countries did not

- produce all their food supplies,
- manufacture or exchange industrial products, and
- collaborate to solve their common problems.

By contrast, during the centuries before 1498, and despite mamluks and foreign invasions and epidemics, the people of the Arab world were integrated by having to produce

- the camels and boats needed by their transport systems, and
- many of the products that they exchanged.

And despite their disunity, they found ways to reconcile in times of need to defend themselves against a common enemy.

Local demand for local products and services created employment for the population. Naturally, the alternative of living on imported products and services destroyed a considerable proportion of national employment.

When independent Arab governments emerged from colonial rule, their political leaders sought to build the machinery of government. The process was "assisted" by the departing colonial powers.

Ministries of Education, Health, and Planning rapidly emerged. With the assistance of UN agencies, these ministries were shown how to use foreign consulting and contracting firms to "accelerate the acquisition of technological capacities." Countries such as India, Indonesia, China, and the Latin American states were all in the same boat, but they all seem to have sought to acquire technology and to develop national capabilities at a high speed.

Science and Youth Unemployment

The Arab countries today face a major and novel challenge: two-thirds of their population is below the age of 25. In most countries this would be considered a blessing, as this is the age for peak creativity and labor productivity.

The Arab world has one of the highest unemployment rates in the world, estimated in the range of 15 percent to 25 percent. The Arab youth bulge is estimated to reach 80 to 100 million by 2020. Thus the Arab world not only faces unemployment of its poor but also increasing unemployment of its educated youth.

How Others Have Done It

It is common knowledge that clean drinking water and sewage disposal are critical items for sound health. We all need good health to be productive at work. The technologies for doing so, if one focuses on rural areas, are low in cost and simple to adopt. The poor, with little help and training, can themselves undertake the work. Such work creates jobs and develops skills.

First, one must solve the problem of clean water and sewage disposal. Simple, sound, and easy-to-use methods for handling sewage and solid waste are available. Naturally, with time, communities would like to use more efficient methods. With regard to alleviating poverty, the first step is to show concern and dedication for its removal, and then to adopt quick, efficient, effective, and sustainable measures.

Second, one must solve the problem of housing. It is possible to build cheaply by using the labor of the poor and local materials as much as possible. The housing should be simple, clean, pleasant, and healthy to live in.

Resolving the twin problems of clean water supply and housing is essential to health, family life, and the formation of stable and productive communities.

Simple and basic consulting and contracting services can be developed in impoverished communities. These can be acquired, hands-on, in the planning and execution of water supply, transport services, sewage systems, and housing projects. Upgrading measures to make urban slum areas healthy and livable are pursued in many countries. Such policies can be easily learnt and diffused in the region.

The entrepreneurial capabilities associated with these activities then become a capital resource. Very rapidly, these capabilities can then be used, by the community, to develop their irrigation systems, terrace their fields, improve rural transport, and so on.

As time goes on, the consultants emerging from such experiences could receive additional training, and thereby embryonic "rural" firms will begin to grow in size and expertise. Their children should be enabled to enroll in universities and have jobs when they return home. The challenge of poverty eradication is all about solving problems in a self-reliant manner.

Anybody who has looked at the statistics of agricultural output will be stunned by the generally low level of yields and productivity of land, labor, water, plants, and animals. Yet, the science of agriculture is an open book. There are hundreds of schools of agriculture in the Arab world, and they have trained tens of thousands of engineers and technicians. There is no doubt that Arab agriculture has progressed over the past 50 years, yet it is clear that it still has a long way to go. The problem is not the lack of human capital, expertise, R&D, and knowledge. The problem and the challenge is partly the management of extension services and the limited interest in farmers and rural areas.

Micro-finance, extended loans by local shopkeepers, and municipal programs can all make contributions that are reimbursable. The farmer has every chance of earning, from improved output, the cost of the investment. Since the Arab countries import half their food requirements, they already have a large internal market to absorb expanding agricultural output.

The Language of Poverty Alleviation

The subject of poverty has become acceptable to be discussed, as it enjoys a UN Millennium Declaration. Until recently people in both developed and developing countries did not wish to be reminded, or spoken to, about poverty. One of the achievements of the UN Millennium Declaration is to make this a normal topic of discourse.

The status of the literature on poverty alleviation has benefited considerably from international support. Countries are told that they are not advancing because of the gaping technology divide that is depriving them of both new and old technologies.[3]

The ESCWA report on the subject goes on to say that in order to bear fruit, national efforts aimed bridging the technology divide will need to:

- formulate comprehensive national science and technology policies and relevant implementation strategies;
- adopt new institutional forms, including technology parks and technology incubation schemes;
- design new measures to reduce or recoup the cost of the brain drain from developed countries; and
- capitalize on expatriate Arab science and technology manpower.[4]

Healing the Technology Systems of the Arab World

Thanks to information technology and to the new science of self-organizing criticality, it should be possible to mobilize, at low cost, existing resources for the benefit of all.

The Arab countries, between 1970 and 2000, have invested some $3 trillion on technology improvements. During the 2000–2010 decade, another $2 or $3 trillion have been invested. GCC investment plans for the coming five years total more than $2 trillion; the rest of the Arab countries are also investing an equal amount.

If appropriate technology and employment policies had been adopted, the design and execution of projects worth $3,000 billion currently under planning and execution during 2010–2013 would be more than adequate to eliminate poverty, resolve the youth unemployment time bomb, and expand the economies of all the Arab countries.[5]

We learn that the total value of projects under execution or in bidding stage was around $900 billion in the UAE (2009) alone.[6] In Saudi Arabia, investment plans for the following few years are estimated at some $500 billon. It is, of course, unlikely that these could be less than those of the UAE. Among these, there are two oil refineries in the pipeline, each costing some $10 billion. The press estimates that 50 percent of the fabrication for these projects will be undertaken locally, thus creating local work.[7] Obviously, it is good news that things are changing for the better.

Elementary economics tells us that the multiplier factor for the projects under way is nearly 4 to 5; which means that through sound planning and policies the Arab world could increase its GNP very substantially during the following decade.

In other words, Arab countries need to learn how to manage the implementation of their development programs by utilizing productively their own human capital while learning as fast as possible from the rest of the world. Very often major international firms will have to be used as trainers and teachers rather than as turnkey operators. Such approaches have been extensively used in Asia and Latin America.

Arab scientific elites have, since Shibli Shumayyil,[8] been urging governments to come to terms with science and technology. Yet, there has been no serious response to date, despite the enormous demand in the Arab world for the products of science.

What does Empowerment Entail?

A society that can utilize its human resources productively is enriched and enjoys a happier, more stable, and more dignified life. We need to recognize that poverty impoverishes everybody in society, rich and poor alike. This arises from the loss of an important national asset.

Science and technology enable us to provide the required skills and support systems at a modest cost. In fact, the Arab world possesses all the assets needed to achieve such an objective in record time.

Enabling the Destitute to Acquire Skills and Resources

Helping the poor by sending a team of consultants to villages to train locals, or sending thousands of children from farming communities to college, will be nonstarters. No country has the resources to finance such costly approaches on a scale sufficiently large to make a difference. Such activities can complement but not replace the recommended hands-on approach.

What are needed are approaches that rely to a high degree on science, and on the poor for undertaking the necessary tasks with assistance. These should start with technologies that can be quickly learnt and lead to immediate impacts: constructing clean water systems, wastewater disposal, rural roads, and storage facilities for agricultural products to reduce farm losses; manufacturing devices for the mechanization of irrigation water systems; improving the efficiency of water use; introducing simple telecommunication systems; undertaking manufacturing in rural areas; designing simple equipment for moving products—possibly starting with improved designs of animal carts and river boats in Sudan—and improvement of agricultural methods.

Such programs should be undertaken with the participation of the local population. The program should enable rural entrepreneurs to

- start simple consulting and contracting organizations,
- develop marketing outlets that provide credit to farmers to purchase equipment and supplies, and
- supply advisory services supported by an Internet link to national extension services.

The region already has the agricultural engineers and agronomists, though some of them may be working in other occupations. Most Arab countries have agricultural extension systems. Many of these can be readily improved through modest investments in Internet facilities and the continued training of key officers. Efforts must be made to mobilize and upgrade whatever local talent is available. Rural areas in the Arab world have schools, colleges, agricultural rural extension services, and so on. All of these organizations possess talent that can be efficiently mobilized and tapped to provide new services.

Rural municipalities, strengthened by well-trained university graduates, can boost such efforts (see chapter 11). Arab universities could readily develop a one-year postgraduate program to train university graduates to undertake research and handle a wide variety of issues that confront rural areas.

The Challenge: To Focus National Resources to Enable the Poor

Neither the technologies required nor the financial requirements should pose serious challenges to development in the Arab countries. The real difficulty and challenge is how to reach the poor without wasting available resources on intermediaries.

The Arab world's high dependence on imported technological services and expatriate labor deprives its inhabitants of opportunities to utilize the normal economy to pull themselves out of their poverty trap.

The ideal way to respond to the poverty challenge is through the progressive incorporation of the poor in the national and regional labor force. In this way they will become an integral part of the national economy.

All Arab countries undertaking large-scale investment programs can pursue policies that could help to eradicate poverty through the incorporation of their own and regional labor in their national labor market. Needless to say, they would give priority in employment to their national labor. What is needed here is to adopt on-the-job labor training programs throughout the Arab world.

The Japanese have excelled in rapidly bringing the output of unskilled labor to Japan's high standards. Learning and diffusing similar practices throughout the Arab world should not be an impossible task.

The Arab countries with surplus labor should make a serious and sustained effort to upgrade the skills of their labor to increase their productivity and competitiveness at par with expatriate labor now being employed.[9] They can introduce reliable skill certification systems that give confidence to employers who recruit Arab labor. Skill certification will also provide workers with professional mobility.

Naturally, the process will take a few decades to complete. But, as we have seen in Japan, Korea, and now China, once the process starts, it does not stop. The benefits to Arab governments and investors will be spectacular. They will not only have their projects cheaper but will also feel some satisfaction that they have undertaken a public good at little cost to themselves.

Arab countries now have a wide variety (probably thousands) of vocational and technical schools, a large number (possibly 500) of universities, research stations (thousands), ministries of education and health with adequate basic planning capabilities, and so on. Improving the standards, efficiency, productivity, and effectiveness of the existing facilities should be feasible given the services of a small number of capable and creative managers; obviously this can be done only with political support. With modest effort, all existing organizations can be systematically upgraded.

The poor and the farmer are poorly connected to formal government services, which are normally neither friendly nor supportive. Existing systems normally assume that there is a demand side capable of asking questions and framing answers. This is, of course, not the reality. A more friendly and enabling environment is needed to stimulate the process.

Thus, what is required is to work at the level of the poor to endow them with services that are easy to access. The interface between the poor and the formal governmental system is obviously critical. Existing municipalities may be enabled to deploy local government services with a view to enabling the rural population.

CHAPTER 10

BUILDING ORGANIZATIONS: LEARNING, ADAPTING, ACCUMULATING, INTEGRATING

Introduction

Thinkers are constantly creating new ideas. To benefit from this creativity, a society needs to constantly "build" new types of organizations. In other words, the conversion of new ideas into new services and products often depends on a diversity of new organizations.[1]

Building organizations concerned with science and technology is not easy. They require, above all, well-trained personnel who can identify problems and design solutions. Graduate schools have become powerful research centers capable of performing the difficult task of incubating the human capital necessary for these operations.

Wherever we look, we find societies inventing and deconstructing organizations that deal with science and technology, and they all seem to be doing it in different ways. Whether it is dealing with the science of medicine or transport, one finds some countries having difficulties in handling the process while others sail through easily.

Civil engineering facilitated the modern distribution of potable water and has made the safe removal of sewage possible in large urban centers. All industrial countries have been able to organize themselves to provide these services to large and small urban centers. Third world countries still face difficulties in building organizations for the application of these essential technologies.

The GCC countries are the only Arab countries that provide a supply of clean water to all their people and dispose safely of their sewage from most urban centers. They have done so by utilizing both international and Arab consulting and contracting services. Lebanon, though it has a plentiful supply of clean water and capable consulting and contracting firms, has been reluctant so far to solve its water and sewage problems in an environmentally safe manner. It dumps raw sewage in its rivers and the beautiful Mediterranean, polluting the beaches and undermining its tourism industry as well as the health of its population.

Americans have been battling for a long time for and against establishing publicly financed national medical services similar to those adopted in Europe. At the same time, major US companies are deconstructing American industry and transferring their factories and research laboratories to China. They then import the output of their Chinese-based factories back home.[2] The process of building organizations in China, following their deconstruction in the United States (where high unemployment currently prevails), appears easier than agreeing in the US Congress to adopt a national health service. (Partial agreement was attained in Congress on March 2010.) Clearly, some actions are easier to implement than others.

Our concern in this chapter is with how and why countries build, or do not build, and utilize, essential organizations.

Chapters 10 and 11 are devoted to discussing some of the difficulties that arise in building organizations. The construction of organizations needed to produce, innovate, and regulate science and technology is discussed here. Chapter 11 will be devoted to the municipality, which has emerged as the leading organization for the application and regulation of science and technology at the level of the citizen.

Enabling Organizations

A highly differentiated range of organizations enables the production and application of science and technology. These include organizations that are concerned with basic research as well as those that deal with codes, standards, quality control, testing materials, and equipment. I add to this set of critical organizations statistical offices, because these provide the data that enables national planners to take stock of the technological and economic state of their country and thus manage its development more effectively.

Enabling the Individual Researcher

The creative force in science, technology, and innovation is the individual. Thus, the frontline organization in science is the research organization. In order to increase their usefulness, from the earliest times, these had to be "integrated" into the practical issues facing their communities.

Once a significant number of scientists undertake research in a society, they find it necessary to form scientific societies. The relevance of these societies was discussed at length earlier. It was emphasized that scientific societies play critical roles in determining the performance, direction, and quality of science in a country. They are also instrumental in the diffusion of science in their societies, and they play a critical role in enabling the scientific community to communicate authoritatively both with their own society and internationally.

National scientific societies intermediate between the individual scientist, the community, government, and funding agencies. They do so by providing a semi-independent authority to evaluate the claims put forward by individual scientists concerning the relative importance of different activities. They are of paramount importance in weeding out mediocrity, as well as in achieving national consensus on critical issues

Whether we are dealing with the safety and quality of food, medical products, or the safety of motor vehicles, a whole range of measures is needed to protect the citizen. Alas, Arab countries have not yet adopted all of the organizations that are necessary to secure these benefits. We are thus at risk of buying fraudulent drugs; consuming agricultural produce that may be poisoned by banned pesticides; occupying buildings that collapse, with or without the assistance of earthquakes, because of corrupt behavior by bureaucrats and contractors.

To enable the various practitioners of science to undertake their business, either of discovering new science or of applying it, society has to make possible the "building" of a range of organizations to fulfill specific functions to the satisfaction of all concerned parties.

The Why, What, and How of Building Organizations

The organizations concerned with the production of science are very focused, and they have to provide specific services to enable the researcher to undertake his or her task.

I discussed earlier how the growing complexity and scale of R&D led industrial countries to adopt collaborative research organizations. These organizations range from facilities at universities, to research centers, specialized laboratories in industry, research activity in the military establishment, and others. In all of these cases the organization has to provide physical facilities ranging from libraries to equipment, staff, personnel, funding, personnel policies, communication facilities, and so on. Ultimately it is a matter of funding, and of the authority to undertake and manage the desired research activities.

There are considerable differences in the nature of the organizations when it comes to basic and applied research. Naturally, both activities are needed. Much applied research is undertaken in industry, in consulting and contracting firms, hospitals, agricultural research stations, government ministries, and branches of the armed services.

Basic research is fairly international, and, as we have seen earlier, collaboration among scientists plays an increasing role in its pursuit. In many areas of basic research—for example, in the areas of nanotechnology, solid-state physics, carbon compounds, molecular biology, and many others—basic research and its application are almost simultaneous.

Industrial countries have, over the past few decades, set up a considerable range of funding organizations to support scientific research. The process is simple and transparent. Legislators review the budgets of these funds annually. Budgets are constantly adjusted to take account of inflation, advances made, international competition, and national security.

Funding activities are closely associated with the enabling organizations and are intrinsic to their design and functioning. The annual debates conducted in national parliaments and scientific societies on the subject of research funding are open to the public and covered by the national press.

Scientific societies are involved in promoting their line of research. Their periodicals publish extensive evaluations of past performance and assess weaknesses and strengths. It is rare that there are such public debates and studies in any Arab country.

In industrial countries the role of politicians and political leaders is restricted mainly to obtaining public funding for agreed national priorities. Political leaders derive great pride in being facilitators of these programs. Needless to say, the economies of industrial countries are visibly dependent on research activity. The political leadership of advanced and advancing countries publicly acknowledges, with pride, this dependence on scientific research. This is equally true of the United States, Korea, China, India, or Brazil.

In industrial countries, intellectuals of all persuasions, scientific societies, and political leaders may question the necessity of undertaking a specific type of research. A small country cannot cover all fields to the same level as a large one, such as the United States, Japan, or China. Thus, a small country has to choose carefully the research programs it wishes to sponsor.

"Leading small countries" devote considerable attention to the quality of their researchers as well as to making sure they have a presence in all the major fields of science. Small countries seek parity with larger countries in the quality, and not the quantity, of their research work.

Naturally, an ambitious large country needs to be involved in all major areas of science. There is a price to pay for failing to do so. For example, for ideological reasons the USSR did not go for molecular biology when the field began to grow rapidly. Its politicians did not wish to acknowledge that heredity plays any role in the differential performance of people. As a result, Russia entered the field much later than others, and is still lagging in research in this field.

The graduate school has remained the major base for all varieties of basic research and for a considerable range of advanced applied work. Graduate schools maintained their importance because they combine the abundance of bright and active young persons with a multidisciplinary environment. Graduate schools remain the major centers for the education of scientists. During the nineteenth and early twentieth centuries generous support for scientific research in industrial countries was available to both private and public universities.

Arab countries have resisted the establishment of graduate schools, and they have suffered accordingly. The first Arab graduate school is being established in Saudi Arabia in 2010. Time will tell if the conditions provided will result in the hoped-for performance.

Scientific and legislative establishments in leading industrial powers go through exhaustive annual and public assessments of the performance of their educational and research organizations. Through these studies they evaluate what they are undertaking in relation to the economy and national security. These studies and discussions involve scientists, economists, politicians, and military and security experts. Thus, the why, how, and what are never a matter of somebody dropping in from outer space and "selling" an "idea" to a political leader, followed by the appointment of a foreign consulting company and a contractor to implement the idea.

Why, How, and When Did Some European Countries Build Their Organizations?

In Europe the ongoing process of building new cultural and scientific organizations was initially driven by contact with Arab expansion before the tenth century. Europe benefited from access to scientific literature available from the Arab world. Arab professors, apparently from Spain, appear to have been employed by the new European universities. European pursuit of knowledge intensified with the advent of the Ottoman conquests in Eastern Europe.[3]

The European Renaissance and the Industrial Revolution both gave a massive push in the same direction. National security, revolutionary changes in the sciences, and social and political revolutions were frequent partners in the process of building new research organizations throughout Europe.

During the late eighteenth century the educational and scientific organizations in most European countries were dominated by the church and monarchies. At the time of the French Revolution there were, in the country, 21 universities and a high international standing in many scientific fields.[4]

Revolutionary change in France produced criticism of existing academic organizations. Between 1789 and 1795 various committees of the revolutionary government hampered the work of these organizations. This revolutionary fervor also hindered medical education.

France was being attacked by several European powers wishing to abort the Republican Revolution. The shortage of doctors led to a crisis in the armed forces defending the country. This resulted in pressure being applied by the armed forces to overcome the ideological disputations concerning the content and objectives of the educational system. A new system of medical education was rapidly cobbled together to respond to the emergency.

At the same time, the French Revolutionary Government founded l'École Polytechnique under the auspices of the army. The objectives of l'École were essentially to train high quality army officers. This objective was crucial to the performance and endurance of this organization. It procured the leading scientists and mathematicians of France to teach at l'École, such as Lagrange, Lazare, Carnot, Bertholet, Laplace, Ampere, and Fourier, names that are still alive in modern scientific literature.

L'École Polytechnique supplied well-trained officers to the Republican army. Napoleon was able to do a great deal of conquering with these capabilities.

The graduates of l'École Polytechnique have been, and continue to be, of crucial importance throughout the French economy. Emphasis on quality and excellence guaranteed the endurance of this organization and crowned its services to France.

As mentioned earlier in this book, Napoleon's defeat of the Prussians in the battle of Jena led the Prussians to investigate in depth the causes of their defeat. They concluded that Napoleon's strength was knowledge-based and was derived from training in the sciences. This led them to invent the graduate school as the appropriate response. *German graduate schools transformed and accelerated German development in science and technology. Graduate schools remain the primary tool for addressing this class of problems.*

The development of American higher education from the colonial period to modern times reflects an interesting pattern.[5] The motivation for establishing the nine colonial colleges, between Harvard College in 1636 and Dartmouth College in 1769, was the training of clergymen and the provision of basic education. There was a burst of new colleges before the war of independence and up to 1862. This was in response to population growth and the western expansion of the American colonization of North America. Many of these colleges were established by graduates of the colonial universities and modeled after them.

The Land Grant College Act of 1862 (also known as the Morrill Act) is considered to have initiated a new era. The federal government awarded the states land to be used to establish agricultural colleges. The colleges that were founded incorporated the applied sciences into the system of higher education. Their initial emphasis was on mechanical engineering and agriculture. They progressively developed to become indistinguishable from other universities. The founding of Johns Hopkins in 1876 as a graduate school was a turning point in American higher education.

Philanthropy, personal initiatives, state and federal governments, all contributed to the "building" of American organizations of higher education.

American students went to Europe in substantial numbers during the nineteenth century. Britain and Germany were the main centers of attraction, with German graduate schools being a favorite. Between 1810 and 1910 some 1,200 American students did postgraduate work at the University of Göttingen. Of these, 200 studied chemistry.[6] These graduates were instrumental in the transfer of knowledge from a leading European center of research to the United States.

When Japan sought to respond to the challenges that it faced from colonial powers, it had no scientists. But it still managed to "build" the organizations required using limited resources, foreign study by Japanese students, and the employment of foreign professors. Much can be done with very few people when there is a political leadership that understands what is at stake. In all these cases the emphasis on the quality of the activities undertaken was crucial to success. Mediocrity in education is a corruption of the scientific enterprise and denies the country the benefits of its efforts.

Serious, heated public debates took place in the countries undergoing rapid expansion of their systems of education. These debates were concerned with the quality of the education systems, access to the education system, the different systems needed, and the constant reforms and adjustments required. Intelligent governments return to the same issue every now and then to reposition their education system to serve new national needs.

Studies of "technology diffusion" appear to lead some who are adept at it to believe that there is a sequential view of development. They seem to believe that a country is exposed to technology before it educates its human capital accordingly, and it then adopts the desired technology. The fact is that all societies possess human capital even if their education systems are underdeveloped. Intelligent persons possess sufficient knowledge to be able to recognize what needs to be done, and they are capable of devising ways to do it. But recognizing what needs to be done and possessing the human capital to do it does not mean that what has to be done is always done.

Let us take the example of the simple technology of providing potable water to every home and removing the sewage produced in urban and rural areas. All the Arab countries have had an abundance of engineers to design ways to perform these tasks. Yet, apart from the GCC countries, no other Arab country has solved this rather simple but essential problem. Many, if not all, Arab countries (excluding the GCC countries) suffer much ill health resulting from polluted drinking water and raw sewage polluting their rivers, aquifers, and agricultural land. Needless to say, ill health has a direct and massive impact on well-being, labor productivity, and economic output.

The delays in adopting such basic technologies have nothing to do with the availability of local human capital and comprehensive knowledge of the technologies available. They also have nothing to do with monetary resources. Judging from public announcements (in March 2010) concerning the expenditure on hashish consumption in Egypt (apparently in excess of the annual revenue from the Suez Canal), or on cosmetic surgery in Lebanon (now the leading country in this procedure worldwide), one can easily deduce that neither human capital, lack of technology, nor lack of financial means are factors in such a pattern of behavior.

I am not aware of systematic studies to find the reasons for the failure to overcome basic problems associated with water in the Arab world. The fact that Arab countries occupy the driest region in the world has always been a major factor in their history. The Pharaonic, Mesopotamian, and early Arab civilizations were all dedicated to resolving water problems.

The lag in acquiring petroleum-related technologies, in an area where oil was recognized as an important resource for millennia and exploited for more than a century, is another interesting case. Hundreds of thousands of "local" engineers have been educated in all aspects of chemical, electrical, mechanical, and civil engineering, as well as geology and petrology. Clearly, technology does not diffuse spontaneously—even if there is an apparent need as well as a profusion of human capital.

The Arab Case

There were less than ten universities in the Arab world before 1950. The development of higher education took off when Arab countries secured their independence. To the credit of the political leaders who took over from colonial powers, they devoted considerable resources to expanding all levels of education. Some 450 or more universities of various sorts are now in existence. Alas, their quality of educational programs and the supreme importance of research faculty have not been major considerations to date. The systems of Arab higher education have suffered greatly from these two deficiencies.

Despite these limitations, the Arab countries have invested in the education of a considerable number of students. They have given more attention to quality in the establishment of professional schools in engineering and medicine than in other fields.

Moreover, during the past 60 years some 200,000 Arabs have earned PhD degrees abroad. A large proportion of these emigrated due to lack of demand for their services at home. Emigration enabled them to acquire further experience and standing in their respective fields. Today the Arab countries could easily mobilize thousands of leading scholars—scientists, engineers, and doctors—to initiate high quality universities.

Surprisingly, there are no tendencies toward improving higher education by utilizing national intellectual resources. This is not the procedure currently pursued in establishing new universities in the Arab world. Scholarship, quality, research, and knowledge are still not prime considerations. And in general, little public attention is paid to the establishment of new universities. The processes adopted to establish new universities do not subscribe to an obsession with quality and the advancement of learning.

The foreign universities that were brought in substantial numbers into the Arab world are meant to transfer the standards of Harvard, Cornell, and others. However, recent American literature on these universities indicates that they are unable to attract their home campus professors abroad. These offshore universities often depend on short-term appointees. The temporary nature of academic appointments and the failure of university faculties in Arab countries to develop scholarly networks in their local communities make it impossible for these organizations to integrate into their new environments. A key feature of Western universities is their close relationships with their host communities.[7]

A successful university is meant to be an integral part of the social, cultural, and political fabric of a society. Arab countries have not facilitated the comprehensive integration of foreign professors into their social fabric.

The Achilles Heel of Science in the Arab World

The expansion of the system of higher education led to a high rate of growth in the number of graduates. The labor market underwent massive expansion without an organized effort to impose standards, define priorities, or regulate activities of new practitioners.

Standards are currently applied through the mechanistic equating of degrees, with limited attention paid to creativity and competence. The absence of scientific societies concerned with advances in science means that a new graduate has no practical way to maintain his or her competences. No public authority enables public intellectual discussions on the sociocultural functions of these new scientific workers or defines and regulates their social and cultural responsibilities. This inhibits scientists from developing a voice and a platform in their countries on these professional issues.

Needless to say, wages are important; and this has become a topic of major concern for most professional groups. This emphasis on wages, and the avoidance of fundamental policy and cultural issues, has undermined the essential reasons for the existence of the professions.

The formation of the necessary scientific societies is not difficult when the political economy is clement and supportive of group formation. There have been very few studies of this critical subject. The evidence is in the poverty of existing organizations.

Longueness provides a seminal account of the current state of some of the unions and syndicates that have emerged.[8] Clement Henry Moore has also shed light on these issues as they arise among Egyptian engineers.[9] Larzilliere examines Jordanian organizations.[10]

Only time will tell whether Arab societies will be able to develop a political class capable of responding to current challenges.

The formation of scientific societies is, of course, within reach of the Arab world. What is lacking are

- a favorable political culture that supports freedom of association,
- public discussions of the issues facing these societies, and
- research facilities to empower scientists and scholars.

Incipient Awareness of a Sense of Crises

The essential instruments for the development of the Arab countries have been in an unsatisfactory condition for a long time. Yet, neither governments nor the public have been willing to recognize this reality.

When the four UNDP Arab Human Development Reports appeared in 2002–2005, there was a ripple of concern that such information was published. The reactions to the reports were mixed, and it gave rise to a minor debate.

There has been no serious public debate on the issue of development and no Arab government has sought to inform its society of the emergency nature of current conditions. Most of the actions that have been taken are along the lines of bringing in more foreign universities and more turnkey projects at all levels of education. In other words, most of the actions taken do not lead to the improvement of national capabilities to cope with the crises.[11]

Interestingly, the subject became sufficiently topical for Arab rulers, at their summit meeting in Kuwait in 2009, to request the Secretariat of the League of Arab States to prepare a report on the current status of Arab development.

When the preliminary draft report was circulated within the Arab League Council, there was shock and disbelief.[12] Radwan El-Sayed reviewed the reactions of Arab governments to the draft report by evoking, in a gentle manner, the prevailing political economy. He found that governments are not yet ready to discuss the central issues publicly. Surprisingly, Arab rulers are more inclined to deepen the crises by importing more foreign organizations than in promoting local understanding of the nature of the crises and involving the community to solve these critical problems.

The literature on what is wrong with any Arab country is now so considerable that any government interested in rectifying prevailing conditions can learn a lot from reading commercially available reports. Even the annual reports of the World Economic Forum (WEF, an organization established to promote business profitability) could shed light on the problems afflicting the Arab countries.

For example, the latest WEF annual report states that there are nine pillars necessary to drive productivity and competitiveness among nations. Five of these involve science, technology, and human capital directly.[13]

- The first pillar, called Institutions and Measures, considers as critical ethics and corruption, and undue influence (judicial independence and favoritism in decisions of government officials).
- The fifth pillar, concerned with higher education and training, measures the quality of higher education and on-the-job training.
- The seventh pillar is concerned with technological readiness.
- The eighth pillar is concerned with business sophistication, with emphasis on the technical aspects of production, such as networks and supporting industries, and the sophistication of the operations and strategy of the firm.
- The ninth pillar is concerned with innovation and deals with the quality of scientific research institutions, expenditure on R&D, the relationship between universities and industry, and so on.

One would have imagined that the participation of political leaders and the business community in the annual conferences of the WEF should already have resulted in a number of obvious reforms in the indicated areas. But, clearly, attendees of WEF meetings do not read its reports.

Organizations and Their Historical Context

The organizations under consideration in this chapter came to life because scientists and political leaders in the industrializing countries found that the scientific enterprise could not proceed without them.

Since the Industrial Revolution, the rate of knowledge growth has been so large that political leaders have become intensely aware of the advances in science. Industrial countries responded to international competition by improving the quality of their capabilities. The political leaders of these countries became deeply conscious of the enormous damage to their countries that can be caused by procrastination.

As late as 1900 the availability of higher education in industrial countries was still on a limited scale. Since then, there has been a steady expansion in facilities, improvement in quality, and increase in the numbers of students.

The quality of higher education has been important to scientists from the earliest times. However, as the number of students and professors increased, the management of standards called for more dedicated and transparent organizations. These trends concerning education, standards, and testing have continued to develop to this day; the quality of education remains a major public concern in industrial and industrializing countries.[14]

Toward the middle of the twentieth century, industrial societies began to recognize that unless they were careful in the way they use science they could suffer from its unintended consequences. For example, the early workers who handled radioactive substances and X-ray died from cancer. At that time, X-ray and radioactive materials were thought to be endowed with magical curative properties. The impact of pollution on our local and global environment has been recognized so late because of the influence of economic interest in not doing so. Current global concern with pollution and global warming is well known.

From the beginning, scientists were concerned with the management of the quality and standards of their publications. They achieved this through the establishment of prestigious scientific societies that published high quality periodicals. These periodicals were tightly managed to maintain high standards.

Bruce Alberts, editor in chief of *Science*, discusses the importance of improving editorial standards to make science as creatively productive as possible. He also refers to joint efforts by the editors of three gatekeeping publications (*Science*, *Nature*, and the *Proceedings of the National Academy of Sciences*) to develop procedures for identifying articles that undermine these high goals.[15] This editorial highlights the need to be constantly vigilant for any deviations from high ethical standards.

Scientific societies in industrial countries are deeply involved in alerting their communities to the requirements of scientific activity, as well as to the implications of scientific advances.

The myriad scientific and technological advances made during the nineteenth century required standardization and quality control. This led industrial countries to establish national bureau of standards, which played a critical role in bringing order to the chaotic varieties of products and measurements. These standards were also needed to enable manufacturers to market products that could work when used together and were safe to use.

Naturally, quality control is also necessary to protect the consumer from purchasing faulty and useless products. Food and medical products received special attention: powerful organizations were established to protect consumers and also to prevent and/or manage epidemics when they did occur.

Collateral Organizations

In addition to organizations that were strictly science-based, a host of other types of sister-organizations emerged that assured linkages with the economy and the consumer. Governments realized that they needed accurate and up-to-date statistical information on economic activities to be able to plan successfully. Thus, national statistical offices were established in all industrial countries. The best such offices were independent of government control, though in receipt of public funding. Statistical offices provide the essential information needed to construct meaningful policies. Without such information a government will be piloting the economy in the dark.

A comparison of the statistical offices of Arab countries with those of European and Tiger countries shows how far they are from possessing useful planning statistics.

Standards and codes have become a powerful factor in modern governance. The degree to which they are implemented in a country is an important measure of the quality of government and the standing of that country. It means, for example, that people can be sure of the measurements used in shops; feel safe from fear of earthquakes because appropriate seismic design measures are enforced; and know that the food that they eat has been tested for chemicals that lead to ill health.

Standards and codes are not only of importance internally but are also the cornerstone of international trade. Discrimination against foreign products on the basis of standards is acceptable under WTO rules. Third world countries have to improve their standards and quality control to be able to export their products.

Legal organizations and institutions are of importance in all aspects of trade in technology as well as in the domain of technology transfer.

In the United States, Ralph Nader inspired the formation of thousands of specialized consumer-protection societies. Some were concerned with the quality of bread; others were concerned with the safety of cars, energy use, and pollution of the environment. These societies led to the formation of organizations to protect Americans from abuse and had considerable impact on US legislation concerned with consumer protection.

The above are illustrative examples of organizations that were based partly in science and partly in trade, the law, and other social institutions.

Underdeveloped countries that do not participate in the setting up of national and international organizations to deal with codes, standards, and regulations of trade lose out, not just because they do not have a voice in the matter but also because they do not benefit from the discussions and research involved in determining the solution to such problems.

As usual, the most advanced countries are the ones that shoulder most of the work and secure most of the associated benefits from these activities.

Instruments for the Application of Technology

When the Pyramids, the Ma'rib Dam, the Great Wall of China, and Le Canal de Midi (or Le Canal des Deux Mers) were constructed, the projects were managed by their owners, and not via external consulting and contracting organizations. In premodern times the number of large-scale projects at any one time in any particular country were very few indeed, and it did not pay to develop independent capabilities for executing them.

The owners of these projects were responsible for the design, construction, financing, maintenance, and distribution of the benefits from these "investments."

The prominence of large consulting and contracting firms emerged with the invention of modern transport systems, such as canals, roads, naval transport, and railway systems. The development of large-scale water and agricultural projects involved the construction of dams, canals, land terracing, and transport systems, and it thus necessitated large-scale engineering.

Over the past two centuries, the number of macro-projects in any economic sector have become so large that it made sense to separate the know-how needed to undertake them from ownership and use of the completed project. Thus, today the people who build a structure do not, usually, own it.

Consultants and contractors are associated with a project for a short period of time, usually about two to five years. This new type of association implies a trade relationship between those who design and construct and the ultimate owner. Naturally, a range of legal issues arise in such a relationship. Though a project may require only few years to design and construct, the responsibility of designers and builders may last for a century. Insurance must be available to protect the different parties involved from various contingencies.

Suitable instruments have to be devised to protect the designer, the contractor, the legal owner, and the supplier of construction materials. A major project may "fail" for one of a variety of reasons. The legal system must provide mechanisms for identifying the guilty party (if any) and impose a just resolution; otherwise the various parties will not be able to enter into relationships that end in the desired structure. All of these organizations are part of the science and technology support infrastructure.

Naturally, all large-scale projects involve a large number of consulting and contracting organizations working together. These collaborative activities cannot exist without an elaborate supporting environment of legal, financial, political, statistical, research, and testing services. In response to these requirements, industrial countries developed the necessary support services to make the execution of such projects feasible.

An interesting example of how a project may fail, but can be brought back to life, is provided by the history of the Egyptian barrage, al-Qanatir al-Khayrriyyah. The construction of this barrage was initiated by Muhammad Ali in 1833. The engineering management was provided by Linant de Bellfonds, who established a committee to plan and manage the process of construction. Progress on the project was erratic as a result of an epidemic that decimated the corvée labor. It was "completed" many years later, in 1861, under the management of Mougel, another French engineer.

When, after its completion, engineers tried to hold the Nile water in it, the dam moved; in other words, its foundation was not strong enough for the dam to retain the water. The barrage project was a near failure.

After the British occupation of Egypt in 1882, it became known that similar problems had been successfully overcome in India. British engineers in India had invented the technology of grouting: pumping cement under the foundation in order to cement the base of the dam to its foundation.

Cromer, the effective ruler of Egypt at the time, was anxious to generate greater revenues to recover the foreign debt of Egypt. He imported British engineering expertise from India in 1884; the problem was finally solved by 1890. In 1896 Major R. H. Brown, inspector general of irrigation in Lower Egypt, provided a brief history of the barrage and how it was made viable thanks to British Indian engineering experience.[16]

In order to solve difficult problems it is not enough to have good engineers; they have to be organized in a manner that can benefit, if need be, from international experience. Engineering organizations have to be research minded to be able to identify problems and solutions. Good engineering work calls for a continuous flow of knowledge between engineering organizations that may be located in different countries. A society whose scientists are not enabled to collaborate is impoverished: Egypt had to await British occupation to benefit from its own dam.

Cromer was part of the British imperial civil service, and thus he had access to information about the type of dam construction problems that arose and had been solved in India by British Royal Engineers. Today, scientists have access to information systems underpinning all scientific activities. It is now easy for them to know about progress made elsewhere.

The enormous extent of scientific activities means that there are few problems that have not been experienced somewhere. Yet, one cannot expect every engineer to be personally familiar with all this universally extensive experience. This is the importance of being "connected" via the appropriate information systems.

Most of these information systems are commercially available for a fee. However, most scientists and engineers in Arab countries do not have access to these information services. This lack of connection to information resources naturally limits their capabilities. The net result is that it makes them dependent on importing international firms to deal with local problems instead of accessing the knowledge needed to solve the problems themselves.

Local Conditions and the Application of Science

The application of knowledge, to be useful for a particular country, must be consistent with its environmental and economic conditions. Some areas of the world are prone to earthquakes, flooding, tsunami threats, landslides, hurricanes, and so on. Specialized organizations such as municipalities have to be enabled and equipped to regulate the use of every site under their responsibility. Otherwise thousands of people may unnecessarily die when an earthquake strikes or when a flood occurs.

This does not mean that industrial countries have perfected their defenses against disasters due to natural causes: in the United States the events precipitated by hurricane Katrina in New Orleans in 2005 led to the loss of 1,836 lives and an estimated $81 billion worth of property. This indicates that the requisite organizations have not been perfected anywhere. The events in Japan at the Fukushima reactors show how another advanced country failed to protect itself from the vagaries of nature.

Similarly, the ability to benefit from the available science of agriculture depends on local research to adapt relevant information to local conditions. Farmers have to be provided with appropriate support and facilities to enable them to benefit from the relevant sciences.

The Nile Delta of Egypt is now threatened by the consequences of climate change. It covers an area of 28,000 square km of farmland.

Two-thirds of Egypt's population lives in the Delta, which produces 60 percent of Egypt's food supply. It has a coastline of 270 kilometers, large parts of which are less than a meter above sea level, with some areas lying below it. Climate experts expect a one-meter rise in sea level within a century. Such a rise will lead to the destruction of 20 percent of the Nile Delta. If the worst scenario of climate change is realized there will be a 14-metre rise in sea level, with practically the entire Delta getting submerged.

Coastal erosion is currently destroying the edge of the Delta at a rate of almost 100 meters a year. Clearly, there is a serious risk to a vital portion of Egypt, and thus one should expect an equally serious response.

Corruption

Many technological activities are prone to corrupt practices. Corruption is an activity that is global in its spread. There was corruption in the Tiger economies, but it did not exclude the possibility of acquiring technology. Countries desirous of protecting themselves from the ills of corruption need to monitor and regulate these activities in order to make sure that buildings are built safely, the scales at the grocers are accurate, medical products on sale are not spurious, food has not been adulterated with chemicals known to harm health, and so on. Undertaking all of this regulatory work, though basically simple, ends up being a complex matter.

The cost of enforcing standards is still less expensive than the damage caused by natural hazards and corrupt practices, when thousands may perish in floods or earthquakes, or suffer ill health from vegetables and fruits sprayed with banned pesticides.

Corruption in construction has led to the collapse of buildings built to subminimum standards, inflicting a considerable number of casualties. Establishing the necessary organizations to regulate the use of technology and to make sure that standards are adopted and implemented is vitally important.

Fighting corruption is important for many reasons. The most obvious is that corruption results in the death of innocent people and considerable economic loss.

Surprisingly, some Arab countries award the responsibility for approving the proposed design of a structure to the union of engineers. Since most of these buildings are designed and constructed by members of such unions, there exists a conflict of interest. It is not outright corruption but clearly facilitates it.

Corruption increases transaction costs, sabotages competition laws, and eliminates the possibility of the client being able to choose a suitable solution to her problem.

In well-organized countries, public organizations are empowered and staffed to take care of these issues. Independent scientific, professional, and governmental bodies regularly investigate the activities of organizations responsible for regulating the use of technology.

Most of the Arab countries have not framed adequate laws and measures to protect them against sources of harm. The setting of standards and the imposition of regulatory services empowered to apply quality control testing on all products are essential activities in the fight against corruption.

Concluding Remarks

The purpose of this chapter was to highlight the importance of a wide spectrum of organizations supporting the processes of producing and applying science and technology. It was also to stress the fact that the Arab countries have still to invest a great deal of effort to build these organizations. Such organizations contribute far more to society than they cost, and they have considerable influence on smoothing the process of development by reducing or eliminating corruption.

To summarize, the growth of science over the past two centuries was associated with the rapid growth of appropriate and evolving organizations. These organizations played massive roles in local, national, regional, and global scientific activity. Arab countries have a long way to go to establish this class of organizations, despite possessing the resources to do so.

CHAPTER 11

MUNICIPALITIES, SCIENCE, AND TECHNOLOGY

Introduction

Municipalities are instruments of governance. They provide a powerful tool for the decentralization of government and for improving its performance. They are instruments for the dissemination of central government services on the local, rather than national, scene.

Municipalities were not developed in opposition to central government, but rather as an extension of its power and services. Initially, government appointed its officials to manage municipalities. As governments became more representative of their populations, they sought to democratize the governance of their municipalities. Municipalities provide a valuable feedback channel that informs central government of what the population seeks and needs.

Arab governments have been attempting to decentralize for some time, but the process has been proceeding at a slow pace. Furthermore, it has been dominated by a top-down approach, giving little chance for local communities to transmit their own views and needs to the central government.

Roula Majdalani discusses three interrelated issues falling in the domain of decentralization: structural adjustment; the so-called crises of the state; and democratization.[1] The difficulties facing developing countries in the pursuit of decentralization are increased by international organizations that prescribe structural adjustment. Structural adjustment promotes so-called liberal policies that aim to facilitate the entry and profitability of foreign investments. What is promoted is neither helpful nor liberal.

The current approaches to decentralization fail to take into consideration the heavy inheritance of technological dependence and foreign technological domination of the economies of developing countries. What developing countries need above all else is to free themselves from technological bondage and develop a coherent and efficient economy whose priority is to serve their own citizens.

The destruction of Arab economic system based on trade and transport was achieved by its dismantling, in a short period of time, during the seventeenth century.

The integration of the economies of the Arab world depended on the place of regional and international trade in the economy of each Arab state. The local and regional economies participated actively in the economic system by contributing the instruments needed for pursuing international trade: the camels and the dhows, the khans, and the financial and legal systems. Their dismantling resulted in socioeconomic fragmentation at both the national and regional levels. Needless to say, mass unemployment resulted in all sectors of the Arab economy.[2]

The Asian experience, from that of Japan to the current approaches of China, Korea, and others, is clear: first strengthen the economy by developing national scientific and technological capabilities. The reason that this "recipe" has universal validity is the commonality of the reasons for the collapse of Asian and African economies: they failed to acquire in time the new technologies to defend themselves against Western aggression and exploitation.

The strong motivation in democratic societies for the development of municipalities originates in the conviction that a community involved in the solution of its own problems adds value to its efforts. The contributions to local welfare that a representative municipality makes are so significant that, once experienced, it would be difficult for a community to resist the benefits of democracy and decentralization.

In the early phases of the formation of a new nation, all technological capabilities are embodied in nascent ministries. These new ministries normally have limited resources committed to the diffusion of their services. Yet, well-staffed and managed municipalities can provide a low-cost conduit to ministries to distribute their services at the local level. All ministries can benefit from facilities that diffuse their scientific and technological capabilities to rural areas and small towns.

In this chapter we are concerned with a dimension that is of considerable importance to the application of science and technology. The transfer of technical capabilities to citizens enables them to better utilize their own resources and to solve their developmental problems. The economic returns of these efforts are almost immediate, through increased agricultural output, better health services, more support to SMEs, and a more productive use of human capital.

Central Government and Municipalities

In the postindependence Arab world there were efforts to develop the relationships between central government and municipalities. Central government sought to appoint a representative, followed by the appointment of community leaders, to serve as advisers to the powerful delegates from central government. In most cases the delegate and the local elites rarely had the necessary expertise to effectively represent local views, needs, and demands. Interest was focused on control and taxes rather than on helping the local community to improve and accelerate its rate of development.

Egypt underwent numerous "reforms," beginning during the nineteenth century, concerning local government. Most of these appear to have been cosmetic changes to the relationships with local representatives.[3] Lebanese municipalities enjoy electing their officers. But in most cases Lebanese municipalities are devoid of the professional capabilities needed to address and solve local problems.

The slow pace with which Arab municipalities are developing reflects the complexity of the process and the attachment of central government to total control.

The municipalities of Arab capital cities appear to have attained a relatively high level of development. For example, the Amman municipality, with 11,578 employees in 1999, is able to run much of its business on its own. But even there only half of the municipal council is elected; the other half is appointed.[4]

It is noteworthy that so far the delegation of authority covers mostly traditional responsibilities such as self-governance with respect to the distribution of potable water, sewerage services, and the like. The responsibilities for these basic municipal functions is still shared between municipalities, ministries of planning (when these exist), ministries of construction or public works, ministries of finance, and so on. This fragmentation of responsibilities increases the difficulties of managing such issues and increases their cost. The day when municipalities will be fully responsible for all services in their areas appears to be still far off. But, without well-defined attribution of responsibilities it will be difficult to streamline the current chaotic relationships as well as endow municipalities with the authority of borrowing, charging and collecting fees, and settling their loans.

Arab municipalities have still to win the responsibility to

- contribute to the cultural and educational life of their local populations,
- improve the economic environment to support local firms,
- promote forward and backward linkages among economic actors in their municipal area,
- become involved in attracting investment to their region,
- be concerned in the agricultural sector,
- be concerned with environmental issues,
- sponsor incubators, and
- enable local entrepreneurs and other services.

Functions and Services that Municipalities Need to Provide

In chapter 10 I alluded to the vital roles municipalities play in the modern state as implementers and regulators of technology, in the reduction of transaction costs and enforcement of standards, and in quality control. This is in addition to their critical role as the local government in the socioeconomic domain.

Municipalities can contribute significantly to all phases of planning, monitoring, and regulating activities concerned with construction activities; transport services; health care; food security; water supply; sewage and garbage disposal; public recreational places; cleanliness in public eateries, groceries, bakeries, restaurants, and hotels; support for SMEs; attraction of investment to municipal areas; protection of the environment; fire hazards and safety; public health, and so on. It is clear that the scope that is available to municipalities to promote scientific approaches to daily life is both considerable and at a basic level.

Much of the work undertaken by municipalities in a modern state is of a technical nature and subject to rules and regulations. Municipalities do not set standards or codes; they apply what has been established by national technical organizations (see chapter 10). Similarly, the social policies that they apply are established by the central government; municipalities merely carry out these policies. The move toward e-government in some Arab countries should facilitate and reduce the cost and effort needed to provide efficient municipal government.

The personnel working at municipalities have a dual role: applying rules and identifying local needs. This involvement in the application of rules and standards can provide feedback for the organizations that set these rules: municipal workers can identify cases where rules and standards are not appropriate and propose modifications. Thus, they serve, on a daily basis, to verify the validity of rules and standards and recommend, when necessary, modifications.

Municipalities employing properly trained staff are able to identify and mobilize local resources embodied in schools, academic and vocational institutions, shopkeepers serving rural areas, and among floating technicians and tradesmen.

The municipality, in this age of the Internet and mobile phones, could link, at low cost, rural areas and small towns to numerous central government services to obtain their share of available knowledge and expertise.

Development, Central Government, and Municipalities

In any country, there are two ongoing developmental processes. The dominant one is top-down. The bottom-up process is usually much weaker, and it grows in strength as democratization progresses.

The top-down process starts with central government and large corporations. These develop and adopt policies and plan and construct major infrastructural projects and industries. Government is ultimately responsible for all policies concerning the economy, employment, science, education, trade, and so on. Modern governments have learnt that to be effective they need an instrument to bring these policies and activities, initiated by a remote central government, to the doorstep of their citizens.

An interesting and successful example of rural development is provided by the manner in which the government of France deployed its engineers in rural areas during the nineteenth century. Daniel Grinrose describes the integrative manner in which a large proportion (some 70 percent) of the engineers of the Corps des Ponts et Chaussees was involved in provincial services. They were involved in small rural and urban areas designing, planning, and implementing small projects. These young university graduates also intermarried with the daughters of the notables in the local communities that they served. Thus there was a process of affiliation and long-term integration between these agents of development and the local communities.[5]

A critical factor in the success of the deployment of these engineers is the support that new appointees received from colleagues that preceded them. The young engineers thus became rapidly integrated in their new societies. Ringrose notes that "the senior officials kept a close watch over the process and encouraged behavioral and social standards that enabled the engineers to fit into a respectable society anywhere in France."

What Ringrose does admirably is exhibiting and discussing the many different supportive participants and institutions involved in this process. The process appeared to be the result of a central plan; it was in fact an effective response to "local concerns and local institutions."

Even in a small country there are great many differences among different groups in the population. Some towns may be the center of a great deal of agricultural activity while others may have some industry or operate tourist services. These different communities might wish to give their educational and recreational services different slants and emphases. Their municipalities may wish to promote economic activities in sectors favored by local advantage.

Before the Industrial Revolution, agriculture was the basis of progress in society. Today the rural economy in a modern state is no longer totally dependent on agriculture, as it may also have rural industries and rural tourism.

These trends in development are obviously complementary, and it is natural to expect them to work toward a coherent relationship.

Urban municipalities can play important roles in the large-scale planning needed to attract global activities such as the Olympics, international artistic activities such as the annual Edinburgh Festival or the London Caribbean Festival, expositions and trade fairs, and so on. For example, the Paris and London expositions of the nineteenth century played a powerful role in globally announcing and diffusing knowledge about the Industrial Revolution.

Local governments in industrial countries have played important roles in bringing major cities back to life after their economic base collapsed. Elected municipal governments can play diverse and important roles irrespective of the size of the community and the nature of the challenge.

The Urban–Rural Gap

Over the past three centuries the combined development of industrialization and urbanization has led to an increasing economic gap between urban and rural areas. Rural areas worldwide have been disadvantaged by the rural–urban technology gap.

Four parallel processes helped to close this gap in industrial countries:

- The shrinkage of agricultural labor to less than 5 percent of the national labor force helped to improve per capita income in rural areas.

- Quality public sector services in education and health became available to the rural population.
- From the early nineteenth century there was public sponsorship of large-scale application of science to agricultural activities.
- The location of industrial and other economic activities in rural areas.
- Rural areas, near cities, attracted substantial populations that commuted to work.
- There was, and continues to be, a massive subsidy for agriculture in both North America and the EU to enable rural populations to enjoy the same standard of living as their urban counterparts.

From the twentieth century the status of rural areas no longer took second place.[6] They had their own local governments, associations, and organizations. In fact, in many industrial countries, universities, industries, and research organizations sought to be located in more affordable and pleasant rural areas rather than in large cities.

Furthermore, since municipalities were granted the power to secure payment for the services they provide to their populations, they have been able to borrow money to finance projects in their jurisdiction and recover the cost from the revenue generated.

Arab universities could have contributed to developing municipalities if they had established postgraduate programs and undertook research on rural societies. This has not taken place to any significant degree.

All in all, rural areas in the Arab world have not had adequate support to help them break out of their isolation and poverty. This is why a serious effort is needed to empower municipalities to modernize.

Science and Rural Areas

There are a number of serious problems facing municipalities in rural areas. For one thing, Arab countries have so far not fully mechanized and modernized their agricultural sectors. As a result, the productivity of land, labor, and water use are below par. Since the leading activity in rural areas in the Arab world is still agriculture, and since Arab agriculture is still in need of much investment and development, there is enormous scope to attract agriculture-related research and industrial activities to rural areas.

Arab rural areas have not yet attracted industries or companies to locate their headquarters and offices there. To do so, they need to improve their schools, hospitals, parks, transport services to cities, and create a more supportive and pleasant social and physical environment.

The effort required to achieve such a goal is obviously beyond the means of an average small town. We learn from European experience that the formation of an association of municipalities could enable small towns and rural areas to plan collectively (see later in this chapter) to address such challenges.

There is an expectation that the use of solar energy in the Arab world will be on a grand scale. The centers of production of solar energy will be in rural areas, and this should lead to considerable employment opportunities. This may not be the case unless local governments take the necessary measures to prepare rural populations for such opportunities.

Clearly, there is no end to new and emerging industries awaiting the Arab world. All of these could contribute to a positive response to rural challenges.

Science and Arab Agriculture

We noted in chapter 3 that Arab agriculture improved, during the past half century, faster than that of China and India, and health services did penetrate the rural areas, improving standards.

The bonding of the Arab states, their food security, and environmental protection all require an intensive concern with agriculture. A focused scientific interest in water is a must if the Arab world is to be able to combine its diverse resources successfully.

Despite the shortage of water and large expanses of deserts, the Arab world has adequate land and water to grow its food if it uses available scientific knowledge optimally. It is unlikely that Arab countries can overcome their current political problems without the development of their agricultural sector. Municipalities can play a decisive role in upgrading the scientific and technological infrastructure of rural areas.

Cadres and Multiple Approaches to
Municipal Development

Numerous approaches are available to accelerate municipal development. European municipalities established an international association with a view to promote international twinning with cities around the world. Such twinning could provide Arab municipalities with excellent opportunities to learn how their foreign counterparts function.

National universities can play an important role in researching the subject. Training professionals capable of serving these municipalities effectively is much needed. At the moment, national universities do little research or training in this domain.

Competent, creative, and dedicated leadership played important roles in the development of municipalities in Western countries. Professionals specializing in municipal affairs were a major factor in this process.

Perhaps the first important measure to be adopted was to enable municipalities to evolve in competence. The further empowerment of municipalities depended on themselves: they had to build competences despite limited resources. Building such capabilities is not simple. Municipalities in different countries approached their challenges in slightly different ways. They all had to find methods of collaborating in order to secure the know-how that they needed at a cost that they could afford.

During the past 50 years municipalities in industrial countries have become active agents in attracting industries and entrepreneurs to rural areas. Agricultural labor, made available by the mechanization of agriculture, served to attract urban-based industries to rural areas where they had access to low-cost labor. This process is yet to be initiated in the Arab world.

Municipal Associations

Small municipalities in industrial countries discovered that they solely could not afford to engage all the services that they needed for development. They noted, however, that since the problems each of them faced were essentially similar, they could share the cost for the consulting services required. They thus established municipal associations to share their resources to cope with these challenges.

Some, like the Dutch municipalities, established their own legal, consulting, and contracting firms, as well as their own bank to finance their projects.[7] In this manner municipalities were able to serve small populations effectively. This was a dramatic development: all municipalities, regardless of size, could access high quality services jointly procured.

A municipal association, supported collectively by all municipalities, could have sufficient resources to plan and campaign on behalf of its members. It could encourage central governments to locate branches of ministries, universities, hospitals, and new organizations in rural areas. Similarly, it could campaign for, and create, services to encourage small and medium-sized industries to move out from large cities.

Thus, the formation of municipal associations not only enabled municipalities to serve their population base but also gave them a voice at the national level. They were therefore able to intervene constructively at the level of central government.

Problems and Challenges Facing Arab Urban and Rural Populations

The literature on Arab municipalities highlights the many problems that they confront. These problems cannot be addressed with the tools and means at the disposal of either the municipalities or central government. Both need additional support from academic research and science.

Lebanese and Palestinian municipalities have already forged a limited degree of association formation. There is little doubt that collaboration between all of these parties, along with the sponsorship of vigorous research programs, could help to resolve current problems.

The underutilized research capabilities available in Arab countries could easily be mobilized to accelerate the development of municipalities. The research topics are ideal for MA or MS programs. This should give the social sciences and humanities-oriented Arab universities practical and useful academic objectives.

There is a considerable range of technical, legal, managerial, financial, social, and economic issues to study. These studies do not require special facilities, besides good libraries and data.

Much material is already available on Arab municipalities. Past records of the varied and unsuccessful efforts toward decentralization provide a rich supply of information on current systems. These models could be studied with stakeholders and a better understanding of the types of acceptable solutions obtained.

Then there is a small but growing literature on many different types of municipal problems. Seteney Shami has produced an admirable contribution in *Capital Cities*.[8] This rich collection of papers falls essentially outside the domain specifically addressed in this book. Yet, as the paper of Montasser Kamal[9] shows, the most elementary application of science and technology at the municipal level involves politics and participatory activity. Politics and governance is the vehicle through which science and technology are transmitted to the citizen. The challenges are surmountable and their resolution will make significant contributions to the quality of life and GNP at little cost.

CHAPTER 12

FUTURE PROSPECTS

Introduction

I have presented in this book information on the available scientific resources of the Arab countries and reflections on the factors that are preventing their productive application. I have mentioned that there have been numerous efforts to overcome some of these problems and that so far the efforts have failed to reach a satisfactory conclusion.

Many countries and societies face challenges in their efforts to benefit from advances in science. For example, though Britain was the leading scientific and industrial country in the world for more than a century, it missed out on benefiting fully from the great discoveries made by some of its scientists such as Michael Faraday and James Clerk Maxwell.

Faraday discovered how to generate electricity. But British investors were not interested in developing electric power generation. Britain, instead of electrifying the world, was electrified by Edison (United States) and Siemens (Germany).

Maxwell discovered the physics for the generation of radio waves and communication. Yet the pioneers in its application were Germans and Americans.

The reason that I am citing these events is to emphasize that great scientific research can have limited industrial and economic benefits to the country of the discoverer. It is the country that "adopts" the science and implements it as a technology that reaps the economic and technological rewards. The Soviet Union invested heavily in science and engineering, but this failed to prevent its collapse. The USSR failed to enable their scientists and technologists to innovate and serve the civilian economy.

The difficulties faced by European countries have, during the past 30 years, received increasing attention. The EU has been making great efforts to overcome their difficulties in innovating.

The challenges that the Arab countries face are the product of a long historic process. Thus, Arab countries suffer from a large backlog of unresolved problems. The entrenched political economy has resisted adaptation to the conditions imposed by the industrial revolution and its sequels. To date, the efforts made are not commensurate with the challenges that face them. The limited scale of collaboration among scientists in the Arab countries increases their difficulties. Hence the stalemate continues.

Opportunities Not Taken

It is well known that development is the result of a combination of inputs: human capital; knowledge; political, cultural, financial, and material resources; and luck. Since the early nineteenth century, these inputs were not often available simultaneously in any single Arab country. Yet, as I will illustrate below, they did occur at unexpected times. When circumstances accidentally arise that facilitate development, a country needs an attentive leadership to seize the opportunity. I have noted the importance of chance opportunities in chapter 1.

The ability of a society to benefit from an unexpected opportunity is dependent on complex cultural and political processes, which call for exceptional leadership.

Egypt missed such an opportunity during the first half of the nineteenth century. It had a small population of 3 million, an underdeveloped agricultural sector with excess land and water, and a world market for its agricultural products and cotton. Cotton at the time was a major industrial raw material. In addition to all of this bounty, Egypt was on the trade route to India, the chief imperial domain of the British Empire. It also had easy access to the world of knowledge and had educated a number of its youth in Europe. Yet it failed to capitalize on these advantages. Instead, it pursued a policy of conquests that it was ill equipped to undertake successfully, and thus ended up in 1882 essentially as a British colony.

As the Arab countries secured their independence in the 1950s they were presented with opportunities. They needed to develop their own entrepreneurial, political, and organizational capabilities and learn how to resume collaboration with each other.

Egypt and Lebanon were the two countries that had by the 1950s acquired a range of modest knowledge-based capabilities that could have enabled them to accelerate their progress and provide regional leadership. They had the most developed universities and medical schools in the region. In fact, they had half of all the universities and also a tradition of foreign study and travel. Egypt was then in the process of developing its science base and its industrial capabilities. The Nakba of 1948 had given a powerful jolt to the Arab world.

For illustrative purposes, I will sketch the critical events that took place in Lebanon. As mentioned in chapter 7, Lebanon was, during the 1950s and 1960s, already a hotbed of entrepreneurial initiatives. Its relatively high degree of personal and economic freedom was an important contributing factor.

Lebanon was, and continues to be, a confessional state. Its government accepted limited responsibility for social development. In 1960 a relatively small proportion of the population could afford educational and medical services.

The Gulf populations were still under British "occupation" and had no access to educational and medical services. But, by the 1950s, income from oil revenues provided the resources to enable some of them to access educational and health services in Lebanon and Egypt.

In 1951 Yousef Beidas, a Palestinian refugee in Lebanon since 1948, established, along with three partners, International Traders. This was a currency trading house, which became known as Intra Bank. Intra Bank focused on providing financial services to Gulf countries. It grew in strength and was among the first Arab banks to open a branch in Switzerland and to realize the importance of capital.

The election of Fouad Chehab as president of the Republic of Lebanon in July 1958 opened the windows of opportunity for Lebanon.[1] Chehab was aware of the nature of the prevailing Lebanese political economy and sought to humanize and empower it. The government of Lebanon sought the consulting services of the Institut de Recherches et de Formation en vue de Development (IRFED) in France with a view to modify and improve prevailing conditions.

The adoption of new concepts of economic planning, social justice, and national unity impinged on the prevailing political economy. There was resistance from the confessional ruling classes to changes in the political economy. Yet, despite the opposition to Chehab's efforts, much was achieved.

The Chehab period was characterized by the expansion of public education at the primary and secondary levels, as well as the establishment of a national Lebanese University, which is now the largest such institution in the country.

Beirut was already the home of two foreign universities, the American University of Beirut (AUB) and the University St Joseph (USJ), both of which had established medical schools. The Second World War years had constrained both of these universities severely. The 1950s and 1960s saw them trying to identify new directions and take new initiatives. The AUB was ahead of the USJ in these pursuits.

The AUB board of trustees embraced these opportunities in 1955 by inviting Professor Charles Malek to chair a university planning committee to prepare a report promoting the development of the liberal arts and humanities at the university.

Malek's committee submitted its first interim report on April 10, 1956. The report argued that the AUB was not a university, and to become one it must establish a doctoral graduate school. The vision adopted in this report was the promotion of all fields of knowledge, with emphasis on the sciences and the humanities.

Following the submission of the second interim report on December 9, 1956, the School of Arts and Science was invited to develop a ten-year program. There was change and improvement, but it was limited and at a slow incremental rate. It was insufficient to respond to the needs of the region for science and technology (S&T).

In 1960 the board of trustees appointed a committee of seven AUB professors under the chairmanship of Professor Constantine Zurayk to prepare a report entitled *The Future Role and Needs of the University* (1961). The report again unhesitatingly recommended a regional outlook with a focus on postgraduate education and research.

There was an obvious and potential demand at the time from the Gulf countries for a wide variety of services that Lebanese organizations could supply. The Middle East region was emerging from a long period of colonialism, and its future looked as bright as the abilities of its citizens. The areas undergoing rapid growth were education, construction, agriculture, transport, industrialization, consulting and contracting services, and health services.

These market demands drove the growth of entrepreneurship in Lebanon discussed in chapter 7. Naturally, entrepreneurs with limited financial resources could not set out to solve the emerging problems. Hence the importance of Intra Bank and the pioneering efforts of President Chehab to establish an enabling environment cannot be overemphasized.

Interestingly, three movements seemed to converge: the Chehabist reform movement; the Beidas effort to increase the availability of Gulf financial resources to serve local and regional development; and a new spirit of scholarship and creativity that was taking shape at the AUB.

However, by 1966 everything began to crumble. Intra Bank was forced into bankruptcy despite its considerable assets; it stopped making payments on October 14, 1966. The collapse of the bank brought the Lebanese economy to a halt and sent shockwaves throughout the Middle East. Intra Bank accounted for 15 percent of the total bank deposits and 38 percent of deposits with Lebanese-owned banks. Beidas's dreams of financing self-reliant development in the region were crushed.

Observers questioned why the Lebanese Central Bank, which had been established in April 1964, did not provide liquidity to Intra Bank during the run on the bank. Press commentators believed that this was due to the influence of politicians and rivals who were unhappy at the influence and power of Palestinian-born Beidas; others believed that the reaction was motivated by sectarian attitudes.[2] The full story of the collapse of Bank Intra is yet to be told.

The importance of Beidas is that he had established a link between Lebanon and the new wealth of the Gulf states. Needless to say, this connection was broken, to the detriment of Lebanon and the region.

Subsequently, various confessional groups successfully thwarted the Chehabist movement, and AUB development never amounted to more than a modest improvement of its undergraduate program.

Consequently, Lebanon missed benefiting from the 1973 massive increase in oil prices, which was another unexpected opportunity. In addition, a long and bloody civil war broke out in April 1975.

The economic returns from the 1973 rise in oil prices could have helped solve Lebanon's socioeconomic problems. It could have established the bonding of its economy with that of the GCC and also served to develop a modern knowledge-based society with rich possibilities for the region.

The missed opportunities of Egypt are as spectacular, since it had far more resources and a strong government. If Egypt's nascent industrial and research capabilities had developed to respond to the GCC, Algeria and Libya's expanding demand could have transformed both the Egyptian economy and the economic framework of the entire region.

Egypt was, for example, ready and willing to support the developmental process of Algeria after it won liberation from France. The causes of the failure of these efforts are still awaiting study.

Many political analysts note that external influences sought to abort these opportunities. There is no doubt that adversaries are always present, but being helpless in their presence closes the door to emancipation. The science of politics is supposed to provide the know-how to manage such situations.

Positive Recent Approaches

Needless to say, there are constant efforts throughout the region to over-come its chronic state of underdevelopment.

The pioneering work of Rima Khalaf Hunaidi at UNDP, resulting in the publication of four UNDP Arab Human Development Reports (2002–2005), induced increasing attention to the subject of development.[3] Yet, public reactions to these efforts are still too limited.

During the past decade, the Arab countries that are traditionally in the lead, such as Egypt, Iraq, Syria, and Algeria, have been kept busy by internal crises and unresolved regional problems. These countries barely took notice of these UNDP Reports. The leaders of the GCC countries, however, have responded more positively to the UNDP initiative. GCC governments sought to adopt new educational policies to deal with the issues raised. We have seen some consequences of these efforts reflected in an increase in their research output.

One of the notable initiatives is that of Shaikh Mohammed bin Rashid Al Maktoum, ruler of Dubai, who established a major foundation whose focus is on knowledge. This initiative gave rise to hope and expectations.

The first annual Arab Knowledge Report 2009 (henceforth, The Report) published by Mohammed bin Rashed Al-Maktoum Foundation was prepared in collaboration with UNDP and published in 2010. It is based on contributions by a number of researchers working across the Arab world.

The Report aims to provide a comprehensive outlook on the prevailing situation. It treats many dimensions of knowledge, culture, freedom, democracy, illiteracy, gender issues, and the use of the Arabic language.[4]

One of the most notable differences between The Report and this book is the former's limited reference to the *active agents* of a knowledge society. It states: "Knowledge is freedom and development and there can be neither knowledge nor development without freedom."[5] By contrast, this book focuses on scientists and on scientific activities. The political economy matters because it acts directly on scientists and entrepreneurs concerned with the pursuit and application of S&T.

The Report treats gender issues as persisting and related to human rights and freedom. In this book it is taken for granted that illiteracy, gender issues, and the use of Arabic language are serious matters. However, they are considered to be no longer major obstacles. Female university enrolment and female employment are at credible levels in leading Arab countries. Thus, males and females face similar issues in most Arab countries, and gender issues are part of the package of difficulties.

Collaboration among Arab scientists has been shown in this book to be severely limited. Yet, The Report does not address this crucial issue. There has been some 1,000 research papers published on aquifers by Arab scientists in quality periodicals during the past decade. Yet, few scientists collaborate to enable them to bring their expertise to serve the entire region.

The benefits of scientific capabilities *available* in a few Arab countries are not available to all the 21 Arab countries. The poor level of collaboration between the Arab countries is a key factor in sustaining the region in its current state: each country has to rediscover the same S&T instead of benefiting from the knowledge that is already available in any one Arab country. The collective use of knowledge contributes to its deepening and improvement.

The Report does not focus on the role of the essential instruments for the application of S&T such as consulting and engineering design organizations. The critical importance of national technology policies and how these policies determine the use and application of national and regional capabilities in S&T are not examined.

The Report refers to the numerous "agreements of Arab Heads of States" to overcome these difficulties, but it does not go into the reasons why there is so little change despite these agreements.[6]

Chapter 5 of The Report dwells on the subject of Arab Performance in Research and Innovation. Figure 5.1 in The Report cites an "innovation system index." Numbers are ascribed to the Arab countries. Yet, on page 189 of The Report we learn that: "Due to the lack of detailed and reliable data, it is difficult to conduct a comprehensive evaluation of the capacity of scientific research institutions for innovation."

The Report is an attempt to sketch the Arab knowledge scene. It is hoped that successive reports that the Al-Maktoum Foundation intends to sponsor will eliminate shortcomings of earlier ones. It will be difficult to reap the benefits of this Foundation's efforts without a massive campaign to improve statistical services and promote research in science policy in the region.

Successes and Challenges

The main challenges facing Arab countries are how to become self-reliant and how to benefit from available resources. The account presented in this book discussed the factors that are critical to the success of the scientific enterprise. It was shown that the acquisition of S&T is a relatively simple matter because it depends on a small number of highly motivated, skilled, and creative persons. Fortunately, nature has guaranteed that every society is amply endowed with such persons. However, building the organizations needed to benefit from acquired knowledge is demanding, and it depends on major changes in the prevailing political economy. Alas, scientists rarely have understanding of, or influence on, their national political economies.

I had indicated that several Arab countries might be on the threshold of a major transition. Several Arab countries have been trying for some time to industrialize, but without success; they have been unable to adopt the necessary measures that would usher them into a period of socioeconomic–cultural growth. Arab political leadership has not been able to manage the political changes needed to move forward.

Arab R&D Output

Since independence, several Arab countries were able to organize and develop their research programs. Some countries, such as Egypt, maintained a steady and expanding output during this period. Egypt's initial share in 1967 was 67 percent of the total Arab output. The population of Egypt is 25 percent of that of the Arab world. Egypt has increased its output over this period 17.6-fold.[7] In other words, the rate of growth of R&D output in Egypt was substantially lower than that of the average rate for the Arab world.

Lebanon suffered serious setbacks during its civil war, but it partially recovered by 2000. Kuwait has also recovered from the devastating Iraqi occupation. Sudan, however, has not recovered the status it occupied in the early 1970s.

Interestingly, the GCC and Maghreb countries (Morocco, Algeria, and Tunisia), which were not R&D active before 1970, have since taken center stage. The GCC assumed the leading position in research output from 1993 until 2007, after which the Maghreb countries began to compete for the top position.

The GCC's share of total Arab output peaked at 36 percent (of total Arab output) in 1998. It then remained steady at around 29–31 percent for the next decade. The GCC is the leading Arab region in terms of per capita R&D output.

The R&D output of the three Maghreb countries steadily increased, from 8 percent in 1967 to 28 percent (of total Arab output) in 2006. The Maghreb now competes, neck and neck, with GCC countries for the position of leading R&D producer in the Arab world.

Iraq, Jordan, Lebanon, and Syria have suffered from wars of various types. Their share of R&D was about 10 percent in 2007. Given enough commitment to development, they certainly could constitute an important base for R&D in the future.

The rest of the Arab countries contributed 8 percent in 2007, an increase from 7 percent in 1967.

Israeli R&D output grew 11-fold over the 1967–2007 period. In 1967 its output was 2.5 times the total Arab output. This ratio declined over the years until it reached 0.87 in 2006 and 0.57 in 2010. The per capita output of Israel, relative to the Arab world, was 58 times larger in 1967 and declined to 26 times in 2010. Needless to say, there is an enormous gap in knowledge between Israel and the Arab world.

Unlike the other regions, the GCC depends on a substantial number of expatriates (both Arab and non-Arab) to generate its output. If the GCC countries develop their immigration laws to absorb expatriate human capital, then they may be able to adopt an American-style approach and build a stable scientific community irrespective of ethnic origin. At the moment, this is not the case. As a result, developments in the GCC are precarious.

Likely Trends in Research Output

By 2005 some Arab countries were making serious efforts to advance in the research domain. It is likely that a small number of Arab countries will assume and retain leadership in R&D output during the next decade. It should not be surprising if Tunisia and/or Saudi Arabia were to increase their R&D output each by a factor of 10 over the next decade.

Saudi Arabia's output grew dramatically over the 1967–2010 period. This growth was in the range of 310–500 times, depending on the starting point.[8] The Saudi growth, unlike that of Egypt, has been irregular, growing ten-fold over one decade and hardly at all over another. Saudi Arabia has enormous potential for growth. It has high quality human capital that, given the space and resources, could rapidly transform the national economy.

No Arab country has yet developed a national S&T system in order to build a knowledge-based economy. So far, Egypt, Saudi Arabia, and Tunisia have shown signs that they are moving in this direction. Egypt has frequently aspired to do so but never took the last step. All three countries have an abundance of human capital. Overcoming the difficulties in building a knowledge-based economy by any of these three countries in the near future will probably be the most dramatic political step taken by any Arab country in the postindependence period.

As a consequence of the considerable investment in human capital by Arab countries, the construction of national S&T systems will be contingent *only* on reforming the political economy.

What the Arab world needs today is not five-star universities, hospitals, or research centers, as much as a five-star enabling environment. It has the scientists, markets, and resources with which to undertake the transition, but not the political culture to do so.

R&D Output and Takeoff

It was argued in this book that third world countries will be able to take off developmentally and research wise when they reach the level of 25 publications a year per million inhabitants. One finds that Korea went through this stage when it passed ahead of the Arab countries in 1985; and later China did so around 1995. In both cases these advances were the result of a long-term commitment to science and industrial development.

It is interesting to note that countries could be committed to development without being committed to industrial development. These two types of development are not similar. Most, if not all, Arab countries are committed to the former but not to the latter. One could have industries à-la turnkey without industrial development.

The major difference between the two types of development is the extent of technological dependence. A commitment to industrial development automatically eliminates the use of methods that deepen technological dependence and highlights the necessity of developing a national S&T infrastructure.

Interestingly, some Arab countries (for example, Egypt) had attained the critical takeoff level long before the 1970s, but they did not take off. Several Arab countries are long past the critical level of 25 publications per million inhabitants. The reason given for this failure is that the Arab countries have neither established a national S&T system (thus creating little relationship between R&D and the economy) nor adopted a national commitment to industrial development. This dissonance is ascribed to their prevailing political economy.

Obstructions to Takeoff

The economies of the Arab countries are heavily fragmented. This extreme fragmentation is the result of a millennium of setbacks. The dramatic increase of mamluks in the Imperial Army brought about by Caliph al-Mu'tassim followed by the move of the army and the court to the new city of Samarra was a turning point. This resulted in the dominance of mamluks in politics, the court, and the military. The mamluks had no loyalty to the population or to the caliphate; in fact, they took control of the caliphate and appointed their choice of the moment as the rulers. The mamlukization[9] of Arab political culture has been fairly comprehensive. The past millennium saw numerous setbacks, invasions, epidemics, and countless civil wars.

European technological advances began to be imposed on the region after 1498 with the arrival of the Portuguese in Gulf waters. Between 1498 and 1800 there was a massive process of economic and technological dismantling of the Arab economy, followed by 150 years of destructive direct occupation. During the 1498–1950 period the advances in S&T were used to consolidate foreign control of the region. This process continues to this day.

The political elites ruling the Arab countries between 1498 and 1950 failed to respond to the technological and scientific advances taking place around them.

The machinery of current Arab governments lacks cross-linkages within and between national organizations. They also lack accurate and up-to-date statistical information needed to understand their predicament and to plan effectively. As noted earlier in this book, these patterns of behavior are a direct outcome of the political economy.

Since the GCC and the Maghreb countries, historically, suffered least from the mamluk political culture, they may turn out to be the first to be liberated from the black hole created by the Caliph al-Mu'tasim. Their success may help heal others from the trauma that has afflicted the Arab world for a millennium. The countries that were devastated by the mamluks were those included in the arc stretching from Iraq to Egypt.

Obstacles and Difficulties in Adopting National Policies of Self-Reliance

Until the beginning of the twenty-first century, Arab governments devoted less of their GDP to scientific research than *most other nations*.[10] This is a well known fact, and there is nothing to add to it.

However, since 2005 there appears to be signs of change, though it is not yet commensurate with the challenges faced. China has been increasing its annual investment in R&D at the rate of 20 percent. It has been deepening its scientific capabilities, self-reliance, and national S&T

infrastructure since its successful national revolution. There is nothing comparable to this in any Arab country.

As a collateral to the self-sterilizing economic policies adopted by Arab governments, limited attention has been paid to the sources of procurement for their projects. Some 70 to 80 percent of the trillions of dollars invested by Arab countries are spent on the importation of services, materials, and equipment. The effort made to overcome this dependence is marginal.

These counterproductive patterns are an outcome of how ministries are organized, decisions are taken, commissions are collected, and foreign influence on Arab development is exercised.

As a consequence of the sustenance of this pattern of technological dependence for the past two centuries, the prevailing patterns of behavior have become entrenched. It will take considerable effort to overcome these traditions.

The oil and gas sector uses an enormous amount of basic chemical and mechanical technologies. These are modern nineteenth-century technologies. The Arab countries have invested heavily to educate, both at home and abroad, hundreds of thousands of engineers in all of these fields. There are probably more than 1.5 million Arab engineers around the world, and this number is growing at an estimated 7 to 10 percent annually. Yet, despite these human resources being available, there is little effort made in the Arab world for seeking industrial capabilities.

The oil sector imports much of the inputs needed to produce and export its oil and gas. There are vast opportunities for technological acquisition and for employment of Arab labor in this domain. Every major item that is imported by the giant oil and gas industrial projects is specially made for them.

President Gamal Abdel Nasser could not have nationalized the Suez Canal if Egyptians had not been available to operate it. The full benefits—embodied in local employment—of the oil and gas industry is contingent on comprehensive participation in the design, manufacturing, and operation of its installations.

In December 2009 the government of Iraq awarded a large number of contracts to international firms to develop its oil and gas fields. Analysts estimate that "it will be spending capital on oilfield services, in 2011 alone, five times that of Saudi Arabia, Bahrain, and the UAE, Oman, Qatar and Kuwait combined."[11] Clearly, Iraq has the opportunity today to use its economy as a powerful tool to promote the formation of a knowledge-based society. It has a huge pool of high quality engineers and scientists. It could also benefit from a rich supply of scientists, engineers, and technologists from many other Arab countries. But Iraq is not pursuing such objectives.

The oil and gas sector is not an exception to the general trend followed by the Arab countries. Arab countries continue to export crude phosphate and phosphoric acid (manufactured in 100 percent imported industrial plants). They have failed to develop the downstream phosphate-based industries that could increase the value added derived from the manufacture of crude phosphates and create jobs for tens of thousands of technicians, chemists, and engineers.

European countries, when confronted by the rapid technological advances in Britain during the eighteenth and nineteenth centuries, sought to secure the capacity to manufacture, rather than buy, their desired products. Some countries, especially France and (even more so) Germany, invented new organizations to expand research and to speed up the rate of increase in the availability of national expertise in order to facilitate the processes of invention and innovation.

In other words, the basic policy that underpinned the efforts of these countries was the desire for "self-reliance," as expressed in their ability to acquire and/or invent the necessary science rather than purchase its products. Interestingly, years later, Japan spontaneously adopted the same attitude. It made its decision totally based on evidence from its own history. The early history of the Arabs provides clear evidence for the importance of the principle of self-reliance.

During the Umayyad and early Abbasid periods the Arabs pursued the same policies as those adopted later in Europe and Japan. It is thus noteworthy that today they are averse to doing so. The Umayyad caliph Hisham ibn Abd el-Malek was called the *muhandess* (the engineer) because of his personal interest in the adoption of advanced water technologies. Arab merchants and soldiers are known to have been on the lookout, during their conquests and travels, for new technologies and products. This is how many new technologies and crops were acquired, and how the Arabs learnt to make paper, gunpowder, military uniforms using asbestos to enable them fight battles with naphtha, and many other products.

Collaboration among Scientists

The subject of collaboration of Arab scientists has been discussed at length in this book on three levels: national, regional, and international. All three levels are important to all countries.

On the national level there is some collaboration between scientists in different national research organizations. Here the most notable field for collaboration appears to be in medicine and agriculture.

From an analysis of the research output of Arab countries, it appears that some—such as Tunisia, Kuwait, and the UAE—are diffusing R&D capabilities throughout their governmental organizations.

There are some signs of weak cooperation in the field of engineering between researchers in industry, consulting and contracting firms, and university professors. Collaboration between research scientists in universities, hospitals, and pharmaceutical firms appears to be limited.

The lack of regional collaboration between scientists in the Arab world is, of course, a major setback. As a result, each country can only depend on the little science it possesses, and not on the substantial resources available to the entire Arab world. This inability to collaborate regionally reduces the ability of scientists to serve the Arab world.

Science is a universal activity, and scientific advances are pursued all over the world. It is thus important for scientists to be acquainted with global scientific activities and to be well supported by information systems. A great deal of the knowledge that scientists acquire of ongoing R&D is through meeting other scientists at conferences and through collaboration.

As far as international collaboration is concerned, one finds a broad range of patterns among the Arab countries (see chapter 6). Scientists in the Maghreb countries appear to be the most active and show a high level of collaboration with European (mostly French) scientists. The level of collaboration of scientists in the Mashreq (with the exception of Lebanon) varies from 14 to 25 percent of their output. Egypt and Saudi Arabia have not shown signs of steady growth in their rate of international collaboration (details are provided in chapters 5 and 6).

A deficit in national and regional scientific societies inhibits Arab scientists from debating national scientific issues and developing strategies and organizations to facilitate collaborative investigations. Scientists develop collaborative relationships as a result of informal encounters during meetings sponsored by scientific societies. It has been shown that Arab scientists have limited opportunities to attend international or national scientific meetings.

The weaknesses of Arab scientific societies are also evident in their shortcomings in contributing to the development of the scientific capabilities of their members.

We have noted that Arab R&D has a weak presence in frontline research areas. This is a serious matter. Normally, scientific societies are the agencies that highlight weaknesses in scientific activities, propose suitable solutions, and lobby both public and private sectors to raise funds to overcome these weaknesses. The absence of such activities by national scientific societies means that there are no organizations drawing the attention of governments to such matters.

The nonexistence of serious scientific societies in the Arab world is partly the result of[12]

- the constraints on freedom of association,
- lack of public support to sustain scientific societies,
- the difficulty that Arabs face in travelling in the Arab world due to the restrictions imposed on visas awarded to Arab citizens by Arab governments,
- the limited scale of R&D, and
- the low income of university professors.

Current Moves

Worldwide, governments have adopted strong measures to support the formation and growth of national scientific societies in order to empower their scientific community and to rationalize the societies' international standing as well as relationships with the public.

As discussed at length in chapter 4, the nexus of relationships between universities, science, and enterprise in a country is dominated by self-organizing criticality. The disruption of the relationships between the components of the triad greatly reduces the benefits that can be derived from human capital.

After recently "investing" $5 trillion, via international firms, one finds little trace in the Arab countries of added knowledge or techno-logical development. GCC countries have been sold the notion that they need to go for renewable and nuclear energy, at a cost of tens of billions of dollars. They can still make very significant contributions and save substantial capital by reducing the (multibillion dollar a year) waste they are inflicting on themselves by not ensuring the concept of efficiency and productivity in their economies.

Ineffective heat insulation in GCC buildings (leading to excessive use of air-conditioning in the hot summer months) and leaks in the water dis-tribution systems cost billions of dollars a year in capital investments and cooperating costs (in power stations and desalination plants). These are only a few examples of the inefficiencies resulting from a lack of attention to economic productivity. Improving heat insulation of buildings and reducing water leaks will also reduce carbon dioxide production.

It is notable that the Kuwait Institute of Scientific Research (KISR) recognized the importance of energy efficiency in buildings in the 1960s and commissioned the development of codes and standards to cope with the insulation problem. As far as I remember, KISR offered its system, at zero cost, to any interested sister country.

It is notable that the Japanese have a water-leak level in their water distribution systems of the order of 3 percent. All their water systems are run by municipalities, and not by private companies. The data and studies on water-leaks (of the order of 50 percent) in the GCC countries are widely known.[13]

Along the same simple and obvious line of thinking, the GCC countries could improve the productivity of employed nationals and save billions of dollars spent on employing expatriates. In this manner they could empower their own populations to be more attentive to their national economies.

They would probably quickly discover that the GCC could save billions of dollars annually by utilizing their own engineering capabilities (which are already considerable) and labor (tens of thousands have graduated from a wide variety of vocational and technical schools) to provide services in facility management. This is a very basic technology. It requires skills that could be acquired at the numerous vocational and technical schools now existing in the GCC.

Similarly, other Arab countries could mobilize their unemployed labor and engineers to maintain their historic buildings, brighten their urban environment, and transform their agricultural sector. Introducing concepts of productivity into the Arab world could do wonders to the economy and to how people view their countries.

Concluding Remarks

Judging by the experience of Arab youth in 2011, the challenges that the Arab countries face are formidable. Yet, enormous capabilities in S&T are already available to most Arab countries. If Arab youth succeed in transforming the prevailing political economy, they will be able to enjoy the creative transformation of their countries.

NOTES

Acknowledgments

1. *Science and Science Policy in the Arab World*, published by Centre for Arab Unity Studies 1979 and Croom Helm, 1980; and *The Arab World and the Challenges of Science and Technology: Progress without Change*, published by Centre for Arab Unity Studies, 1999.

1 Background

1. These numbers, as we shall see, are approximate.
2. "10 Emerging Technologies 2009," *Technology Review* 102, 2 (April 2009), 37–54.
3. For a report on the ongoing debate in Germany on this issue, see Carter Dougherty, "Debate in Germany: Research or Manufacturing," *New York Times*, August 12, 2009.
4. See Alvin and Heidi Toffler, *Revolutionary Wealth* (Currency Doubleday, 2006), 94.
5. Ibid., part 6, 146ff.
6. Gavin Weightman, *The Industrial Revolutionaries: The Making of the Modern World* (Grove Press, 2007).
7. It is speculated that the steam engine may have been invented earlier by Pharaonic priests and that knowledge of this invention was available to Hero of Alexandria at about 10 to 60 CE
8. It seems that cats became domesticated around 1450 BC and were used at that time to protect granaries in Egypt. See, for an interesting account of the cat in Egypt, Jaromir Malek, *The Cat in Ancient Egypt* (London: The British Museum Press, 2006), 54–55, Revised Edition.
9. Research concerning the conversion to steam shipping was already well under way. See Christine Macleod, Jeremy Stein, Jennifer Tann, and James Andrew, "Making Waves: The Royal Navy's Management of Invention and Innovation in Steam Shipping, 1815–1832," *History and Technology*, 16 (2000), 307–333.
10. Naomi Klein, *The Shock Doctrine: The Rise of Disaster Capitalism* (Allen Lane, 2007).

11. Ibid., 15.
12. Mayssun Succarie, "Winning Hearts and Minds: Education, Culture and Control," PhD dissertation, Berkeley: University of California, 2008.
13. For example, there was not a single Arab university in the top 500 universities list before 2008. See Said El-Sidiqqi, "Arab Universities and the Quality of Scientific Research," *al-Mustaqbal al-Arabi* 350, 4 (2008), 70–93. By 2011 a few Egyptian and Saudi universities joined the top 500 universities in the Shangai list.

2   R&D in the Arab World

1. The literature on R&D in the Arab countries is a lively subject and does receive attention, but there is little effort to improve the available data. Furthermore, there are no bibliographical compilations of sources.
2. The reader is directed to the footnote to ★Table A (★Appendix 1) on the accuracy of this data.
3. I have discussed the output during this period in my *Science and Science Policy in the Arab World* (Croom Helm, 1980).
4. ISI is often referred to as the Web of Knowledge and/or Science Citation Index. It is owned by Thompson Reuter.
5. This table, along with all other tables preceded by an asterisk, may be found online at http://us.macmillan.com/sciencedevelopmentand sovereigntyinthearabworld/ABZahlan.
6. The shift in the slope of the curve in figure 2.1 at 1995–1996 shows the extent of the difference in SCOPUS and ISI counts. SCOPUS gives higher counts than ISI, probably because it includes more of the periodicals published in the region.
7. See footnote to ★Table A in ★Appendix 1 for further details. The Jordan and Lebanon data show substantial advances; however, it was found that much of the increase from these two countries arises from errors resulting from the inclusion of sources not based in Jordan or Lebanon.
8. See E. B. Worthington, *Middle East Science: A Survey of Subjects other than Agriculture* (London: His Majesty's Stationary Office, 1946).
9. It is often forgotten how recently the United States established its great organizations of advanced scientific research and education. It did not have significant graduate schools until the First World War. These were established by emigrant scientists and by American students who pursued their graduate work in Europe (mostly in Germany, the inventor of the graduate school). For comparison, it is useful to note that some 100,000 Arab students are enrolled in OECD postgraduate schools. During the period of the initial rapid growth of American graduate schools (1880–1914), the newly established US graduate schools graduated some 14 PhD students for each American who studied abroad for a PhD (Unpublished work by A. B. Zahlan on foreign study of American students, 1880–1914).

Considerable private donations to support the establishment of US graduate schools were made to both the "old" universities (Harvard, Yale, and Princeton) and to pioneer the establishment of graduate schools and new universities. Interestingly, research in the United States was spontaneously integrated into the economy. Self-reliance was already an American trademark.

10. The expression "technology-free turnkey contracts" is used throughout the book to imply that a particular contract did not involve the acquisition of technology by relevant organizations in the host country.

11. This affiliation gives us the numbers we obtain from the citation indices, whether ISI or SCOPUS.

12. In 2005, some 684 publications (47 percent of the total) were wrongly included in the listing of Lebanon and some 153 (13 percent of the total) were included in those of Jordan. These errors were corrected in *Table A (*Appendix 1). This anomaly arose from a systemic error caused by the search engine.

13. Papers that fall in two or more subject areas are counted once under each area.

3   R&D and Its Functions

1. See A. B. Zahlan, *Acquiring Technological Capacity: A Study of Arab Consulting and Contracting Firms* (Macmillan, 1991).

2. Nicholas Nassif, *The Republic of Fuad Chehab* (Dar al-Nahar: Institute of Fuad Chehab, 2008).

3. Searches for titles of publications using key words have limitations. Furthermore, using only the publications of two years (2000, 2005) for the search emphasizes fluctuations in research output per subject area in small research communities. The results yield a worst case scenario. The reality should be slightly better. A survey of a decade of output would naturally give a better assessment.

4. "The GCC Likely to Pump $200 Billion into Renewable Energy," *The Emirates Business 24/7 Newsletter*, July 8, 2009.

5. It is noteworthy that during the 1970s the Arab countries had a booming program in solar energy. See M. Ali Kettani and M. A. S. Malik, *Solar Energy in the Arab World: Policies and Programs* (Kuwait: OAPEC, 1979). This Report has 199 pages of information on these activities. But this effort seems to have evaporated leaving little trace. The current efforts have no relation to hundreds of earlier projects. The earlier programs were propelled heavily by local expertise.

6. This work by Moza al-Rabban, director of ARSCO, was undertaken to investigate mechanisms for networking researchers in the Arab world. I am grateful to Dr. Al-Rabban for this contribution.

7. Jeffrey Mervis, "An Insider/Outside View of US Science," *Science*, 325 (July 10, 2009), 132. The survey inquired into a wide variety of American perceptions concerning US science.

8. C. N. R. Rao. "Science in the Future of India," *Science*, 325 (July 10, 2009), 126.

9. Travel by Arabs within the Arab countries is far more controlled than travel by foreigners.

10. Arab universities graduate some 100,000 engineers annually in various fields. The accumulated number of Arab engineers is of the order of 1.5 million or more. The absence of adequate statistical information leaves us in the dark as to their actual location and employment.

4   Science, Universities, and Enterprise

1. Clement M. Henry and Robert Springborg, *Globalization and the Politics of Development in the Middle East* (Cambridge University Press, 2001), provide the type of analysis that exhibits the functioning of the triad subject to political culture. Some readers may disagree with some of the analysis presented by Henry and Springborg; what I would like to highlight here is the nature of the processes that determine triad output. Kevin Murphy, Andrei Shleifer, and Robert W. Vishny provide a concise explication in "Why is Rent-Seeking So Costly to Growth?" *American Economic Review* 83, 2 (1993), 409–414. A seminal paper on the dynamics of the processes is provided by William J. Baumol, "Entrepreneurship: Productive, Unproductive, and Destructive," *Journal of Political Economy* 98, 5, pt. 11 (1990), 893–921. These different approaches provide a useful explication of how triad relationships are dominated by the political economy.

2. A. B. Zahlan, "Established Patterns of Technology Acquisition in the Arab World," in A. B. Zahlan and Rosemarie Said Zahlan (eds), *Technology Transfer and Change in the Arab World* (Pergamon Press, 1978), 1–27.

3. Linant de Bellefonds was a self-taught engineer who devoted his life to working in Egypt during the nineteenth century. He was essentially a high-ranking civil servant in the government of Muhammad Ali. He has written a comprehensive study of the civil engineering history of the canals and lake systems of Egypt from their beginning during the Pharaonic period to the end of the period during which he served in Egypt. His account provides details and on-site observations that are both interesting and unique: Linant de Bellefonds Bey, *Memoires sur les principaux travaus d'utilité publique executes en Égypte depuis la plus hautes antiquité jusqu'a nos jours*, ed. Arthus Bertrand (Paris, 1972–1973).

4. A. B. Zahlan, *Science and Science Policy in the Arab World* (Croom Helm, 1980), 37.

5. In fact, much of the information presented in this book seeks to demonstrate that the Arab countries have had, and continue to have, massive opportunities to activate their triads, but they constantly reject the option.

6. A. B. Zahlan, "The Integration of Science and Technology into Development Planning," in *Proceedings of the Workshop in the Development Planning and Management Process in the ESCWA Region* (United Nations, 1994), 5–34.

7. A. B. Zahlan, "Technology: A Disintegrative Factor in the Arab World," in Michael C. Hudson (ed.), *Middle East Dilemma: The Politics and Economics of Arab Integration* (Columbia, 1999), 259–278.

8. See A. B. Zahlan, *Science and Technology in the Arab World: Progress without Change* (in Arabic) (Beirut: Centre for Arab Unity Studies, 1999).

9. Ronald Wee and Andrew Ma, *Report on the Establishment of a Productivity Council and a Trade & Tourism Council in Egypt*, Project of the Government of the Arab Republic of Egypt, United Nations Development Program (UNDP), 77 pages, March 1995.

10. The Economic Research Forum sponsored a conference on June 17–18, 2009 on Access and Equity in Financing Higher Education in Arab Countries. The Proceedings were published in 2011 in *Prospects* 41, 1 (2011). Ahmed Galal and Taher H. Kanaan were guest editors of the issue.

11. In fact, the sums are larger because these figures do not include the figures for Algeria, Libya, and Qatar. See *Statistical Report: Arab Regional Conference on Higher Education*, Cairo, May 31, 2009, UNESCO Regional Bureau for Arab States, Beirut.

12. Henry and Springborg, *Globalization and the Politics of Development*, 148.

13. In the literature concerning the Arab world there is often confusion on this point. For example, a UNESCWA report entitled *Towards an Integrated Knowledge Society in the Arab Countries: Strategies and Implementation Modalities*, UN, 2005, exhibits such confusion when it relates the high level of net imports of technology to the limited availability of R&D (see 43).

14. A vigorous debate is under way in Germany, the largest exporter in the world preparing to cede its place to China because of a shift to research. See Cartier Dougherty, "Debate in Germany: Research or Manufacturing," *New York Times*, August 12, 2009.

15. William W. Lewis, *The Power of Productivity: Wealth, Poverty, and the Threat to Global Stability* (University of Chicago, 2004).

16. See Henry and Springborg, *Globalization and the Politics of Development*, for illustrations.

17. This is why a large proportion of university graduates are unemployed. Arab workers are unemployed and yet more than 30 million workers are imported from outside the Arab world.

18. Henry and Springborg, *Globalization and the Politics of Development*, chap. 2, esp. 52.
19. Anybody who feels that such incompetent measures prevent foreign powers from managing and controlling the activities of an Arab country will be well advised to read the extensive report by the Right Honorable Sir Richard Scott, entitled *Report of the Inquiry into the Export of Defence Equipment and Dual-Use Goods to Iraq and Related Prosecutions*, submitted to the UK House of Commons, February 15, 1996.
20. According to Wikipedia the expression "chaordic" was coined by Dee Hook to reflect a coexisting state of chaos and order. The idea is that this state of affairs facilitates orderly change. The Internet provides considerable information on this term.
21. I am grateful to Mrs. Kaoru Makhlouf for this information.
22. Don Tapscott and Anthony D. Williams, *Wikinomics* (Portfolio, 2006).
23. On March 14, 2010 there were 6,780,000 entries derived in a Google search for "rankings of universities."
24. See, for details, El-Sidiqqi, Said, "Arab Universities and the Quality of Scientific Research," *al-Mustaqbal al-Arabi* 350, 4 (2008), 70–93.
25. Ken Adler, *Engineering the Revolution: Arms and Enlightenment in France, 1763–1815* (Princeton, 1997). See also the excellent review of the book by Brett D. Steele, *History and Technology*, 16 (2000), 403–412.
26. The shortage of information on the subject of quality is a common complaint. See, for example, Nasser Jassem El-Sane and Mohamad Adnan Wadie, *Education and the Labor Market in the Arab Countries* (Arab Planning Institute, 2003), 107–108. The authors devote only one page to the subject of quality, due to lack of information.
27. See William Hinton, *Iron Oxen: A Documentary of Revolution in Chinese Agriculture* (Vintage Books, 1970) for a beautiful example of how a very difficult task can be simplified and undertaken successfully.
28. A. B. Zahlan, "Technology, Institutions, Organizations, Connectivities and the Diversification of the Real Economy," in *Proceedings of the Expert Group Meeting, Economic Diversification in the Arab World, Beirut, 25–27 September 2001* (United Nations, 2002), 347–368. See also Henry and Springborg, *Globalization and the Politics of Development*.
29. A. B. Zahlan, "The Impact of Technology Change on the Nineteenth-Century Arab World," in Charles E. Butterworth and I. William Zartman (eds), *Between the State and Islam* (Woodrow Wilson Centre and Cambridge University Press, 2001), 31–58.

5   Scientific Collaboration in the Arab World

1. B. Godin, M. P. Ipperseil, "Scientific Collaboration at the Regional Level: The Case of a Small Nation," *Scientometrics* 36, 1 (1996), 59–68.

2. A small sample of contributions is provided here: Pam Waddell, *The Role of Research Conferences in Developing European Collaboration in Science and Technology*, SEPSU Policy Unit No. 9, March 1994, Science and Engineering Policy Studies Unit of The Royal Society and The Royal Academy of Engineering. See also E. E. Vogel, "Impact Factor and International Collaboration in Chilean Physics: 1987–1994," *Scientometrics* 38, 2 (1997), 253–263.

3. This subject received extensive treatment in the report prepared under the aegis of ALECSO in 1989. ALECSO Committee for the Development of Science and Technology in the Arab Nation, *A Strategy for the Development of Arab Science and Technology: The General Report and the Sectoral Strategies*. Abdallah Wassek Chahid (Chairman), Elsharif Hajj Sleiman, Abd el-Wahab Bouhdeba, Mohamad Razzouk Kaddoura, Ahmad Abed el-Rahman el-Aqeb, Antoine Zahlan, Adnan Badran, Mohamad Othman Khadr, Ussama el-Kholy, Saleh el-Athel, Issam Naquib, and Musa Muhammad Amr. Centre for Arab Unity Studies, Beirut, 1989 (In Arabic).

4. http://www.nytimes.com/2010/12/15/business/global/15chinawind .html?_r=1&nl=todaysheadlines&emc=a2&pagewanted=all.

5. www.cirs.net.

6. Roula Khalaf, James Blitz, Daniel Dombey, Tobias Buck, and Najmeh Bozorgmehf, "The Sabotaging of Iran," *Financial Times*, February 11, 2011.

7. Shehab M and Vignola G, "Mechanical Design Considerations for SESAME Main Subsystems," in *IEEE Particle Accelerator Conference*, Vols 1–11 (IEEE Particle Accelerator Conference, 2007), 833–835.

8. Salah W., del Rio M. S., and Hoorani H., "Ray Tracing Flux Calculation for the Small and Wide Angle X-ray Scattering Diffraction Station at the SESAME Synchrotron Radiation Facility," *Review of Scientific Instruments* 80, 9 (2009), Article Number 095106.

9. I discuss the importance of the Arab construction industry in two books: A. B. Zahlan, *The Arab Construction Industry* (Croom Helm, 1983); also published in Arabic by the Centre for Arab Unity Studies (Beirut: CAUS, 1983); and *Acquiring Technological Capacity*, also published in Arabic by Centre for Arab Unity Studies (Beirut: CAUS, 1990).

10. The number of papers was divided by two because each coauthored paper is counted once under each of the cooperating countries. Cooperation with non-Arab countries does not lead to double counting.

11. The following observations depend on the assignment of a nationality to the names of the authors of the various papers; errors are likely. The guess-estimates are assumed to be reasonably accurate. The general conclusions made are unaffected by possible errors of assignment.

12. More detailed information on R&D regional and international collaboration pre-1995 is provided in Zahlan, *Science and Technology in the Arab World.*

13. Climate Research Branch, Meteorological Service of Canada, 4905 Dufferin Street, Downsview, Ont. M3H 5T4, Canada; Climate Change Research Group, Universitat Rovira i Virgili, Plaza Imperial Tarraco, 1, E-43005 Tarragona, Spain; Turkish State Meteorological Service, P.O. Box 401, Kalaba 06120 Ankara, Turkey; Department of Hydrometeorology of Armenia, 54 Leo Street, Yerevan 375002, Armenia; National Hydrometeorological Department, Ministry of Ecology and Natural Resources, Hydrometeorological Service, Haydar Aliyev pzt 50, Baku 370073, Azerbaijan; Bahrain Meteorological Service, P.O. Box 586, Manama, Bahrain; Hydrometeorological Department of Georgia, Agmashebelli 150, Tbilisi, Georgia; Atmospheric Science, Meteorological Research Centre, P.O. Box 14965–114, Tehran, Iran; Iranian Meteorological Organization, P.O. Box 13185–461, Tehran, Iran; Iraqi Meteorological Service, Baghdad, Iraq; Department of Geophysics and Planetary Sciences, Tel-Aviv University, Tel-Aviv 69978, Israel; Jordanian Meteorology Department, P.O. Box 341011, Amman-Marka, Jordan; Kuwait Meteorology Department, P.O. Box 17, Kuwait; Meteorology Department of Oman, P.O. Box 111, Muscat, Oman; Qatar Meteorological Service, Box 17621, Doha, Qatar; Meteorology and Environmental Protection Administration, P.O. Box 1358, Jiddah 21431, Saudi Arabia; Syrian Meteorological Department, P.O. Box 4211, Damascus, Syrian Arab Republic; Hadley Centre for Climate Prediction and Research, Met Office, Fitzroy Road, Exeter EX1 3PB, United Kingdom; National Climate Data Centre, NOAA, 151 Patton Avenue, Asheville, NC 28801, United States.

14. Waleed El-Shobakky, SciDev.Net, December 25, 2007.

15. Zahlan, "Technology, Institutions, Organizations."

16. The following UNCTAD report discusses and describes the measures taken in detail with respect to the energy sector of Korea: UNCTAD Secretariat with the collaboration of Dr Jin-Joo Lee and Dr H. N. Sharan, *Technology Issues in the Energy Sector of Developing Countries: Technological Impact of the Public Procurement Policy: The Experience of the Power Plant Sector of the Republic of Korea,* UNCTAD/TT60, July 12, 1985.

6 International Collaboration of Arab Scientists

1. Andrew Jack examines the prevailing situation in this industry in "Remedy for a Malady," *Financial Times,* August 15/16, 2009.

2. Jonathan Adams, Karen Gurney, and Stuart Marshall, *Patterns of International Collaboration for the UK and Leading Partners* (summary

report), a report commissioned by the UK Office of Science and Innovation, June 2007.

3. Stefan Wuchty, Benjamin F. Jones, and Brian Uzzi, "The Increasing Dominance of Teams in Production of Knowledge," *Science* 316, 5827 (May 18, 2007), 1036–1039.

4. "Other Countries" consist of Bangladesh, Romania, Armenia, Belarus, China, India, Madagascar, Malaysia, Russia, Senegal, Ivory Coast, and Kenya.

5. The conferences planned for 2011 in Arab countries appear to have increased slightly in number. See http: //www.docguide.com/crc.nsf /web-bySpec; http://www.conferencealerts.com/.

6. The population of China was assumed to be 1,200 million during this period.

7. Please remember that the data used in this section consists of the total number of publications from each of these countries that was available in the SCOPUS data base on the day downloaded. Thus, it is data that covers all previous years and cannot be compared with annual output. This approach was adopted to secure sufficient information to map interorganizational collaboration.

8. The data for this paragraph is based on the annual research output of these four countries and not on the total SCOPUS download.

9. Please note that the total SCOPUS download covers all years up to 2009, while the annual output cited in chapter 2 refers to output during one year.

7 Seeding the Arab World

1. These topics have attracted a large number of distinguished authors, such as Adam Smith, Alfred Marshall, Frank Knight, Joseph Schumpeter, Raymond Vernon, Benjamin Chinitz, William Kerr, Giacomo Ponzetto, Edward L. Glaeser, and others. Their list of publications on these topics would fill a volume.

2. The World Bank website http://www.worldbank.org/.kam provides detailed information on KAM.

3. See World Bank KAM website.

4. Robert Koenig, "US Takes Steps to Use Science to Improve Ties to Muslim World," *Science*, 326 (November 13, 2009), 920–921.

5. Murphy, Kevin, Andrei Shleifer, and Robert W. Vishny, "Why is Rent-Seeking So Costly to Growth?" *American Economic Review* 83, 2 (1993), 412.

6. It is taken for granted here that an entrepreneurial society will have a wide range of profitable activities. The science and technology contents of these activities may vary considerably without reducing the entrepreneurial implications of the activities.

7. For a discussion of the emergence of Dar al-Handasah, see Zahlan, A. B., *Acquiring Technological Capacity: A Study of Arab Consulting and Contracting Firms* (Palgrave Macmillan, 1991); also in Arabic (Centre for Arab Unity Studies (CAUS): Beirut, 1990).

8. Mohamed El Arbi Chaffai, Patrick Plane, and Dorra Triki Guermazi, "TFP in Tunisian Manufacturing Sectors: Convergence or Catch-up with OECD Members?" *Middle East Development Journal* 1, 1 (2009), 123–144.

9. According to Wikipedia the expression "chaordic" was coined by Dee Hook to reflect a state of chaos and order coexisting harmoniously. The idea is that this state of affairs facilitates ordered change. The Internet provides considerable information on this term.

10. This is not a full account of the tentative relationships between promoters of science and technology and business activity in the Arab world. Almost every Arab government has some activity in this area. Yet the total outcome is still very limited considering the enormous potentialities of the Arab market.

11. Mark Waite, "Study Shows Green Energy Jobs Growing at 2.5 Times Higher Rate," available at www.pahrumpvalleytimes.com/2009 /Jun-26-Fri-2009/news/296069774html.

12. The establishment of the Maktoum Foundation in Dubai is a move in this direction.

8   Science and National Security

1. The history of this process remains to be written. This is an interesting area that has received limited attention. It is possible to argue that the Pharaonic temples were centers of R&D. It is here that the discovery of ammonia (named after Ammon) and steam engines (probably used to operate the heavy temple doors), among many others, probably took place. The temple priests made significant contributions to the science of chemistry and engineering. Similarly, temples in Assyria and elsewhere were probably sites for the conduct of R&D. Arab astronomical observatories were also centers of R&D that made considerable contributions to the development of timekeeping and the understanding of natural laws. The establishment of the naval research center under Prince Henry the Navigator could also be claimed to be the first deliberate R&D program designed to achieve a specific technical and military objective.

2. Eugene B. Sokolnikoff, *The Elusive Transformation: Science, Technology, and the Evolution of International Politics* (Princeton University Press, 1994).

3. John Francis Guilmartin Jr., *Gunpowder and Galleys: Changing Technology and Mediterranean Warfare at Sea in the Sixteenth Century* (Cambridge University Press, 1980).

4. For a detailed discussion of this development see Zahlan, A. B., "Technology: A Disintegrative Factor in the Arab World," in Michael C. Hudson (ed.), *Middle East Dilemma: The Politics and Economics of Arab Integration* (Columbia University Press, 1998), 259–278.

5. The extent of dematerialization is extensive: by 1900, raw materials accounted for only 25 percent of the US GDP; the share of raw materials declined to 7 percent in 1970. See Richard Auty, "Materials Intensity of GDP," *Resources Policy* (December 1995); V. E. Spencer, *Raw materials in the United States Economy, 1900–77*, Bureau of Census Technical Paper No. 47, Washington, DC, 1980. Minerals alone accounted for 7 percent of GDP in 1900 and only 1.7 percent in 1977. Information quoted in Jeffrey Madrick, *The End of Affluence: The Causes and Consequences of America's Economic Dilemma* (Random House, 1995), 66.

6. *World Bank Development Report 1995: Workers in an Integrating World* (Oxford University Press, 1995), 119.

7. Ibid., 29.

8. World Economic Forum, *Global Competitiveness Report* (Geneva, 1998).

9. World Economic Forum, *The Global Competitiveness Report 2006–2007: Creating an Improved Business Environment*, Augusto Lopez-Claros (editor) (Macmillan, 2006).

9 Science and Poverty

1. Lewis, William W., *The Power of Productivity: Wealth, Poverty, and the Threat to Global Stability* (University of Chicago, 2004), 11.

2. Adel A. Sabet, "UAR Commitments to Science and Technology," in Claire Nader and A. B. Zahlan (eds), *Science and Technology in Developing Countries* (Cambridge University Press, 1969), 187–239.

3. See ESCWA, *Forum on Technology, Employment and Poverty Alleviation in the Arab Countries and the Consultative Committee on Scientific and Technological Development*, Beirut, July 16–18, 2002, esp. 15.

4. Ibid., 16.

5. There are no reliable statistics on investments in capital formation in the Arab world. Clearly the $3,000 billion figure is below what other quoted figures imply. The UAE and Saudi Arabia alone have projects under implementation and bidding of the order of $1,400 billion. The figures used in this book are often from newspapers. The fact is that the sums being invested are staggeringly large; if spent according to known and well-tested methods, these investments should transform the scientific and technological conditions prevailing in the Arab world.

6. See http://www.ameinfo.com/223978.html; AME Information, February 14, 2009.

7. See "Saudi Construction Sector Is Surging: Al-Rashid," in Trading
Market.Com, December 12, 2009, published by *Arab News*, Jeddah,
Saudi Arabia, Distributed by McClatchy-Tribune Information Services.
8. A medical doctor and leading Egyptian nineteenth-century scientist
who was concerned with the role of science in society. One of his
important contributions was *Kitab Falsfat al-nushu' wa-al-irtiqa*, Matba'at
al-Muqtataf, 1910; see also Susan Laila Ziadeh, "A Radical in His Time:
The Thoughts of Shibli Shumayyil and Arab Intellectual Discourse
(1882–1917)," PhD thesis, University of Michigan, 1991.
9. Arab labor has to become, through training, more productive to justify
higher wages.

10   Building Organizations: Learning, Adapting, Accumulating, Integrating

1. Historically, most of the temples in ancient Egypt and Iraq undertook scientific research of relevance to their societies. The library in
Alexandria during the Hellenistic period was also a center of research.
Thereafter, private and public support increased, and Arab-Islamic
civilization supported a wide range of such activities at universities
and hospitals and by independent scientists. The research effort of
Prince Henry the Navigator of Portugal was probably one of the first
modern long-term "applied" research programs. Its objective was to
develop transoceanic ships capable of sailing in the Atlantic Ocean.
Prince Henry sought to enable Portugal to project its naval power in
Gulf waters in order to undermine Arab domination of world trade.
The Royal Society in London, during the tenure of Michael Faraday,
was a great research organization in both basic and applied science.
Thomas Edison, in the United States, is credited with establishing the
first industrial research laboratory.
2. Keith Bradsher, "China Drawing High-Tech Research from the US,"
New York Times, March 17, 2010.
3. There is some literature on the relationships between the Arab and
European civilizations during that period. The subject is attracting
some attention from researchers.
4. For information on these conditions, see Robert M. Stamp, "Educational
Thought and Educational Practice during the Years of the French
Revolution," *History of Education Quarterly* (Fall 1966), 35–49; David
M. Vess, "The Collapse and Revival of Medical Education in France: A
Consequence of Revolution and War, 1789–1795," *History of Education
Quarterly* (Spring 1967), 71–92; A. Brunot and R. Coquand, *Le Corps
des ponts et chaussées*, Editions CNRS, 1982.
5. The account presented is based on A. M. Carter (ed.), *American Universities
and Colleges*, 9th ed. (American Council on Education, 1964).

6. H. S. van Klooster, "Friedrich Wohler and his American Pupils," *Journal of Chemical Education*, 21 (1944), 158–186.
7. *International Higher Education*, published by the Boston College Center for International Higher Education. Cf. n.11 below.
8. Elizabeth Longuenesse, *Professions et société au Proche-Orient* (Presses Universitaires de Rennes, 2007).
9. Clement Henry Moore, *Images of Development: Egyptian Engineers in Search of Industry* (MIT Press, 1980).
10. Larzillière, Pénélope, "Organisations professionnelles et mobilisation politique en contexte coercitif : le cas de la Jordanie," *Critique Internationale*, 48 (2010), 183–204.
11. *International Higher Education*, 58 (Winter 2010), published by the Boston College Center for International Higher Education, contains articles by Philip G. Altbach, Rosa Becker, Spencer Witte, and Vik Naidoo on transnational higher education. Clearly, the Arab countries account for a substantial proportion of all such colleges. The authors voice their concern about the assumptions that underlie these campuses.
12. Radwan El-Sayed, "The Arab Development Problem and Political Management," *al-Sharq al-awsat*, December 25, 2009.
13. Source: World Economic Forum, *Global Competitiveness Report 2006–2007: Creating an Improved Business Environment*, ed. Augusto Lopez-Claros (Macmillan, 2006).
14. In the United States there are annual national tests for various school grades to assess progress being made and the problems that need to be faced. See, for more details, Alice C. Fu, Senta A. Raizen, and Richard J. Shavelson, "The Nation's Report Card: A Vision of Large-Scale Science Assessment," *Science*, 326 (December 2009), 1637–1638.
15. Bruce Alberts, "Editorial: Promoting Scientific Standards," *Science*, 327 (January 2010), 12. The abuses discussed by Alberts are common place in periodicals published in the Arab world.
16. The barrage became a tourist attraction, and the contribution of Brown was highly appreciated by visitors. R. H. Brown, *History of the Barrage at the Head of the Delta of Egypt* (F. Diemer, 1896).

11 Municipalities, Science, and Technology

1. Roula Majdalani, "The Governance Paradigm and Urban Development: Breaking New Ground?" in Seteney Shami (ed.), *Capital Cities: Ethnographies of Urban Governance in the Middle East* (Center for Urban Community Studies, University of Toronto, 2001), 13–32.
2. By comparison, the US automobile industry (including manufacturing, servicing, and Repair & Maintenance) employs one of every five workers in the country. It is most likely that during the seventeenth

century, Arab transport employed a similar proportion of Arab labor in "manufacturing the camels" and running the system.

3. For an interesting historical sketch of the Egyptian experience, see Najwa Khalil, with Howaidi Adli, Majadi Abdel-Ghani, and Hassan Salameh, *Istetla' ra'a awina min al-jamhour al-khas fi nizam al-idara el-mahalia* (National Center for Social and Criminal Research, Department for the Measure of Public Opinion, 2004).

4. Decentralisation and the Emerging Role of Municipalities in the ESCWA Region, E/ESCWA/HS/2001/3, February 2001, Beirut.

5. Daniel Ringrose, "Work and Social Presence: French Public Engineers in Nineteenth-Century Provincial Communities," *History and Technology* 14 (1998), 293–312.

6. Irwin et al. discuss the transformations of the economies of American rural areas over the past century. Not only are rural areas more prosperous than urban areas today but they are also no longer dependant on agriculture as the major component of their economy. Elena G. Irwin, Andrew M. Isserman, Maureen Kilkenny, and Mark D. Partridge, "A Century of Research on rural Development and Regional Issues," *American J. Agr. Econ.* 92, 2 (2010), 522–553.

7. For a brief description of the Dutch approach, see Arthur Wiggers, "A National Association of Local Authorities: Its Role and Function," in A. B. Zahlan (ed.), *The Reconstruction of Palestine: Urban and Rural Development* (Kegan Paul International, 1997), 142–148.

8. Seteney Shami (ed.), *Capital Cities: Ethnographies of Urban Governance in the Middle East* (Center for Urban and Community Studies, University of Toronto, 2001).

9. Montasser M. Kamal, "Cairo: Exclusive Governance and Urban Development in Egypt," in Seteney Shami (ed.), *Capital Cities*, 54–66.

12   Future Prospects

1. See the Fouad Chehab website: http://www.fouadchehab.com/en/?loc=presidency.

2. An analytical account of the Intra Bank crises is provided by Hanna Asfour, *Bank Intra* (published in Arabic; Beirut, 1969). Dr. Asfour, an economist and a lawyer who specialized in financial matters, provides a detailed and balanced account of the factors that contributed to the collapse of Intra Bank. The collapse of Intra provides an excellent example illustrating the importance of the rule of law, and of regulatory services. It also illustrates the importance of legislation in development.

3. See, for example, Nadji Safir, "Les sociétés musulmanes face aux défis de la science: une crise systémique de créativité," *Le Monde Diplomatique*, November 20, 2010.

4. The Report does not seek to make up for the deficiencies of the *UNDP -AHDR-2003: Building a Knowledge Society*. See A. B. Zahlan, "Arab Societies as Knowledge Societies," *Minerva*, 44 (2006), 103–112.
5. *The Arab Knowledge Report*, 220.
6. Ibid., 184; Box 5–1, 186.
7. The average of the outputs during 2006–2010 was divided by that of 1967–1971 to average fluctuations.
8. During the period 1967–1971 Saudi Arabia produced an average of 54 publications. If we divide the average for the period 2006–2010 by that of 1967–1971 we obtain a 310-fold increase.
9. By this, I mean the absence of any authority of the population to choose who rules over it.
10. See UNESCO data.
11. Source: Gerson Lehman Group, December 17, 2009, available at www .glgroup.com//NewsWatchPrefs/Print.aspx-45450.
12. It is clear that these points apply differently to different countries.
13. See, for example, Global Water Intelligence, *Desalination Markets 2005–2015, A Global Assessment and Forecast, 2005*; Water Global Intelligence, *Water Market Middle East*, January 2005; Global Water Intelligence, *Water Reuse Markets 2005–2015*, 2005. There are more recent publications than these.

BIBLIOGRAPHY

Adams, Jonathan, Karen Gurney, and Stuart Marshall. *Patterns of International Collaboration for the UK and Leading Partners* (summary report). London: Office of Science and Innovation, June 2007.

Adler, Ken. *Engineering the Revolution: Arms and Enlightenment in France, 1763–1815.* Princeton: Princeton University Press, 1997.

Alberts, Bruce. "Editorial: Promoting Scientific Standards." *Science*, 327 (January 2010), 12.

ALECSO Committee for the Development of Science and Technology in the Arab Nation. *A Strategy for the Development of Arab Science and Technology: The General Report and the Sectoral Strategies.* Abdallah Wassek Chahid (Chairman), Elsharif Hajj Sleiman, Abd el-Wahab Bouhdeba, Mohamad Razzouk Kaddoura, Ahmad Abed el-Rahman el-Aqeb, Antoine Zahlan, Adnan Badran, Mohamad Othman Khadr, Ussama el-Kholy, Saleh el-Athel, Issam Naquib, and Musa Muhammad Amr. Beirut: Centre for Arab Unity Studies, 1989 (in Arabic).

Al-Rashid. "Saudi Construction Sector is Surging," in *"Trading Market.Com,"* December 12, 2009, published by *Arab News.* Jeddah, Saudi Arabia. Distributed by McClatchy-Tribune Information Services.

Altbach, Philip G., Rosa Becker, Spencer Witte, and Vik Naidoo contributed articles to *International Higher Education,* 58 (Winter 2010), Boston College Center for International Higher Education.

Asfour, Hanna, *Intra Bank: Case and Lessons,* published by the author. Beirut, 1969, in Arabic.

Auty, Richard, "Materials Intensity of GDP: Research Issues on the Measurement and Explanation of Change," *Resources Policy* 11, 4 (December 1985), 275–283.

Baumol, William J. "Entrepreneurship: Productive, Unproductive, and Destructive." *Journal of Political Economy* 98, 5, part 11 (1990), 893–921.

de Bellefonds Bey, Linant. *Memoires sur les principaux travaus d'utilité publique executes en Égypte depuis la plus hautes antiquité jusqu'a nos jours,* editeur Arthus Bertrand. Paris: 1972–1973.

Bradsher, Keith. "China Drawing High-Tech Research from the US." *New York Times,* March 17, 2010.

Brown, R. H. *History of the Barrage at the Head of the Delta of Egypt.* Cairo: F. Diemer, 1896.

Brunot, A. and R. Coquand. *Le Corps des ponts et chaussées.* Paris: Editions CNRS, 1982.

Cartter, A. M. (ed.). *American Universities and Colleges,* 9th ed. Washington, DC: American Council on Education, 1964.

Chaffai, Mohamed El Arbi, Patrick Plane, and Dorra Triki Guermazi. "TFP in Tunisian Manufacturing Sectors: Convergence or Catch-up with OECD Members?" *Middle East Development Journal* 1, 1 (2009), 123–144.

Chehab, Fuad. http://www.fouadchehab.com/en/?loc=presidency.

Dougherty, Cartier. "Debate in Germany: Research or Manufacturing." *New York Times,* August 12, 2009.

Editors. "The GCC Likely to Pump $200 Billion into Renewable Energy." *The Emirates Business 24/7 Newsletter,* July 8, 2009.

Editors. "Emerging Technologies 2009." *Technology Review* 112, 2 (April 2009), 37–54.

El-Sane', Nasser Jassem, and Mohamad Adnan Wadie. *Education and the Labor Market in the Arab Countries.* Kuwait: Arab Planning Institute, 2003.

El-Sayed, Radwan. "The Arab Development Problem and Political Management." *al-Sharq al-awsat,* December 25, 2009.

El-Shobakky, Waleed. SciDev.Net. December 25, 2007.

El-Sidiqqi, Said. "Arab Universities and the Quality of Scientific Research." *al-Mustaqbal al-Arabi* 350, 4 (2008), 70–93.

Fu, Alice C., Senta A. Raizen, and Richard J. Shavelson. "The Nation's Report Card: A Vision of Large-Scale Science Assessment." *Science,* 326 (December 2009), 1637–1638.

Gerson Lehman Group. www.glgroup.com//NewsWatchPrefs/Print.aspx-45450.

Global Water Intelligence. *Desalination Markets 2005–2015, A Global Assessment and Forecast, 2005; Water Reuse Markets 2005–2015.* UK: Oxford, 2005.

Godin, B. and M. P. Ipperseil. "Scientific Collaboration at the Regional Level: The Case of a Small Nation." *Scientometrics* 36, 1 (1996), 59–68.

Guilmartin, John Francis Jr. *Gunpowder and Galleys: Changing Technology and Mediterranean Warfare at Sea in the Sixteenth Century.* Cambridge: Cambridge University Press, 1980.

Henry, Clement Moore. *Images of Development: Egyptian Engineers in Search of Industry.* Cambridge, MA: MIT Press, 1980.

Henry, Clement Moore and Robert Springborg. *Globalization and the Politics of Development in the Middle East.* Cambridge: Cambridge University Press, 2001.

Hinton, William. *Iron Oxen: A Documentary of Revolution in Chinese Agriculture.* New York: Vintage Books; Random House, 1970.

Irwin, Elena G., Andrew M. Isserman, Maureen Kilkenny, and Mark D. Partridge. "A Century of Research on Rural Development and Regional Issues." *American J. Agr. Econ.* 92, 2 (2010), 522–553.

Jack, Andrew. "Remedy for a Malady." *Financial Times,* August 15/16, 2009.

Kamal, Montasser M. "Cairo: Exclusive Governance and Urban Development in Egypt," in Seteney Shami (ed.), *Capital Cities: Ethnographies of Urban Governance in the Middle East*. Toronto: Centre for Urban and Community Studies, University of Toronto, 2001, 54–66

Kettani, M. Ali and M. A. S. Malik. *Solar Energy in the Arab World: Policies and Programs*. Kuwait: OAPEC, 1979.

Khalil, Najwa, with Howaidi Adli, Majadi Abdel-Ghani, and Hassan Salameh. *Istetla' ra'a awina min al-jamhour al-khas fi nizam al-idara el-mahalia*. Cairo: National Centre for Social and Criminal Research, Department for the Measure of Public Opinion, 2004.

Klein, Naomi. *The Shock Doctrine: The Rise of Disaster Capitalism*. London and Chicago: Allen Lane, 2007.

Koenig, Robert. "US Takes Steps to Use Science to Improve Ties to Muslim World." *Science*, 326 (November 2009), 920–921.

Larzillière, Pénélope. "Organisations professionnelles et mobilisation politique en contexte coercitif: le cas de la Jordanie." *Critique Internationale*, 48 (2010), 183–204.

Lee, Jin-Joo and Dr H. N. Sharan. "Technology Issues in the Energy Sector of Developing Countries: Technological Impact of the Public Procurement Policy: The Experience of the Power Plant Sector of the Republic of Korea," UNCTAD/TT60, July 12, 1985.

Lewis, William W. *The Power of Productivity: Wealth, Poverty, and the Threat to Global Stability*. Chicago and London: University of Chicago, 2004.

Longuenesse, Elizabeth. *Professions et société au Proche-Orient*. Rennes, France: Presses Universitaires de Rennes, 2007.

Macleod, Christine, Jeremy Stein, Jennifer Tann, and James Andrew. "Making Waves: The Royal Navy's Management of Invention and Innovation in Steam Shipping, 1815–1832." *History and Technology*, 16 (2000), 307–333.

Madrick, Jeffrey. *The End of Affluence: The Causes and Consequences of America's Economic Dilemma*. New York: Random House, 1995.

Majdalani, Roula. "The Governance Paradigm and Urban Development: Breaking New Ground?" in Seteney Shami (ed.), *Capital Cities: Ethnographies of Urban Governance in the Middle East*. Toronto: Centre for Urban Community Studies, University of Toronto, 2001, 13–32.

Malek, Jaromir. *The Cat in Ancient Egypt*. London: The British Museum Press, 2006, 54–55.

Mervis, Jeffrey. "An Insider/Outside View of US Science." *Science*, 325 (July 2009), 131–132.

Mohammed bin Rashid Al Maktoum Foundation and UNDP. *Arab Knowledge Report 2009*. Dubai, 2009.

Moore, Clement Henry. *Images of Development: Egyptian Engineers in Search of Industry*. Cambridge, MA: MIT Press, 1980.

Murphy, Kevin, Andrei Shleifer, and Robert W. Vishny. "Why is Rent-Seeking So Costly to Growth?" *American Economic Review* 83, 2 (1993), 409–414.

Nassif, Nicholas. *The Republic of Fuad Chehab*. Dar al-Nahar: Institute of Fuad Chehab, 2008.

Rao, C. N. R. "Science in the Future of India." *Science*, 325 (July 2009), 126.

Ringrose, Daniel. "Work and Social Presence: French Public Engineers in Nineteenth-Century Provincial Communities." *History and Technology* 14 (1998), 293–312.

Sabet, Adel A. "UAR Commitments to Science and Technology," in Claire Nader and A. B. Zahlan (eds), *Science and Technology in Developing Countries*. Cambridge: Cambridge University Press, 1969, 187–239.

Safir, Nadji. "Les sociétés musulmanes face aux défis de la science: une crise systémique de créativité," *Le Monde Diplomatique*, November 20, 2010.

Salah, Wa'el, del Rio M. Sanchez, and Hoorani H. "Ray Tracing Flux Calculation for the Small and Wide Angle X-ray Scattering Diffraction Station at the SESAME Synchrotron Radiation Facility." *Review of Scientific Instruments* 80, 9 (2009), Article Number 095106.

Scott, Sir Richard. "Report of the Inquiry into the Export of Defence Equipment and Dual-Use Goods to Iraq and Related Prosecutions, submitted to the UK House of Commons," February 15, 1996.

Shami, Seteney (ed.). *Capital Cities: Ethnographies of Urban Governance in the Middle East*. Toronto: Centre for Urban and Community Studies, University of Toronto, 2001.

Shehab, M. and Vignola G. "Mechanical Design Considerations for SESAME Main Subsystems," in *IEEE Particle Accelerator Conference*, Volumes 1–11. IEEE Particle Accelerator Conference, 2007, 833–835. IEEE is a global association of 400,000 members. The Corporate headquarter is in New York City.

Sokolnikoff, Eugene B. *The Elusive Transformation: Science, Technology, and the Evolution of International Politics*. Princeton: Princeton University Press, 1994.

Spencer, V. E. *Raw Materials in the United States Economy, 1900–77*. Washington, DC: Bureau of Census Technical Paper No. 47, 1980.

Springborg, Robert. "IV. Patterns of Association in the Egyptian Political Elite," in George Lenczowski (ed.), *Political Elites in the Middle East*. Washington, DC: American Enterprise Institute for Public Policy Research, 1975, 83–106.

Stamp, Robert M. "Educational Thought and Educational Practice During the Years of the French Revolution." *History of Education Quarterly* (Fall 1966), 35–49.

Steele, Brett D. "Engineering the Revolution: Arms and the Enlightenment in France, 1763– 1815 (Princeton, Princeton University Press, 1997)." *History and Technology: A Book Review*, 16 (2000), 403–412.

Succarie, Mayssun. "Winning Hearts and Minds: Education, Culture and Control." PhD dissertation, University of California, Berkeley, 2008.

Tapscott, Don, and Anthony D. Williams. *Wikinomics How Mass Collaboration Changes Everything*, Portfolio published by Penguin Group, USA, 2006.

Toffler, Alvin and Heidi Toffler. *Revolutionary Wealth*. New York: Currency Doubleday, 2006.

UNCTAD Secretariat, with Dr Jin-Joo Lee and Dr H. N. Sharan. "Technology Issues in the Energy Sector of Developing Countries: Technological Impact of the Public Procurement Policy: The Experience of the Power Plant Sector of the Republic of Korea," UNCTAD/TT60, July 12, 1985.

UNDP and Arab Fund for Economic and Social Development. *Arab Human Development Report 2003: Building a Knowledge Society.* UN, 2003.

UNESCO. *Statistical Report: Arab Regional Conference on Higher Education,* Cairo, May 31, 2009. Beirut: UNESCO Regional Bureau for Arab States.

UNESCWA. "Decentralisation and the Emerging Role of Municipalities in the ESCWA Region," E/ESCWA/HS/2001/3, February 2001, Beirut.

UNESCWA. "Forum on Technology, Employment and Poverty Alleviation in the Arab Countries and the Consultative Committee on Scientific and Technological Development," Beirut, July 16–18, 2002.

UNESCWA. *Towards an Integrated Knowledge Society in the Arab Countries: Strategies and Implementation Modalities.* UN, 2005.

van Klooster, H. S. "Friedrich Wohler and his American Pupils." *Journal of Chemical Education,* 21 (1944), 158–186.

Vess, David M. "The Collapse and Revival of Medical Education in France: A Consequence of Revolution and War, 1789–1795." *History of Education Quarterly* (Spring 1967), 71–92.

Vogel, E. E. "Impact Factor and International Collaboration in Chilean Physics: 1987–1994." *Scientometrics* 38, 2 (1997), 253–263.

Waddell, Pam. *The Role of Research Conferences in Developing European Collaboration in Science and Technology,* SEPSU Policy Unit No. 9, March 1994, Science and Engineering Policy Studies Unit of the Royal Society and the Royal Academy of Engineering.

Waite, Mark. "Study Shows Green Energy Jobs Growing at 2.5 Times Higher Rate," www.pahrumpvalleytimes.com/2009/Jun-26-Fri-2009/news/296069774html.

Water Global Intelligence. An international consulting firm that specializes in water resources. It undertakes consultancies, publishes reports and organizes conferences on the subject.

Wee, Ronald and Andrew Ma. *Report on the Establishment of a Productivity Council and a Trade & Tourism Council in Egypt.* Project of the Government of the Arab Republic of Egypt, United Nations Development Program (UNDP), 77 pages, March 1995.

Weightman, Gavin. *The Industrial Revolutionaries: The Making of the Modern World 1776–1914.* New York: Grove Press, 2007.

Wiggers, Arthur. "A National Association of Local Authorities: Its Role and Function," in A. B. Zahlan (ed.), *The Reconstruction of Palestine: Urban and Rural Development.* London: Kegan Paul International, 142–148.

World Bank. "Regional Perspectives on World Development Report 1995: Will Arab Workers Prosper or Be left Out in the Twenty First Century?" World Bank, 1995.

World Bank. *World Development Report 1995: Workers in an Integrating World.* Oxford: Oxford University Press, 1995.

World Economic Forum. *Global Competitiveness Report.* Geneva: World Economic Forum, 1998.

World Economic Forum. *Global Competitiveness Report 2006–2007: Creating an Improved Business Environment,* Augusto Lopez-Claros (ed.). Geneva: Macmillan, 2006.

Worthington, E. B. *Middle East Science: A Survey of Subjects other than Agriculture.* London: His Majesty's Stationary Office, 1946.

Wuchty, Stefan, Benjamin F. Jones, and Brian Uzzi. "The Increasing Dominance of Teams in Production of Knowledge." *Science,* 316 (May 2007), 1036–1039.

Zahlan, A. B. *Acquiring Technological Capacity: A Study of Arab Consulting and Contracting Firms.* London: Macmillan, 1991; also in Arabic, Beirut: Centre for Arab Unity Studies (CAUS), 1990.

Zahlan, A. B. *The Arab Construction Industry.* London: Croom Helm, 1983; also in Arabic, Beirut: Centre for Arab Unity Studies.

Zahlan, A. B. "Arab Societies as Knowledge Societies." *Minerva,* 44 (2006), 103–112.

Zahlan, A. B. "Established Patterns of Technology Acquisition in the Arab World," in A. B. Zahlan and Rosemarie Said Zahlan (eds.), *Technology Transfer and Change in the Arab World.* Ocford: Pergamon Press, 1978, 1–27.

Zahlan, A. B. "The Impact of Technology Change on the Nineteenth-Century Arab World," in Charles E. Butterworth and I. William Zartman (eds), *Between the State and Islam.* Washington, DC: Woodrow Wilson Centre Press and Cambridge University Press, 2001, 31–58.

Zahlan, A. B. "The Integration of Science and Technology into Development Planning," in *Proceedings of the Workshop in the Development Planning and Management Process in the ESCWA Region.* New York: United Nations, 1994, 5–34.

Zahlan, A. B. *Science and Science Policy in the Arab World.* London: Croom Helm, 1980.

Zahlan, A. B. *Science and Technology in the Arab World: Progress without Change* (in Arabic). Beirut: Centre for Arab Unity Studies, 1999.

Zahlan, A. B. "Technology: A Disintegrative Factor in the Arab World," in Michael C. Hudson (ed.), *Middle East Dilemma: The Politics and Economics of Arab Integration.* New York: Columbia University Press, 1998, 259–278.

Zahlan, A. B. "Technology, Institutions, Organizations, Connectivities and the Diversification of the Real Economy," in *Proceedings of the Expert Group Meeting, Economic Diversification in the Arab World, Beirut, 26–27 September 2001.* New York: United Nations, 2002, 347–368

Ziadeh, Susan Laila. "A Radical in His Time: The Thoughts of Shibli Shumayyil and Arab Intellectual Discourse (1882–1917)," PhD thesis, University of Michigan, 1991.

INDEX

Page references in **bold** indicate figures or tables.

Arab-Arab collaboration, 86, **87**, 88–9

economic ranking, 143–4

entrepreneurship, 121

graduate education plans, 28, 161

international collaboration, 98, **99**, 200

oil industry investment, 198

potential for nondependent transition, 118

research output, 21, **23**, **25**, 26, 27, **31**, **32**, **33**, 35

research output in priority subjects, 44, 45

research output trends, 195–6

technology investment, 153–4

See also GCC Countries

Sayed, Radwan el-, 167

Science (journal), 169

scientific societies/associations

citizen/scientist connections, 159

competence maintenance and, 166

cultural/political importance, 68

freedom of association and, 3, 65, 68, 201

importance for collaboration, 76, 96, 120

limited scale of, 51, 200

links with collateral organizations, 170–1

necessary conditions for formation, 166–7, 201

quality of scientific publications and, 169

strengthening of human capital, 39

travel to meetings as participation barrier, 65, 96

university/science/industry relationship and, 56, 63, 65, 66–7

Scopus (SciVerse Scopus), 20, 30–1, 35, 43, 85, 102

self-reliance (national/regional), 197–9

in Arab history, 133

as development requirement, 37–8, 148

economy and, 134, 148

knowledge gap and, 2

as motivation for technological advancement, 10–11, 199

oil industry and, 46

political culture and, 132

R&D and, 12, 49, 50

universities and, 56

Sesame Centre (Synchrotron Light for Experimental Science and Its Applications in the Middle East), 81–2

sewage disposal

importance to health and sanitation, 40, 151–2, 157–8, 164

municipalities and, 180

poverty and, 154–5

See also water problems

Shahriyari, Majid, 81

Shami, Seteney, 186

Shleifer, Andrei, 117, 206n1

Shobakky, Waleed el-, 90

The Shock Doctrine (Klein), 13–14

Shumayyil, Shibli, 154

Siemens AG, 187

Singapore

agricultural productivity, 42

economic ranking, 141, 143

education, 140

Singh, Manmohan, 47

small countries *vs.* large countries, 46–8, 70–1, 143, 160–1

Sokolnikoff, Eugene, 129

solar energy production/research, 43, 44, 184

solid state physics, 86

Somalia, 57, **87**, **99**

South Korea. *See* Korea, Republic of

sovereignty. *See* self-reliance

Soviet Union

Cold War, 129

education, 141